STYLE ON A

STYLE ON A SHOESTRING

A Guide to Conspicuous Thrift

Carolyn Chapman

Hutchinson

London Melbourne Sydney Auckland Johannesburg

Hutchinson & Co. (Publishers) Ltd
An imprint of the Hutchinson Publishing Group
17–21 Conway Street, London W1P 6JD

Hutchinson Group (Australia) Pty Ltd
PO Box 496, 16–22 Church Street, Hawthorne, Melbourne, Victoria 3122
PO Box 151, Broadway, New South Wales 2007

Hutchinson Group (NZ) Ltd
32–34 View Road, PO Box 40–086, Glenfield, Auckland 10

Hutchinson Group (SA) (Pty) Ltd
PO Box 337, Bergvlei 2012, South Africa

First published 1984

© Carolyn Chapman 1984

Set in Linotron Baskerville by Input Typesetting Ltd, London

Printed and bound in Great Britain by
Anchor Brendon Ltd of Tiptree, Essex

British Library Cataloguing in Publication Data
Chapman, Carolyn
Style on a shoestring.
1. Dressmaking—Handbooks, manuals, etc
I. Title
646.4'04   TT550
ISBN 0 09 155781 X

Contents

Acknowledgements

I should like to thank the following colleagues, friends and members of numerous organizations for all their encouragement, and the expert and kindly advice without which this book would never have materialized. Particularly Meg Perkins of Sketchley (Tailoring Alterations), Delores del Rio (ex-Harrods Alterations Department) and Yvette Boston – the most Conspicuously Thrifty home dressmaker I have ever met. My thanks also to knitwear designer, Alison Robson, for knitting-pattern alterations and suggestions. On general clothes cleaning and care I owe much to friend and colleague, Barbara Chandler. Her book *How to Cope at Home* provided invaluable reference. On the more esoteric aspects of textile conservation, antique clothes expert Bobby Wornsnop and John Lawson of Picreator Enterprises offered much helpful advice, as did Karen Finch and Greta Putnam of the Textile Conservation Centre – their Hampton Court workshops were a pleasure to visit. For everyday practical information on washing matters I am indebted to Norman Warburton of the Fabric Care Research Association and to Ruth Parkhouse of the Association of British Launderers and Cleaners for her help in compiling a list of specialist drycleaners for the Directory. My thanks also go to Christopher Bellingham-Smith of the Home Laundry Consultative Council and to Pauline Swaine of Lever Brothers for permission to use their respective washing symbols and stain removal guides. The following manufacturers also deserve my heartfelt thanks for providing endless assistance and allowing the reproduction of instructional information, and particularly to Messrs Frister & Rossman for the loan of a Cub 7 sewing machine: Russell Hobbs for permission to use their ironing instructions; Shirley Barnett and Janet Seed of Dylon International Ltd for painstaking checking and instructions on clothes dyeing; Messrs Coats, Milwards, Vilene and Reckitt & Colman products, for permission to use amended charts and other material. I also extend my gratitude to many of the staff at IPC magazines for support and advice and for providing much of the reference material. Other useful sources of information came from Francis Ross and her staff at the London College of Fashion library and the staff at the British Museum Reading Room for locating Nicholas Tomalin's original article on Conspicuous Thrift. I am also obliged to Madeleine Ginsburg of the Victoria & Albert Museum for her fascinating article in *Costume Magazine* on the history of the second-hand clothes trade in England. Last but by no means least, my thanks go to Susan Hill and Valerie Hudson at Hutchinson and to Vanessa and Janet Williams for typing and deciphering a seemingly endless manuscript. My final tribute goes to everyone running Thrift shops, antique dress emporiums and market stalls all over the country – to them I doff my secondhand hat – especially 'Bid' and 'Rene' of the War on Want charity shop in Westbourne Grove who have always made my rummaging for Conspicuous Thrift such a pleasure.

Introduction

This book owes its subtitle to the late Nicholas Tomalin who, twenty years ago, in *Man About Town* first defined Conspicuous Thrift. The 'Swinging Sixties' Conspicuous Thrifter, declared Tomalin, was rebelling against those whose lifestyle had unashamedly embraced Conspicuous Consumption, Waste and Leisure; who displayed their money with Rolls Royces, minks and couture clothes. Conspicuous Thrifters, on the other hand, disdained such vulgarity in favour of Minis, knotty pine kitchens, pseudo-egalitarian denim and pop-designed off-the-peg clothing. Conspicuous Thrift set the trend for junk misers and for weekends spent haunting street markets for bargain bric-à-brac. Tomalin admitted that his inspiration for Conspicuous Thrift was founded in the work of Thorstein Veblen, the nineteenth-century American social anthropologist.

Almost a century has passed since Veblen wrote *The Theory of the Leisure Class*, but its exposé of transatlantic mores, education and finance holds as potent a message for us now as it ever did. Clearly, Veblen's insight into what he termed 'The Pecuniary Culture' was sharpened by a decade's experience as an unemployed academic. He probably established the notion of 'clothes as language' and 'we are what we wear'. Clothes, according to Veblen, are the most immediate barometer of individual financial and social status.

This book, however, seeks to redefine the concept of Conspicuous Thrift dressing in the context of present-day living. Conspicuous Thrifters of the prosperous Sixties were seldom motivated by any puritan desire to save money. Their main purpose was to be different from the vulgar rich. It was always somehow tacitly assumed that pine in urban farmhouse kitchens, the denims and the gingham shirts would be *new*. In those pre-recession days, Conspicuous Thrift was

9

born of optimism, with little thought of dole queues and diminishing world resources.

Today's Conspicuous Thrift has more to do with actual survival. The tendency now is for Conspicuous Thrifters to create an illusory effect of wealth and style while working almost entirely within the confines of old, secondhand and antique clothes that can cost next to nothing. This takes persistence and knowhow. Adept Conspicuous Thrifters have to be thoroughly conversant with all the cheapest sources of secondhand garments. They must also know how to put the craft back into traditional cleaning, sewing and clothes repair techniques as well as old-fashioned valeting. Stylish dressing comes, too, from a working knowledge of costume and textile history and a desire to experiment with new decorative techniques. Expert Conspicuous Thrifters are less squeamish about stains and surface dirt, the indications of previous ownership. In any case, the built-in obsolescence of today's high fashion garments worn by those still wedded to Conspicuous Consumption means that many clothes are discarded after only a few wearings. For this Conspicuous Thrifters should be grateful: other people's wastefulness keeps them in clothing.

Conspicuous Thrift dressing clearly thrives in a climate of eclectic fashion. The dictates of Paris fashion houses or the definitive style labels of 'Sloane Ranger' or 'American Preppy' can now be ignored or selected from at random. Conspicuous Thrifters are far more likely to be inspired by old and new films or by a glut of some item going cheap in a local army surplus shop. Films such as *Cabaret, Annie Hall, Reds* and *Dr Zhivago* and box-office stars such as Humphrey Bogart, James Dean, Elvis Presley, Charlie Chaplin, Joan Crawford and Doris Day have had their influence on Thrift style, too. This kind of dressing cuts across age, class and sex because it is concerned with the wearer finding clothes to suit his or her identity – or to emulate a style he or she admires. It is about saving money, feeling comfortable and looking good in the context of one's own lifestyle. The toddler who wears his brother or sister's hand-me-down patched dungarees, the prep school master who sports patched leather elbows on his tweed jacket, the teenager who wants to emulate Elvis or Marilyn with bandbox original Sixties outfits and the dowager duchess wishing to keep her tiaras sparkling and cashmere twinsets tidy are all Conspicuous Thrifters under the skin.

'Waste not, want not' is certainly the Conspicuous Thrifter's creed. All clothes ever to be discarded are subjected first to careful scrutiny.

Is a particular fabric, set of buttons, zips or a trimming worth salvaging? Can a style be altered or a colour changed? Only if nothing is worth keeping do they ever give anything to a jumble sale or charity shop. The crafty Conspicuous Thrifter goes even further and sells garments in good condition to specialist secondhand clothes shops.

Conspicuous Thrifters also recycle. Their mothers and grandmothers made bras out of lace curtains and skirts out of plus-fours during the Second World War. Thrift dressers today, like peasants from diverse cultures, delight in embroidering, altering and recycling their clothes. With the simplest new dressmaking materials becoming increasingly costly, all ideas are welcome. For this reason, this book includes information on specialist cleaning and repairs; where still more detailed knowledge is required, readers are referred to the appropriate book or organization.

Being unable to afford any kind of wardrobe is a positive disadvantage when it comes to job interviews and carrying out some occupations. Similarly, gala occasions, or indeed any function where for some reason people are obliged to dress 'richer' than they really are, become increasingly difficult for most people. Not being appropriately dressed was always, and is, depressing. The war between Conspicuous Thrifters and Consumers still rages. Conspicuous Thrifters castigate the Wasters as spendthrift, ostentatious, unimaginative and vulgar. The Consumers dismiss their economies as tacky, shabby gentility. Nicholas Tomalin pointed out that Conspicuous Thrifters had a nasty streak of snobbery in their makeup. He attributed this to war-deprived parents who had grown up with the idea that Sixties Conspicuous Consumption was the hallmark of the spiv and black marketeer. It is just possible that the Consumers are piqued at Thrifters making an impression on a shoestring and are somewhat envious. 'Repairs are too time-consuming', and 'It's been worn by someone else', they cry – claims any Conspicuous Thrifter can dismiss by using the latest sewing aids and by keeping their eyes peeled for designer-label clothes. Many is the time I have come across clothes boasting haute couture labels hanging ignominiously with batches of Crimplene dresses in charity shops.

As a confirmed Conspicuous Thrifter from the day I first received my older sister's hand-me-downs, finding any clothes bargain still gives me a lift. Charity shop stories on the 'hidden treasure' theme are legion: someone once claimed to have found £500 stuffed in the toe of a junk shop shoe; Anglo-Saxon gold brooches have been mixed up in trays of junk jewellery.

Finally, having extolled the virtues of Conspicuous Thrift, I should point out its snags – one being that it takes time to search out and overhaul cast-offs. In the words of Nicholas Tomalin: 'It takes money to conceal the waste of money.' Time and money are inexorably linked for most of us, so this truism hits hard. Even if repairs are time-consuming, however, the rewards are genuinely worthwhile and financial savings spectacular. As for the erosion of precious leisure – quite apart from the fact that much restoration work is positively enjoyable – one can work while watching television or travelling. Knitters have been working this way for years. Once hooked on Conspicuous Thrift you'll be well dressed for life.

Carolyn Chapman 1984

1
What to Look For and Where to Go

Most of us know someone who always manages to look like a million dollars but swears they don't spend a thing on clothes. This is the kind of person who scoops the only silver fox fur at a jumble sale and whose Great Aunt Maud has a seemingly endless supply of Twenties beaded evening numbers and Art Deco jewellery. To cap it all, they're usually good seamstresses, have an eye for what suits them and seem to have all day to browse round charity shops! But perhaps they are simply Clever Clothes Hoarders: they store démodé treasures in their wardrobes with tender care and wait for those styles to become fashionable. Whatever anyone else's fashion secrets are, it's your own fashion identity and sense of style that matter, and this can be achieved by anyone prepared to spend time and effort rather than money. Investing in secondhand clothes is probably the most painless way to discover what suits you. It's not going to break the bank if the dress at 55p isn't quite what you want, whereas a dress costing £55 is a very different matter.

Your fashion identity

Looking good in secondhand bargain clothes simply means studying your personal assets. As with all sorts of dressing, it's learning to play up your best points and camouflage the worst that spells success. Mini-skirts on chianti-bottle legs never look good, neither do flabby thighs in tight trousers. Magazines used to give women readers fashion rules as to what suited a certain colouring and a certain shape, but today common sense and a feeling for style are more important. It makes sense, nevertheless, to think about proportions and figure faults, and learn how to make the most of them while

13

playing down your weak points. Colour has a lot to do with visual tricks: avoid cutting yourself in half if you're on the dumpy side (a high percentage of the British female population is small and pear-shaped). Big legs do look best in toning tights and shoes: for example, dark brown or black tights or stockings with dark or black shoes.

Style means, above all, achieving a happy blend between old and new, and teaming up the unusual rather than the predictable. An antique silk camisole top looks great with a milkmaid Victorian petticoat, for example, but it can look even more exciting with Japanese workmen's cotton pants or military leather jodhpurs. A richly embroidered ethnic skirt in a brilliant primary colour looks great with a dinner jacket and black riding boots. If you don't want to be considered a weirdo and know you are a twinset-and-pearls girl at heart, then consider a little dash with, say, fishnet tights.

What to look for

Just how does anyone start collecting secondhand and antique clothes, either as their main wardrobe or to complement new items? Well, first of all, it's a good idea to identify the season's 'look' you like best: either cut out from fashion magazines or from window shopping. Make careful notes of shapes, colours, hem lines and accessories and then hunt around for similar secondhand items that can be adapted by a few sewing alterations or colour changes. Planning a total look is just the same with old and secondhand clothes as with new, so it pays to invest in a few secondhand classics, in good quality fabrics and neutral colours. A Burberry-style trench coat or army-tailored gabardine or poplin mackintosh in fawn, grey, khaki or green is a good foundation; so, too, are Harris tweed overcoats (men's and women's), and riding jackets and tailored pinstripe suits. Well worth considering are men's dinner jackets (and trousers), cricket flannels and morning dress.

After the basics, it's worthwhile collecting the more exotic cashmere and mohair coats and sweaters, beaded cardigans, ball gowns from the Twenties to the Sixties, oriental kimonos, shawls, jackets and dresses, Victorian cotton nighties, petticoats and camisoles, men's silk dressing-gowns and Thirties underwear. Keep an eye out for embroidered and decorative evening bags, good quality calf shoulder bags, crocodile and snakeskin handbags, kid gloves (long and short), strappy evening sandals, leather riding boots, silk scarves, leather belts and costume jewellery, as well as assorted trimmings such as braids, lace and buttons. Look out, too, for couture and designer names such as St Laurent, Jap and Jean Muir – expensive, even secondhand, their clothes are worth buying for their outstanding craftsmanship. Quality makes like Jaeger, Viyella and Cacherel often go for bargain prices in charity shops and jumble sales.

For more detail about what to look for in particular types of clothes, refer to the following chapters:

 8 Lingerie, Nightwear and Baby Clothes
 9 Dresses, Blouses and Skirts
10 Suits, Overcoats and Jackets
11 Children's, Teens and Sports Clothes
12 Knits
13 Fantasy and Special Occasion Clothes
14 Recycled Clothes, Army Surplus and Workers' Clothes
15 Accessories

Note: Conspicuous Thrifters should try to memorize their measurements as well as the measurements of anyone else they may be buying and altering clothes for.

What to avoid

If an item is going to be difficult and time-consuming to repair, it's only worthwhile considering if it's going to be worth a good deal more when properly restored – as in the case of, say, anything beaded or embroidered. Otherwise, if a lot of work is involved it must be something you *know* you'll wear and wear. Clothes damaged beyond repair, however, can provide useful salvage (buttons and fabrics) for mending other things of the same period, 'restoring like with like' being the true conservator's ethic. When buying anything second-hand, do check first of all for any holes, and underarm stains; also lapels, trouser fronts and crotches. Check linings and seams for damage, look out for fraying and splitting – particularly on silk – and give felted sweaters a miss. Make sure, too, that zips and fastenings work. Be prepared to seek professional advice over cleaning and repairs, especially if clothes are antique. Some buttons and sequins will disintegrate, as might delicate old lace and silk.

Some dull metallic braids and furs can be successfully revived at home; other problems such as replacing twisted interfacings in silk ties and dressing-gowns are time-consuming repair jobs (see Chapter 15) and hardly worthwhile. Re-weaving and invisible mending is best undertaken by experts (see Chapter 5). It's practical in any case to assume that most secondhand clothing, apart from cottons, will need drycleaning as care labels will probably be missing or illegible. If in doubt, always dryclean. Check out your local drycleaner's repair and alteration services if you don't feel up to tackling jobs yourself; remember that if an item is too small it's seldom practical (or possible) to let out – taking in is always a better bet. Haberdashery counters stock a good many items to speed DIY sewing repairs (see Essential Sewing Kit, Chapter 2), and with the range of home dyeing and colour-changing techniques available many an article takes on new life simply by changing to a fashionable, exciting colour (see Chapter 7).

Where to go

Jumble sales

Look for listings in parish magazines, and noticeboards in local newsagents and church, town hall, and community centres. Local house sales sometimes sell off contents that may include old clothes. Get into the habit of carrying a tape measure around with you: clothes bargains can turn up in the most unlikely places and if you have no way of measuring it can be difficult to assess size, particularly when labels may be missing or illegible. It pays to arrive early – you may even get a sneak preview if you bring along your own castoffs to sell. Always take plenty of bags with you and be prepared to bargain for a job lot of assorted clothes. Waiting around until the end of the sale can sometimes prove valuable. I've scooped a practically new child's cavalry twill riding jacket made by Moss Bros for 10p, and a man's Pierre Cardin suit for £5.00, items which by some odd chance were left until last.

Charity shops

The charity shops run by organizations such as Oxfam, MIND (the National Association for Mental Health), the Red Cross, War on Want, Help the Aged, the Salvation Army and numerous other smaller agencies throughout the country often prove to be goldmines. Write to the individual charity, enclosing an s.a.e. (see Directory) for details of shops in your area. Do check opening times and days for shops; they are staffed by part-time volunteers and it can be very annoying to journey all the way out only to find the shop closed. If you do see something inviting in the window drop a note through the box and make them an offer.

Dress agencies

'Nearly New Shops' and dress agencies are a cut above charity shops. They usually accept only clothes that are clean and in good condition – no missing belts, broken zips or bad stains. Compared with charity shops, prices are much higher, with donors receiving a proportion of the sale price.

Auctions

Truly professional clothes collectors – or antique costume experts as they prefer to be called – attend costume and textile auctions and fairs held regularly by Phillips, Sothebys, Bonham's and Christies. Large theatrical costumiers also have occasional sales. Here you may well sell your Aunt Maud's beaded frocks at a profit. These auction houses also offer on-the-spot valuations, whereas costume museums do not. Although costume and textile auctions are usually attended by specialist dealers, remember, they have overheads and VAT to think about, so you may be able to afford a little extra as well as getting an opportunity to see the best quality antique clothes available. Don't be put off by high bidding – it is still possible to pick up a bargain in, say, slightly damaged oriental shawls or mandarin underskirts. As a rule, costume museums and dealers only want perfect examples, so flawed clothes often go for a song and can then be altered.

Attending a preview, normally held several days in advance, is essential if you're to make a successful purchase. You won't be allowed to try on the clothes, but at least you will be able to examine at close quarters for marks, stains and fraying. Sale catalogues list estimated prices, and dates and fabrics, but rarely say what is wrong with the items. Do check a 'lot': lace and trimming lots, particularly, can get very muddled by the time everyone has poked at them, and what you bid for may not always be intact by the time you hand your money over. If you do see something and can't make the sale or auction, you can probably leave a written bid stating the maximum you're prepared to pay. The auction staff then bid on your behalf.

You may well get it for less than you thought. Nervous first-time bidders can rest assured that their every nod and wink isn't going to mean they're lumbered with clothes they don't want. Professionals wave a rolled-up catalogue or a hand. The auctioneer will look away and then come back to you to verify. Systems of payment differ from auction house to auction house: a slip of paper may be left on your chair for you to fill in and the clerk will collect it later; otherwise payment is made at the end of the sale, usually to the rostrum clerk or the cashier's office.

——2——
Equipment

Nothing is more irritating than delving for a particular thread or fastening in a giant tangle at the bottom of a carrier bag. Those prepared to take their secondhand clothes bargains seriously need to have all repair and mending materials, gadgets and equipment organized. DIY shops sell useful mini chests-of-drawers with transparent fronts which are excellent for storing thread, pins and fastenings. Conventional sewing workbaskets are usually too small for storing all the necessary fabrics for patching and the battery of gadgets you will need. I store mine in two large picnic hampers lined with quilting with special straps and pockets to keep tape measures, thimbles, etc., neat. Other storage alternatives include lightweight plastic tool boxes and jumbo-size kit bags in lightweight parachute nylon. The latter is useful for storing articles while being repaired; gadgets and sewing gear can be stored in small transparent boxes fitted with compartments – of the type anglers use for fishing tackle.

Essential sewing kit

The following is the essential kit: all items can be found in haberdashers, sewing shops and department stores.

Beeswax

It helps to prevent double threads from parting when sewing on buttons, stitching sleeves into armholes, etc; it also prevents manmade threads twisting and snagging when sewing by hand. After threading the needle and knotting the thread ends, twist the threads into a cord by rubbing the palms together across the threads, then draw the cord through the beeswax which can be bought in small pieces.

Buttons

Stockpile sets of buttons that can be used on a variety of clothes. Real mother-of-pearl buttons (you can tell by the striations on the back) in different sizes are worth collecting; they can be tinted different colours to blend in with your clothes. Sets of small glass buttons are useful as these go with many dresses, blouses and knits, but are not suitable on clothes for babies or small children as they can break when sucked or chewed. Other useful buttons are men's fly and braces buttons in black or brown, and overall buttons in different colours. The latter require no sewing – they clip through and are secured with a small ring. Leather and wooden buttons are also good standbys for coats and jackets, as are metal button moulds which come in a variety of sizes. They can be covered in the same fabric as the garment.

Defuzzer/depiller

This gadget consists of a small comb with metal teeth for removing unsightly wool or manmade fibre balls caused by friction. An electric razor also does the same depiling job.

Elastics

Keep a few lengths of 6 mm and 12 mm (¼ in and ½ in) wide for waistbands and cuffs. Wide stretch elastic in plain colours and stripes makes a decorative alternative to waistbands on skirts and anoraks. Shirring elastic is essential – stitching three rows will pull in out-size waists on old crêpe-de-chine dresses – Frister and Rossman recommend a 5–6 setting and oversewing elastic with a polyester thread using a zig-zag stitch rather than threading elastic direct on bobbin. (See Chapter 8.)

Elastic threader bodkin

These big needles with large eyes and rounded, blunt ends are also good for threading elastic through waistbands and for threading decorative ribbon through knits. They can be used for removing tacking threads, as the rounded end picks up the thread without harming the fabric. They are safer to use than scissors and quicker than unpicking with fingers.

Fasteners

Keep a stock of different colours and sizes. Press studs and hooks and eyes in black and silver finishes are available in 00 (small) to large size 2; clear plastic press studs are useful for fine fabrics, e.g. lingerie and baby clothes, when you don't want anything to show. Proper skirt and trouser fastenings on waistbands are tougher than ordinary hooks and eyes, look neater and are more secure. Velcro tape makes a good alternative to buttons on cuffs and waistband fastenings. It is available in three widths and a good range of colours including black and white, and can be dyed any colour. Use small slip stitches to attach or machine-stitch. Velcro 'Spot-ons' are 20 mm self-adhesive circles that are ideal for small fastenings, i.e. sweater necks.

Hem leveller

Particularly handy when skirts are cut on the bias in lightweight fabrics like chiffon and silk. You will need a friend to use the leveller, while you wear the garment standing on a chair.

Mending and fraying preservatives

Liquid nylon, i.e. Calaton, can be bought to prevent fraying. (See Glossary.) A slight stiffening of the frayed edge occurs when used, but further fraying is prevented (e.g. ladders in tights). Useful on antique silk and chiffon seams. Strip adhesives, e.g. Wundaweb, can be used on dress hems and where seam allowances are smallest, at collar points for example. Bondaweb is also an iron-on adhesive web used for preventing buttonhole edges fraying and patchings; also for making fabric appliqué motifs. All fraying preventatives are washable and drycleanable, but adhesive webs may need re-pressing after several washes.

Pins and needles

Have a box of good quality steel pins, 25 mm for general use, 30 mm for heavy fabric, 16 mm for lingerie and delicate fabrics, and two or three papers of needles in a variety of sizes: (fine) nos 8–10, and (large) nos 3–8. You will also need a pack of assorted crewel and darning needles, and a fine steel crochet hook for picking up threads, for working round corners, and for pulling through snagged threads on fabrics and knits is useful. Brass or stainless steel pins for pinning out will not leave rust marks.

Plastic curve (template)

This sort of plastic curve ensures accuracy when reshaping curves, for example, of a neckline, armhole or sleeve head. Mark out the alterations using tailor's chalk and make use of the curve's markings when drawing identical curves.

Scissors

The best are made from drop-forged steel, heavier than cheaper versions but easy to hold. Check that the finger holes are big enough, keep them sharp, and don't use them for anything else but sewing. A large pair for cutting out fabric, and a smaller pair should be adequate for most jobs; a tiny pair is useful for snipping embroidery work. For those planning large-scale tailoring renovations, it's worth investing in a pair of cutting-out shears with a specially long blade. Pinking shears are useful for dealing with untidy seams – again, buy the best you can afford, as cheap ones wear out quickly and can be uncomfortable to work with.

Seam ripper

An ingenious gadget, and much safer than a razor blade or scissors when unpicking seams and zips or snipping off buttons. When ripping clothes remember to salvage all buttons, hooks and eyes, snap fasteners and zips as these may come in useful for future repairs.

Tailor's chalk and marking pencils

Tailor's chalk sold in special protective containers lasts longer than marking pencils. Use only white chalk which still shows up on white fabrics, as some coloured chalks can be difficult to remove. Pencils should be kept sharp.

Tape measure

Keep both a cloth measure and a retractable steel rule, good for measuring hem heights and loose fabric lengths, and check that they are metric. A one-metre or 50-cm ruler is also useful for marking.

Thimble

Professionals in the sewing game recommend a tailor's thimble (without a top) as this allows ventilation; it is much more comfortable to use over longer periods than the 'closed-end' variety.

Threads

Match your thread to the fabric whenever possible. Even if you are trying to save money on clothes, don't be tempted to economize on threads. Market stalls specializing in haberdashery often offer sub-standard, cut-price reels of sewing (mercerized) cotton which frequently breaks in a sewing machine, or the thread doesn't unwind properly, or it is less than the stated amount. For sewing secondhand clothes economically, use a thread that is suitable for a large range of fabrics. Coats' Drima polyester thread can be used successfully on practically any weight or texture of fabric from fine chiffon to denim, and because it has some 'give' it is also ideal for jersey and knitted fabrics. Tacking cotton is cheaper than ordinary cotton thread and several large reels should come in useful; it should be used for tacking rather than ordinary thread, which is far too slippery and harsh, as it breaks easily without damaging fine fabric. For fine silks, fine wool and chiffons, real silk and silk embroidery thread can be used, but if the garment is antique, take care as a chemical reaction can take place between old silk fabric and new silk thread. When handworking buttonholes use a special buttonhole thread which is thicker, and for sewing buttons to coats use a linen or polyester button thread which has a thick glacé finish. Machine embroidery thread of fine mercerized cotton is also widely available – sizes 30, 50 and 60 are most popular, but finer grades are obtainable. It is good for machine-made buttonholes on fine fabrics. Mediumweight fabrics will probably need buttonholes worked round twice. Skeins of embroidery cotton in primary colours are also useful if you need to do a quick repair or camouflage embroidery. However, skeins of embroidery silk – the kind used in Twenties and Thirties kimonos and Chinese shawls – are harder to come by, although the Royal School of Needlework (RSN) shop stocks a good substitute in au ver a soie's, soie d'alger range as well as a comprehensive range of metallic linen and cotton (lace) threads suitable for repairing antique clothes (see Directory). Crochet cotton is handy for making belt loops. If you've ever wondered why orange Sylko thread looks wrong when you've repaired Levi jeans, the answer is to use Gutermann's no. 887 polyester button thread, which is not orange but dark ochre.

Use short lengths of thread when sewing by hand to prevent knots and wear as it passes through the fabric, particularly manmade fabrics. Never use cotton thread for sewing manmade fabrics as the fibres rub away the thread and wear it out. If you have any technical problem or difficulty obtaining threads, write to the manufacturers (see Directory for details).

Trimmings

Store small items such as sequins, beads, ribbons and pieces of lace tidily (old typing ribbon boxes are ideal); keep small pieces of fabric from dressmaking or recycling ready for patching. Waist-length pieces of petersham ribbon are useful for making quick waistbands.

Hand sewing

1 When unwinding thread, let spool roll in one hand as you draw thread with the other.
2 Use short lengths – never more than 50 cm (approx 1 ft 6 in)
3 Cut your thread – never break it.
4 Always cut on the slant – it makes threading easier.
5 Thread the newly cut end into needle – the old end might be frayed.
6 As a general rule, don't double thread (see Beeswax in previous section).

Your sewing machine

Whether you own an old-fashioned sewing machine or an electronic superstitcher, it is important to understand it and use it properly with the correct extras.

Needles

1 Use good quality needles with sharp points and smooth eyes. Inferior needles have rough spots that can cause the threads to fray and break.
2 Whether sewing by machine or hand, always use as fine a needle as possible.
3 Change your needle regularly, especially when sewing manmade fabrics which tend to blunt the point. Don't forget to use a 'ballpoint' needle for knitted fabrics.

Needle manufacturers make something like 1000 varieties, each in many sizes and point styles. Most common sizes range from 9 to 20

(Singer) – metric nos 65/125 and W & G 0/6 – the difference in size being 1/2000th in per size.

Needles for high-speed sewing often incorporate a supplementary shank, the upper part of the needle, or step, a reinforcement which reduces, significantly, frictional heat as compared to a standard needle with a shaft of equal cross-section.

Long groove needles are used when the blade is for the convenience of the needle thread, from the take-up device, and provide a protective channel in which the thread is drawn through the material during stitch formation. Short groove needles are identified by 'a groove formed a little above and below the eye on the side towards the shuttle, hook or looper. They help in throwing the loop of needle thread.

For practically all woven and knitted textile fabrics, the round or conical point is used, since this type of point tends to spread the fibres of the material apart without damaging them. Fabrics susceptible to damage (e.g. manmades) should be sewn with ballpoint needles. All round-point needles are made with the extreme tip of the point slightly blunted or set, to strengthen the point against breakage or distortion. For leather and other non-fabric materials of low elasticity, a needle with a cutting point is used.

Machine sewing

1 Do read the machine manual carefully. Be sure to follow the instructions for threading your particular machine. Write to the manufacturer for further details if you have queries with a second-hand machine. Make sure you understand the machine before starting a major sewing job.

2 Use Coats' Drima for the thread and for the bobbin. Wind the thread on to an empty bobbin, making sure it is wound evenly.

3 Always sew a test seam to ensure the machine's foot pressure and thread tension are correctly set.

4 If the top layer of the fabric ripples, chances are the pressure is too heavy and must be loosened. If the fabric doesn't feed properly, the pressure may need tightening.

5 If a seam is puckered, the tension is too tight. Loosen the top tension and bobbin screw. On some machines the lower tension is fixed.

6 When straight-stitching the line should look the same on both sides

of the fabric. If it doesn't, loosen the tension on the side where the stitching is tighter. Sew another test seam.

Listed below are the most common causes of things going wrong with your sewing machine:

Thread breakage

1 Improper threading of either top or bobbin thread
2 Starting machine with needle incorrectly positioned
3 Rough spots on needle eye, throat-plate or bobbin case
4 Lint or thread ends around bobbin case
5 Needle too fine for thread and fabric
6 Needle improperly set
7 Bent needle
8 Tension too tight
9 Top thread caught around spool holder

Irregular or skipped stitches

1 Sewing in spurts
2 Needle wrong size for thread or fabric
3 Pressure too light
4 Pulling fabric

Machine stuck

1 Bits of thread caught in bobbin holder

Needle breakage

1 Wrong needle for machine
2 Presser foot improperly set
3 Stitching over pins, zips, etc.
4 Bobbin inserted incorrectly
5 Needle improperly set
6 Wrong size needle for fabric
7 Fabric pulling and causing tension
8 Sewing zig-zag with straight-stitch throat plate

3
Know Your Fabric

The main snag with secondhand clothes is that fabric care labels tend to be illegible or missing, so identifying the fibre for home dyeing, cleaning or stain removal can cause problems, particularly when over 200 mixes and blends exist. For instance, a petticoat may be a polyester/cotton mix rather than pure cotton; a lacy-knit jumper may be 50 per cent acrylic and 50 per cent silk yet look and feel like crocheted cotton; a Forties crêpe-de-chine dress may look like real silk but could be rayon acetate – misleading examples are endless. If in doubt, and your bargain too good a find for amateur cleaning experiments, take it to your local drycleaners. They may not want to accept it – drycleaners, too, prefer today's care labels telling them what solvents to use – but the specialized drycleaners (see Directory), with an on-the-spot special textile chemist, can identify the fabric (and the stain). They will also tell you whether something is likely to wash or dryclean. Cleaners don't take risks (and neither should you), so don't expect miracles. Especially difficult to clean are fabrics with special finishes. Many undergo special treatment in the manufacture to achieve some particular quality. Examples are organdie with its permanent crispness, non-crushable linen, velvet, fabrics that are rain or windproof or those that have been treated (Sanforized) to prevent shrinkage. Some of these finishes may also affect methods of pressing, washing, dyeing or cleaning.

Most old and secondhand fabrics fall into two main groups: first, the natural fibres, including cotton, linen, silk and wool; second, the manmades, like Acrilan, polyester and nylon, each with its own particular characteristics. Whereas today's manmades are derived from a variety of substances such as coal, petroleum, wood and even recycled plastics, the vegetable fibres, from which are made cotton and linen, can stand the most heat in washing and pressing. Animal fibres such as silk and wool respond better to lower temperatures; manmade fibres require very little heat and next to no pressing.

Today's textile experts also claim that the advent of these complex fibre blends have made yesterday's DIY fibre identification completely unreliable. The old method of describing wool as burning like hair is not much help if your mystery wool sample happens to be a blend of wool, nylon and acrylic fibres. Again, textile experts recommend seeking professional advice over flame, moth and shower-proofing processes as there is simply no home-grown method of finding out. Keeping a collection of clearly labelled fabric samples that you know to be *pure* wool, silk or whatever is useful if you wish to carry out a simple *burn test*, i.e. by touching your unidentified sample with a lighted match and comparing the reaction with that of the known sample. The old-fashioned *water test* is also quite useful for determining whether silk has been 'sized'. Simply drip some water onto an area of the silk and leave to dry. If it is sized a ring mark will be formed.

The following FABRIC GUIDE to natural and manmade fibres is intended as a checklist as to their properties, care and use. More detail concerning cleaning, care and dyeing techniques will be given in the four chapters following.

Natural fibres

Cotton

A vegetable fibre which grows as hair on cotton boll seeds.

Properties. Quality varies depending on country of origin: Egyptian fibres are around 5 cm (2 in) long; Indian and North American, around 2 cm (¾ in). All are highly absorbent and stronger when wet i.e. fibre strength increases by 25 per cent. Soft and warm to the touch, it can be bleached or dyed (see Chapter 7). Mildews easily, although can be treated. Other finishes include brushing, glazing and crimping, also processing to repel creases water and shrinkage (Sanforized or Tebilized). Some types such as winceyette and finer cottons can be highly flammable unless specially treated with Pyrovatex, Proban or Timonox. Often mixed with other fibres, e.g. polyester.

Care. Most cotton garments are better for washing; tailored items should be drycleaned. Do not use bleach on resin finishes e.g., glazed or waterproofed. Avoid leaving damp for too long before ironing or mildew may develop. Do not starch items for long term storage. (For restoring colour and whitening see Chapter 4.) Iron while damp on the wrong side with a hot iron; embossed or embroidered cottons should be ironed face down on terry towelling.

Fabrics. Aertex, batiste, broadcloth, broderie anglaise, calico, cambric, cretonne, chambray, cheesecloth, chintz, corduroy, denim, dimity, flannelette, gabardine, galatea, gingham, lace, lawn muslin, percale, piqué, sateen, seersucker, terry towelling, ticking, twill, velvet, velveteen, voile, winceyette, zephyr.

Chief fibre. In overalls and sportswear, secondhand summer wear i.e., dresses, suits, shirts, T-shirts and Victorian underwear.

Sewing. Use mercerized or polyester thread. Machine needle should suit fabric weight.

Linen
A vegetable fibre derived from the stalk of the flax plant.

Properties. Very hard wearing and absorbent with a high lustre. It is naturally mothproofed. Older linen garments may crease and shrink easily but most of today's linen fabrics are treated with resins for crease-resistance and water repellence. A further development with the lighter weights is a stretch linen. Cool and practically anti-static, it can be bleached, dyed and blended with other fibres. Withstands repeated launderings, has a higher tensile strength when wet and does not tear easily.

Care. Washes and drycleans well. Resin finishes can be safely bleached with Dygon (see Chapter 7), otherwise ordinary bleach will do. (Test on spare piece of fabric if unidentified.) Iron while damp at hottest setting on wrong side of fabric. Crease-resistant linens may need a light pressing.

Fabrics. Art linen, crash, damask, lace, lawn, tweed.

Look out for   tropical suits and summer separates, handkerchiefs, lace trimmings.

Sewing.   To cut, pull a thread on the seam to find grain line and use sharp scissors. Use a mercerized cotton thread for stitching; linen thread is useful for linen lace repairs and when glacéd, for sewing on buttons of outer garments.

Silk

An animal fibre from the cocoon of the Bombyx Mori silkworm.

Properties.   As with cotton and linen, the short staple fibres are spun into a yarn. Fabric is highly lustrous, smooth, absorbent and drapes well. Frays easily. Most of today's varieties are woven from continuous filament yarn with the exception of spun and noil silks. These are formed from waste pieces of cocoon; spun silk is smooth but noil is rough. Silk is sometimes weighted and sized for body; lustre is due to the removal of gum-like sericin found in the raw filament. Corresponding weight loss is then compensated for with metallic salts according to type. It can be weakened by perspiration and heavy soiling.

Care.   If labelled washable, it can be gently handwashed at 30°C, but most tailored garments and weighted silk must be drycleaned. Always test for colour bleeding on dark or bright colours and prints. Ideally, clean or handwash after each wearing. Special silk cleaner called Tenestar is recommended (see Chapter 4). Never soak and especially avoid using pre-wash stain removers and biological detergents. Press while slightly damp on wrong side with a cool iron. Do not spot dampen or use plastic spray-on stiffeners as these may mark. Instead, use a lightly dampened pressing cloth. Never soak or bleach with household bleach; white silk can be lightened with hydrogen peroxide.

Fabrics.   Bengaline, brocade, chiffon, crêpe-de-chine, damask, faille, georgette, habutai (jap), jersey, lace, moiré, net, pongee, ribbon, satin, shantung, surah, taffeta, tulle, twill, tweed, velvet.

Look out for   coats, dresses, dressing gowns, gloves, hats, hosiery, kimonos, lace, lingerie, ribbons, head scarves, separates, sewing threads, shawls, suits, ties, umbrellas.

Sewing Tack thin silks, i.e., chiffon, on to tissue paper and sew through both layers. Use silk or polyester thread, fine size needles and dressmaking pins as large sizes leave marks.

Wool

An animal fibre from the sheep's fleece. 'Virgin' wool means pure new wool; merino, botany and lambswool are finer quality than Shetland.

Properties. Two kinds of yarn: woollens made from the shorter fibres and worsteds made from the longer fibres for smoother surfaces. Either yarn can be blended with other fibres, i.e., cashmere, angora, polyester etc., and woven into any pattern. Needs careful handling when wet. Wears well, insulates, crimps and dyes easily. Is damaged by perspiration ('felts') and moths.

Care. Tailored garments and lacy complicated and bulky knits must be drycleaned. Unless labelled machine washable always wash by hand in lukewarm water using a branded product such as Woolite, or Adamite (see Chapter 4). Never soak or use biological detergents or pre-wash stain removers. Do not wring or rub. Responds well to fabric conditioners. Steam press using a pressing cloth on wrong side. Air frequently. Dry flat. Use a depiller for pills. Clean before storage and treat with a moth preventative to prevent further attack.

Fabrics. Bedford cord, bouclé, broadcloth, challis, cheviot, covert, crêpe, felt, flannel, gabardine, jersey, rolo cloth, serge, tweed, twill, worsted, whipcord. Also: non-sheep wool minority hair fibres such as Angora, alpaca, camelhair, cashmere and mohair.

Look out for baby-wear, coats, dresses, gloves, hats, hosiery, knitting yarns, scarves, shawls, suits, sweaters, trousers, underwear, uniforms.

Sewing. Use polyester thread, ballpoint needles and zig-zag stitch if machine stitching jersey or knits.

Manmade fabrics

Acetate

A cellulose ester made from cotton linters or wood pulp mixed with acetic acid.

Properties.   Drapes well, of moderate strength and absorbency. Old acetates may crease easily and be highly flammable but today's are treated for flame and crease resistance. It is naturally moth and mildew resistant. Test on a sample first if home dyeing. Quick drying.

Care.   Wash in cool water, handle gently, do not wring. Iron at low heat, hot irons can make permanent creases. Never spot-clean with acetone or vinegar. Check that pre-wash stain remover is suitable, some are not recommended for pure acetates.

Brand names.   Dicel, Lansil.

Fabrics.   Bengaline, cloque, crêpe-back satin, damask, faille, gabardine, jersey, lamé, linen-look fabrics, moiré, satin, sharkskin, sheers, surah twill, taffeta, tricot.

Look out for   blouses, dresses, evening wear, ribbons.

Sewing.   Most acetates do not shrink or stretch but seams on old dresses etc. may fray, so neaten by pinking or oversewing. Use polyester thread. Hold tricots taut when stitching.

Acrylic

A manmade fibre developed around 1950 and composed mainly of acrylonitrile, a by-product of oil and coal processing.

Properties.   Hardwearing, it resists moths, mildew and fading but stretches and pulls easily. Skirts tend to sag at seats, trousers bag at knees. Warm to touch and quick drying. Usually blended with cotton, wool, nylon or viscose in amounts varying from 30 to 80 per cent. Do not home dye.

Care.   Hand or machine washable according to washability of other fibres in blend. Responds well to fabric rinses and pre-wash stain removers. Wash in warm water, avoid wringing. Dry bulky knits flat. Lightly press if necessary with iron at coolest setting. Drycleanable.

Brand names. Acrilan, Courtelle, Dralon, Orlon, Neospun.

Fabrics. Usually found in blends, i.e. flannel, gabardine, knits, jerseys, fur fabrics for linings or outerwear, also suitings.

Sewing. No special sewing techniques needed, use polyester thread.

Elastane

Elastomeric fibre is made from polyurethane and now replaces rubber formerly used in stretch fabrics.

Properties. Stretchy and fast-dyeing with good resistance to sweat and chlorine. Can be home dyed but depends on garment as dyes react to chlorine.

Care. Handwash gently in warm water, drip-dry. Do not bleach.

Brand names. Lycra, Spandex, Wonder-Lastic.

Look out for foundation garments, keep-fit wear, e.g. leotards, swimwear.

Sewing. Use a polyester thread and machine zig-zag stitch.

Nylon (Polymide)

A continuous filament yarn discovered in 1938, derived from polymer chips.

Properties. Very strong with good elasticity and abrasion resistance. Quick drying. Non-inflammable but melts if burnt. Can be permanently pleated and water repellent. It is mildew and moth resistant. Home dyes well.

Care. Washable in mild soaps and detergents. Discoloured white nylon can be treated with special bleaches (see Chapter 4). Fabric conditioners reduce static and spray-on ironing aids are useful for nylon ciré etc. Most garments need very little pressing with a cool iron.

Brand names.   Bri-Nylon, Celon, Enklon, Perlon, Rilsan.

Fabrics.   Balloon cloth, brocade, ciré, crêpe, damask, flock, fur fabric, gabardine, jersey, knits, lace, net, panne (velvet), piqué, plissé, satin, taffeta, tricot, velvet.

Sewing.   Use fine pins, ballpoint sewing needles and polyester thread.

Polyester

Fibre is derived from petroleum and its by-products.

Properties.   Very strong and fade resistant. Found in a wide range of knitted and woven fabrics, many with easy-care finishes. Often blended with cotton. Useful lightweight easily washed wadding for padding and quilting. Special dyes now exist for home dyeing fabric pastel shades (see Chapter 7); if home dyeing blends, test on fabric sample. Dries quickly.

Care.   Machine or hand wash using hand-hot water, cold rinse, short spin or drip-dry. Wash whites separately. Responds well to pre-wash stain removers and fabric conditioners. Press with a cool iron when damp-dry, spray-on ironing aids help with stubborn creases. Polyester blends can take a warm iron.

Brand names.   Crimplene, Dacron, Tergal, Terlenka, Terylene, Trevira.

Sewing.   Use a polyester thread; zig-zag stitch is useful.

Viscose

Fibres derive from regenerated cellulose; wood pulp or cotton waste. Available from 1910 onwards. It was called rayon until the late Fifties.

Properties.   Moderate strength and absorbency but frays easily and is weaker when wet. Warm, smooth, elastic fibre that drapes softly. White viscose retains its whiteness. Can be treated for creasing and water resistance but burns easily unless flame-retardant finishes are used. Home-dyes well, but test on a sample of fabric first.

Care. Most types are machine washable but older viscose should be hand washed in warm water with liquid detergent. Do not wring. Responds well to pre-wash stain removers, fabric conditioners and spray-on ironing aids. Iron on wrong side of fabric at warm setting. Do not use household bleach or spot-clean with vinegar.

Brand names. Durafil, Sarille, Viloft.

Fabrics. Bengaline, brocade, covert, crêpe, damask, faille (poor quality), flannel, gabardine, jersey, lace, moiré, net, ninon, satin, sharkskin, sheers, taffeta, tricot, velvet.

Look out for blouses, dresses, linings, sportswear.

Sewing. Frays easily so seams in older garments may need neatening. Use pinking shears or oversewing. Use polyester thread and fine pins and needles to avoid making holes in sharkskin.

4
Coming Clean: The Washing Guide

Fastidious souls who baulk at the idea of secondhand clothes usually complain that they 'don't know where it's been', even if the garment has never been worn. No one minds a friend's or relative's castoffs; or trying on clothes in a boutique where they may have been worn briefly by hundreds of potential buyers. Indeed, it's commonplace in today's boutiques to find make-up stains, perspiration marks, and rips and tears in new clothes, let alone secondhand! The reasons why something gets relegated to jumble sale and charity shop are legion, but certainly it is not a question of clothes having been taken off corpses. Remember, too, that once an item has been treated for stain removal and washed or drycleaned a chemical breakdown of the dirt has taken place.

Care labels

This book generally assumes that care labels will be missing or illegible. However, if you are lucky enough to find items with instructions intact, then cleaning is straightforward. Where care labels can be identified, the Home Laundering Consultative Council has issued definitions for labelling. The code is known as the International Textile Care Labelling Code. It comprises the following symbols, each of which is variable.

The washing process

A number and a temperature in the washtub symbol indicates that the article can be washed safely either by machine or hand. The figure which appears above the waterline in the tub represents the full washing process and the figure below the waterline represents the water temperature. The symbol may be accompanied by a box containing written description of the process. There are nine numbered processes in the International Code, but only seven are likely to be used in the United Kingdom. These can be seen in detail on most washing product packets.

Note. A hand in the washtub indicates that the articles must *not* be washed by machine. The appropriate handwash instructions may be added in a box alongside the symbol. The washtub crossed out indicates that the article must not be washed. [The handwash symbol does not mean hand-hot water (washing codes 1–4 stipulate this); it means you should use warm water or test with your elbow as for a baby's bath. Woollens with the Superwash label have been formulated to be machine-washed on Code 5.]

Chlorine bleaching

A triangle containing the letters CL indicates that the article may be treated with chlorine bleach. If it is crossed out, chlorine bleach must not be used. The symbol refers only to chlorine bleach, not to other types of bleach.

Ironing

There are four variations of the ironing symbol. The temperatures shown in brackets are the maximum sole plate temperatures indicated by the dots in the symbol.

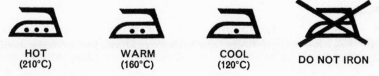

| HOT (210°C) | WARM (160°C) | COOL (120°C) | DO NOT IRON |

Drycleaning

Letters placed in a circle indicate that the article may be drycleaned and which type of solvent may be used. Only the letters A, P and F are recognized. If the circle containing the letters P or F is underlined, it indicates that special procedures are required as these goods are sensitive to drycleaning.

 Normal goods drycleanable in all solvents.

Ⓟ Normal goods drycleanable in perchloroethylene, white spirit, Solvent 113 and Solvent 11.

Ⓕ Normal goods drycleanable in white spirit or Solvent 113.

⊗ Do not dryclean.

Drying

The vast majority of textile articles can safely be tumble-dried. Care labels are used to indicate either that tumble-drying is the optimum drying method for a particular article, or that tumble-drying should be avoided if the article is likely to be harmed by this treatment.

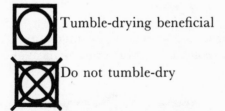 Tumble-drying beneficial

Do not tumble-dry

In cases where the tumble-drying prohibition symbol is used, special positive instructions, such as 'dry flat' for heavier weight knitwear, are given.

Handwashing

Most of the information in this chapter is concerned with hand-washing for clothes that require special attention. My experience with old clothes is that, unless they're bargains that you're prepared to lose, you should never risk throwing Victorian cottons, or indeed anything, into the washing-machine. Much old cotton looks as if it would barely stand up to the mildest handwash! On one occasion a pretty viscose/cotton voile headscarf shrank dramatically despite cool washing in liquid detergent. I spent the next two hours easing it back into shape, but it's never been the same for the experience. Now I have it drycleaned. Similarly, Forties crêpe-de-chine dresses can shrivel alarmingly the moment they touch water; but, surprisingly, most of these do iron back to normal. The golden rule is, when in doubt, cut a scrap from the seam and test first.

I've found it best not to treat very slight discolourations, such as streaks and spots, as these often disappear with correct washing. This happened with a cream silk embroidered Chinese blouse I found for 30p and a child's Arran sweater. As to trying out the old cleaning remedies that Grandmother used, some sound fantastic but some can work. For example, grating a raw potato into the rinsing water to prevent black dye running can be effective. However, to avoid little bits of potato clinging to the fabric put the gratings in a J-cloth, tie it up into a bag and dunk it into the water.

If there is no label, but you know what the fabric is, check the washing instructions in the Fabric Guide (see Chapter 3). If in doubt always handwash under the mildest conditions, using only warm soapsuds. Do not soak, wash through gently and quickly, and rinse thoroughly. Finally, blot off surplus moisture with a towel and dry carefully, flat if possible. If machine-washing, choose the gentlest programme.

Before washing, examine for any tears and stains and treat where appropriate (see Chapter 5). It really is best to do all sewing repairs before washing as it gives disturbed fibres a chance to settle and blend after washing and ironing. Empty everything from the pockets. Close zips and fasteners, as these can snag other items. Tie all long tapes and belts in loose bows and check that surface mud is brushed off trouser turn-ups.

Handwashing is always much gentler than machine-washing, although putting delicate things in a pillowcase or drawstring bag of nylon net (use nylon net curtaining for this) and running the machine on a cool cycle with a detergent such as Persil is certainly the safest way to machine-wash tights and other fragile, 'snaggable', pricey manmade items. But many fabrics today are mixes and blends of other fibres, so it's wise to play safe and wash for the fibre needing mildest treatment. More of today's fabrics than you would think take to the wash tub. Manufacturers and shops tend to label everything 'dryclean only' because it lets them out of dealing with customer complaints over bad laundering. Generally speaking, natural fabrics, such as silk and wool, live a lot longer if you wash by hand. Your best denim jeans and corduroys all come up better for a careful handwash and dripdry. But don't go overboard: if you're in doubt at all and suspect your clothes bargains are antique, seek professional advice. Someone I know once tried to wash a Twenties sequinned jacket and found the gelatine sequins rotted away in the wash.

Water for handwashing generally means a temperature that is pleasantly warm to the hand – 40°C (104°F) – not 'hand-hot' which is 50°C (120°F). You may need to use hotter water, however, for heavily soiled white cottons and silk that won't come clean.

Washing powders

These fall into three basic groups:

1 *Soap products:* for example, Persil, Fairy Snow or Lux flakes. These dissolve easily but are not suitable for flame resistant finishes such as Proban.

2 *Synthetic or soapless detergents:* The heavy-duty powders such as Drive, Omo, Daz and Tide; light-duty liquid detergents such as Stergene; or powders, such as Dreft, which are recommended for preventing colour-fading.

3 *Low-sudsing or low lather powders:* These are specially formulated for automatic washing-machines. Main brands are Daz Automatic, Surf Automatic, Bold, Persil and Ariel Automatics – the last three combine biological action and work on lower, cooler temperatures than the other low lather powders and are best suited to washloads of manmades at lower temperatures. Never use for silks or wool.

Biological detergents are discussed in detail later in this chapter.

If you use heavy-duty handwashing powders, check that they are thoroughly dissolved, or you'll get patchiness. Never pour powder direct on to clothes – today's detergents are far too powerful, containing sodium perborate bleaches and fluorescers which cause almost immediate colour loss. Old, weak fabrics can literally disintegrate in front of your eyes. (You can rub heavily soiled areas with soft white toilet soap or Sunlight soap.) Stir for at least a minute before immersing articles and rinse three times in cold water or your clothes will feel stiff and uncomfortable and look blotchy. If fabrics are old never leave them to soak, and the same applies to all wools and silks.

Colour-fast test

This is essential for old silks and wools and for checking ethnic clothes. Damp a piece of the hem or seam allowance and iron a piece of dry white fabric on to it. If any colour blots off, wash the article separately, in very cold suds, and rinse at once in cool water. Immediately soak up excess moisture with an old towel. If colour is very loose, dry-cleaning is advisable. (Salt in the rinsing water can sometimes reduce colour loss.)

Pre-wash and pre-soaking aids

Absolute 'musts' are Frend, Shout and a packet of Bio-tex. These products are useful on all washable/colour-fast old clothes made of cotton and manmades as they lift off ingrained grease and quite a few stains, notably make-up, grass and tar (see Chapter 5). Similarly soaking in biological powders can remove many a stubborn stain with a protein base. The disadvantage is that neither pre-soak methods can be used on wool or silk as some products contain enzymes that weaken the animal fibre of these materials. Biological detergents do not function at temperatures higher than 60°C (140°F), and hot water in fact sets stains. Greasy-necked silk shirts or sweaters can be treated with Lux soapflakes or Dreft and 1 tablespoon of borax to each gallon of lukewarm water. Dissolve borax and soapflakes in a little hot water, and add to the lukewarm washing water. Add 1 tablespoon of dissolved borax to the final rinsing water. Alternatively use Tenestar, a branded washing product specially formulated for silk. The manufacturers suggest applying a little of the Tenestar solution neat for heavily soiled and stained areas, leaving for 10–15 minutes before washing in Tenestar. Use two capfuls to 5 litres (10 pints) of water.

Adding fluorescers

Adding that little blue bag – Reckitt's have been going since 1890 – isn't so necessary these days as detergents have their own fluorescers. A little goes a long way, but a little added blue can improve that dingy 'creamy' look some white cottons develop after a time. They are available in liquid form to add during machine-wash cycles, or in a final rinse of handwashing.

To soak or not to soak?

Do not soak old or secondhand clothes either of unknown or obviously fragile fabrics, or silks and woollens. The only time soaking is beneficial is for cottons and manmades when dyes are colour-fast and articles more or less new. Check that the washing powder is always completely dissolved before immersing items and that the water temperature is not too hot for the dye or fabric type; the container should be large enough to allow for easy movement. Check too, that whites and coloureds are not soaked together – watch out for tights – these are notoriously unfast, as are some deep-dyed ethnic cottons and inexpensive T-shirts. Same goes for home-dyed articles – it's always wise to wash these separately. Anything with metal fastenings should not be soaked overnight, this can encourage rust and iron mould stains. Some buttons can be affected by long soaking, especially old plastic ones which can dissolve or discolour dramatically.

Fabric rinses

A boon for 'washed-in' clothes, these reduce static, and their action bulks out fibre, preventing nylon and polyester petticoats from clinging. Most, like Lenor, also reduce creases and make ironing easier, particularly silk. Comfort and supermarket own-line brands are pleasantly perfumed, so secondhand clothes smell sweet after treatment. I have had marked successes with many a wornout Forties crêpe-de-chine dress, viscose and silk garments.

Starches and stiffeners

Our ancestors used to starch their clothes for the same reasons we do: to increase the body and crispness of thin, flimsy fabrics and to add greater resilience to wear and soiling. Maize starch used for cottons and linens, however, is not suitable for silk, wool, or manmade fabrics. Nor should starched clothes be stored over winter, as grubs could be attracted. Folding delicate old starched cottons should also be avoided as fibres can wear badly at creases and folds. Traditional starch in powder form can still be bought; it is added to boiling water to form a smooth paste. (One teaspoon of Laundry Borax = 4 oz of starch dissolved in boiling water improves the final gloss and prevents the iron from sticking.) This old method has largely been superseded by today's more convenient ready-mixed starches. While spray-on plastic stiffeners such as Fabulon contain silicones to ease ironing operations, particularly on polyester, nylon ciré and denims and are useful in treating specific areas such as collars and cuffs.

For a *very crisp* finish suitable for overalls, dicky shirt fronts, cuffs and collars use 2 heaped tablespoons of starch to 2.2 litres (4 pints) of water.

For a *medium-crisp* finish: use 2 heaped tablespoons to 2.2 litres.

For a *light* finish suitable for cotton lace trimmings and redressing ostrich feathers use half a tablespoon to 2.2 litres.

Alternative stiffeners

Water rice has been boiled in, is the traditional Japanese starch used for cotton kimonos (Yukata). The Victorians resorted to sugared water and milk for stiffening lace and ribbons. Less sticky is using gum arabic to restore old silk to its former lustre. The following recipe is good for reviving tired silk twill headscarves: 1/2 teaspoons of gum arabic (depending on stiffness required) should be thoroughly mixed to 1 pint of cold water: Immerse scarf in this solution for about 2 minutes gently manipulating fabric. (For further silk washing see Chapter 4.)

Improving dingy whites

Despite the claims of detergent manufacturers, white fabrics can stay depressingly grey or yellowed, especially when washed in launderettes where temperatures may not be high enough for detergent bleaches to work. If your clothes were secondhand bargains, someone else's poor washing is probably to blame; items may have been discarded for that very reason.

Cotton and linen

Examine the fabric of your Victorian nightie, petticoat, bloomers, or whatever, before treating. If the fibres look delicate, if the garment has been darned, or if there is a delicate lace trimming, the following method is not advisable. The same applies to any cotton with special finishes. Pre-soak in Bio-tex detergent, preferably overnight. Wash at the highest temperature you can, and dry outside in the sun if possible. If yellowness persists, wet the article again and soak in hydrogen peroxide. Alternatively, soak the article in Stain Devil rewhitening or Acdo Glo-white solution according to instructions. Finish by rinsing in water with a drop of Reckitt's Blue. For heavily soiled white overalls: Kleeneze, KP4 detergent and Supakleen oxygen-based additive bleach are useful.

Manmades

Acrylics may respond to an overnight soak in a heavy-duty detergent such as Drive, Surf or Radiant. Rinse in a dilute solution of household bleach according to container instructions.

Elasticated fabrics. No really successful method exists to whiten these, but some can be dyed (see Chapter 7).

Nylon responds to Dylon's Nylon White.

Polyester clothes can be treated with Dylon's Cold Water Curtain White which works just as well for white blouses and shirts as it does for net curtains.

Silk

Acdo Glo-white works well with silk garments. Soak for ten to fifteen minutes before rinsing with a touch of Reckitt's Blue. Hydrogen peroxide (one part 20–volume strength to six parts cold water) can also be effective, but exercise caution and soak for no longer than twenty minutes.

Wool

Acdo Glo-white solution (soak for five to ten minutes), or treat with Dylon Super White.

Note. Water softeners are used in hard-water areas to prevent scale building up in washing-machines. Use sparingly, or not at all, as they may yellow silk and wool. Ordinary washing soda, a cheaper method of softening water, has the same yellowing effect.

Special washing, cleaning and care

Silk

1   Before washing, test for colour-fastness. Dip a small piece of the silk in cold or tepid water. Take a piece of white cotton fabric and lay it over the silk, then press with a warm iron. If there is any transfer of colour to the white fabric do not wash the item.

2   Never soak, boil or bleach silk.

3   Never try to remove old stains yourself. Silk threads – light colours only – may be handwashed in tepid water (40°C maximum 104°F) with the addition of a washing product for delicate lingerie, e.g. soapflakes or gentle detergent. Rinse thoroughly three times using hand-hot water for each rinse.

4   Roll the article in a clean dry towel to remove surplus water. Never leave it in a towel or in a crumpled condition. Allow to dry if necessary in an airy place away from the sun and direct heat, but only until the material is slightly and evenly damp.

5   Iron silk on the wrong side while it is still damp with a cool iron, taking special care not to apply too great a pressure over seams. Do not use a steam iron and do not attempt to re-damp locally. Finish off lightly on the right side.

Note.   Be very careful with dark colours – navy, dark brown, bright red. These shades are obtained by the addition of colouring agents and dyeing cannot be fast. If in doubt over any silk, seek professional advice (see Directory).

Lace

Pieces of lace found in markets or junk shops will probably need a good clean before you use them, but the delicate handworked samples need only to be washed very gently. To do this, fill a wide-necked jar with pure soap diluted with warm distilled water and place the lace inside. Shake for a few minutes and repeat the process with clean, soapy water. Rinse in the same way. If the lace is made of silk add ½ teaspoonful of methylated spirit to the rinsing water to give extra gloss. Using this bottle method you don't handle the lace as much, thus reducing the risk of tearing. To dry, roll the lace in a towel and then pin out on a board to dry naturally. Special brass lace pins should be used to avoid rust stains. Pin out any straight edges first so the lace retains its shape. If the lace has been stored, it may be discoloured with tiny brown spots: treat cotton lace with mild household bleach, checking dilution instructions on bottle. For manmade lace, soak in hydrogen peroxide solution (one part 20-volume strength to nine parts water). In both cases inspect frequently as delicate lace may disintegrate if left in bleach for a long time. Rinse thoroughly in distilled water as this prevents iron mould forming. If the lace is limp you can stiffen it in a weak solution of household starch.

Costume conservators soak lace in several baths of distilled water to loosen dirt. Then they wash it in warm water with a few drops of Vulpex (see Glossary) before carefully rinsing in warm water. If it is particularly delicate, the lace is supported by stitching (with large tacking stitches) to a piece of fine lawn or net.

FRAGILE FABRICS
COSTUME CONSERVATORS' TIPS

1 Begin any cleaning of old velvets, tapestries and embroideries by fixing a piece of filtration fabric over and vacuuming through this. A small vacuum cleaner of the type used in car interiors is ideal.

2 Check colour-fastness by making a test on a scrap of fabric.

3 Check fabric has no special finish to give it a glaze or sheen, as these are probably water-soluble and cannot be restored after washing out. The water pattern on moiré silk is formed by running fabric through patterned rollers.

4 Rinse old fabrics in cool, distilled water as this helps prevent iron mould.

5 Smallish, fragile items of clothing can be soaked for approximately one hour in flat photographic developer trays – these support the weight of the fabric and so prevent tension. Change the water three times and if the fabric is not clean use one of the following agents: Lissapol N, or Spirit Soap or Saponaria.

6 Never use very hot water as it will harden and shrink wool and linen, for example. Do not rub or wring old fabrics or use harsh commercial detergents as these may contain harmful bleaches and additives.

7 Remove excess moisture by pressing with a white towel or white blotting paper.

8 Pin out to dry on a board covered with towelling and allow to dry naturally. Never use direct heat or strong sunlight as this may weaken old fabric and fade colours.

9 Home drycleaning can be done in the following way when washing is not suitable: heat potato flour in a double saucepan and spread over fabric surface. Brush off the flour and the dirt before the flour cools.

10 Storage. Cover some large cardboard rolls with acid-free tissue-paper and wrap pieces of lace or silk, for example, around them. Hard folds eventually rot fabric. Do not cover fabrics with polythene as this attracts dust and static electricity, and in some cases can harbour damp.

11 Avoid wearing fragile fabrics in hot sun, or sitting about in them for too long.

12 Don't spray old fabrics with insecticides, such as mothkiller, or treat with moisture and dirt repellent. Long-term effects are not known and dyes may be affected.

5

Drycleaning and Stain Removal

Specialist drycleaners can literally clean anything, and undertake particularly difficult jobs – such as cleaning clothes that have been in house fires. One firm I know took three weeks to clean a suit that had been covered in gloss and emulsion paint – its owner had used it for decorating! Garments, including antique clothes, sometimes need several types of cleaning – they may be trimmed in suede, old lace, sequins or fur with no convenient care label.

Even if your local cleaner cannot cope with a particular job they can probably put you in touch with a specialist firm, one who employs an on-the-spot textile chemist. The important thing in the case of drycleanable items is to tell the drycleaner that the clothes are second-hand and stains are unidentifiable. Textile chemists can usually identify a stain; if they are unable to remove it, they may suggest ways to camouflage.

Don't treat old unidentifiable stains yourself – it often only makes matters worse and a cleaner's job that much harder. Never be embarrassed to tell your cleaner that clothes are secondhand; point out any problems such as stains, fabric rips, holes, 'shine', let-down hem marks. Old fabric care labels may be missing, or faded and illegible, so cleaners may need to make special tests beforehand. However, some stains may defy even the experts. Red lollipop dyes and other sugar-based stains may be invisible until a garment is drycleaned, when they appear as brownish marks having 'caramelized' in the heat. Perspiration stains on the underarms of jackets, blouses and dresses are water-based and can sometimes be treated successfully. Drycleaners have steam guns for dispersing 'ring' marks, but if the fabric is discoloured or faded as a result of deodorant build-up, there's not much hope of restoring its original condition.

The ideal is not to let garments get too dirty in the first place, but of course if they are secondhand you will not be able to do much about it. Trousers should not be worn more than three times before drycleaning, and certainly not on consecutive days. Neither is it wise to skimp on special drycleaning for white or pastel-coloured fabrics; less scrupulous cleaners have been known to toss these into the same machine as coloured garments. At coin-operated cleaners the spirits and solvents are sometimes changed less frequently than they should be, although you may be lucky enough to encounter the first cleaning of the day. Items such as silk blouses can come out looking disappointingly grey when the solvent is exhausted. Coin-ops also don't provide the professional pressing service which makes second-hand clothes look so bandbox. Some cleaners do, however, provide a pressing service without insisting you have your clothes cleaned by them.

If the care label has a drycleaning circle underlined, or contains the letter F in the circle, it should not be coin-op cleaned. It's a good idea to make your own drawstring net bags for putting clothes in. Make them in various sizes (use nylon net curtaining); they are very useful for DIY drycleaning small items such as ties and scarves and items such as pleated skirts and beaded dresses. As with washing, any sewing repairs should be done before cleaning. Subsequent pressing will help to make any mends less visible.

Cleaning equipment

You'll need the following chemicals and cleaners if you want to keep secondhand or new clothes looking good. When you know what the stain is, you should be able to remove it successfully yourself.

1 *Cotton-wool buds* which are useful for dealing with tiny spots.
2 *Cotton-wool* (cheapest variety).
3 *Clean white cotton rags and tissues,* the more absorbent the better.
4 *Grease solvents:*
   i Liquids, e.g. Dabitoff
   ii Aerosols, e.g. Goddard's Dry-Clean. They contain powder to absorb the stain lifted out by the solvent.
   iii Paste/jelly solvents, e.g. K2r Stain Remover.
   iv Turpentine substitute. White spirit and lighter fuel are effective solvents.

v Petrol can be used as an alternative to solvents, but its smell lingers. (Lighter fuel is more manageable, see Glossary.)

5 *Oxygen bleach* Many of the commonly occurring stains require bleaching action to remove them. Heavy-duty washing powders contain an oxidizing bleach, e.g. sodium perborate, which removes stains such as fruit juice, by oxidation. It works at all temperatures, but is particularly effective in the wash at temperatures of 60°C (140°F) and above. A heavy-duty powder can be a soap powder like Persil, a synthetic detergent powder like Surf, Omo or a solvent powder like Drive, or a low sudsing powder for automatic machines like Persil Automatic.

Oxygen bleach such as hydrogen peroxide may be used on wool and silk. Hypochlorite bleach, such as Domestos, may be used on white cottons (without special finishes) and linens, but is not suitable for bleaching Victorian cottons.

Caution

1 Always test for colour-fastness before using bleach.
2 Never use undiluted hypochlorite bleach on any article.
3 Never use hypochlorite bleach on wool, silk, flame-resistant or easy-care finishes.
4 Use in correct dilution, i.e. 14 ml to 1 litre of cold water (½ fl oz to 2 pints) for spot stains and 14 ml to 11½ litres of water (½ fl oz to 2½ gallons) for large stains.
5 Use 20 vol. hydrogen peroxide diluted: one part solution to four parts water.

Stain treatment

1 Treat all stains as soon as possible, admittedly not easy with secondhand clothes. The longer they are left on the fabric the more difficult they will be to remove.
2 If treated quickly, washing powder and water is often all that is necessary. If this does not remove the stain, and alternative treatments are available, try the mildest one first.
3 Apart from those stains which should be soaked in cold water first, it is best to be on the safe side by using only warm suds on other stains.
4 Make sure your chemical or cleaner is fresh: some have only a short active life.

5 Tests must be made to see whether a chemical or solvent is suitable for all colours. Try to do this on an inconspicuous part of the garment or article.

6 Always place the area to be treated over an absorbent cloth. An old piece of towelling is ideal.

7 In order to avoid a ring, first treat an area around the stain, and then work in towards the centre of the stain. Don't rub, use pressure: place a pad of solvent on the right side of the fabric, tissues underneath and on top of stain and press down. Use clean tissues for each pressing, until the stain has disappeared and the tissue comes away.

8 When a stained part of a fabric has to be dipped or soaked in a solution, hold the cloth by this area and then twist the unstained parts to prevent the solution spreading when the stained area is immersed in the solution.

9 If it is the type of stain that is treated with solvent first and by washing afterwards, wash the garment in good rich suds immediately after treatment, before the fluid has dried on the fabric.

10 Keep any cleaning preparations out of children's reach. The cup or basin used must be washed after use. Keep all chemicals clearly labelled and do not put in old lemonade bottles, for example.

11 Many solvents are highly inflammable, and some are poisonous. Treat with care, and never use near a naked flame.

12 Always work in a well-ventilated room and do not smoke.

13 Do not use methylated spirit on acetates or triacetates; or oxalic acid or acetone on nylon and acetates (they will melt). White spirit may be used.

14 Do not add ammonia to hydrogen peroxide for use on wool. Test carefully on coloured fabrics before use.

15 Do not mix chemical and cleaners.

16 Always add acids to water, never water to acid.

Note. A solution of one part of a chemical to, say, three parts water means that whatever is used to measure the chemical is also used for the water in the amounts the figure indicates.

Stains

Adhesives

1 Clear or contact adhesives, such as Bostik or Evostik on fabrics and upholstery should be treated with amyl acetate. Hold absorbent pad on the stained side and dab from the wrong side. Acetate fabric should not be treated with acetone, as it will melt and disintegrate; try white spirit.
2 Latex adhesive on fabrics and upholstery, such as Copydex. If wet, it is removable with damp cloth. If dry, loosen with liquid grease solvent, rub off as much as possible, sponge or launder. A special solvent is available from the manufacturers (see Directory).

Alcohol (beer, spirits, wine, etc.)

Beer stains. Rinse or soak fresh stains in lukewarm water, then launder in heavy-duty detergent. For dried stains launder, then bleach remaining marks on white cottons/linens in hydrogen peroxide solution. Sponge coloured fabrics with a solution 28 ml to ½ litre water (2 tbs to 1 pint water) of white vinegar. Sponge acetates with borax paste mixed according to the packet instructions (see Glossary).

Spirit stains. Rinse with clear, warm water, then launder in heavy-duty detergent at the highest temperature for the fibre type.

Wine stains (including fruit juices). Rinse in warm water or soak and sponge in a warm detergent solution. Wine is an oxidizable stain, which can be removed in a high temperature wash. When high temperature washing or soaking is not appropriate, on wool for example, treat difficult stains with hydrogen peroxide.

Beer (see Alcohol)

Blood

This method also applies to other protein-based stains such as milk, egg, gravy, meat juices, chocolate, ice-cream. Soak in cold water and salt, or warm biological detergent solution. Launder for fibre type. Soak stubborn stains in hydrogen peroxide solution plus a few drops of ammonia. Rinse well. *Note.* Hot water will set stains. Most protein stains are easily removed when fresh.

Boot polish (see Grease)

Candle wax

Lift off surface deposit with fingernail. Sandwich stained area in clean blotting-paper, melt out remainder with warm iron. Keep moving the paper so that the unused sections absorb the wax. Use grease solvent to remove any final trace. On upholstery, melt out wax with moderately hot iron over clean blotting-paper; remove remainder by dabbing with methylated spirit. Aerosol powder sprays may also be used.

Chewing-gum

Harden the gum by placing the garment in a fridge or holding a plastic bag containing ice cubes against it. It can then be cracked and picked off. Use liquid grease solvent (not on proofed articles) or rub in Swarfega hand cleanser. Launder or sponge with warm water. Polyclens Plus paint brush cleaner and appropriate Stain Devil remover are also effective.

Chocolate (see Blood)

Coffee, tea

These stains can usually be washed out in good rich suds. Put into soak, or wash, as soon as possible. Difficult stains should be treated with hydrogen peroxide or appropriate Stain Devil remover.

Creosote, tar

Scrape off surplus. Treat small stains with a pre-wash stain remover, such as Frend or Shout; leave for 1 minute; dab area with cotton-wool, or a grease solvent or petrol over absorbent pad (caution: solvents and petrol are inflammable). Wash thoroughly to remove final traces of stain. If the fabric is not washable, professional cleaning is essential.

Dyes

There are no simple rules. For many coloured fabrics and particularly for fabrics which are not washable, professional treatment is needed. Soak white and fast-coloured fabrics (not wool, silk or fabrics with flame-resistant finishes) in a solution of heavy-duty detergent. Treat any remaining dye on white articles with a dye-stripper such as

Dygon. Follow the manufacturer's instructions for dye stain removal. Bear in mind that if the dye is on a coloured article, the original colour may be affected by the dye-solvent treatment.

Egg (see Blood)

Fats (see Grease)

Flower

This also applies to grass stains. Sponge with methylated spirit. For bad stains, warm the spirit first by placing the open container in a bowl of hot water away from any naked flame. Wash through in good, rich suds. To remove green colouring, moisten with glycerine then wash. Alternatively, use a pre-wash stain remover such as Frend or Shout.

Small grass stains on cricket flannels may respond to K2r Stain Remover. If not suitable for washing they should be cleaned professionally.

Fruit juice (see Alcohol)

Grass (see Flower)

Gravy (see Blood)

Grease

These methods also apply to fats and oils, including boot and shoe polish, lipstick, wax polish.

Heavy stains should be treated with a grease solvent such as Frend or Shout before washing. Alternatively, soak in a washing solution of solvent detergent such as Drive; a subsequent washing at the maximum temperature recommended for the fabric should remove most grease stains.

Professional advice may be needed for fabric unsuitable for washing, but it may help to spread talc over small marks, brushing off as it absorbs grease, and repeating until finally brushing clean. Alternatively, use an aerosol spray (such as Goddard's Dry-Clean) or press with a warm iron over clean blotting paper.

Hair lacquer (see Nail varnish)

Ice-cream (see Blood)

Ink

Washable ink. Sponge or rub under cold water. Launder in heavy-duty detergent.

Permanent ink. Dab with a pad soaked in methylated spirit. Wash in detergent solution. Large areas must be professionally drycleaned.

Ballpoint. Dab lightly with cotton-wool moistened with methylated spirit, or use grease solvent. Sponge with warm water or launder. Have delicate fabrics or bad marks cleaned professionally.

Felt-tip ink. Dab small marks with methylated spirit and treat as for ballpoint ink. Felt-tip on wall coverings may be sponged with neat Handy Andy, dishwashing liquid, or methylated spirit.

Duplicating machine ink. Treat with castor oil, then wash if possible in strong detergent solution. Repeat several times if necessary.

Iodine

Wash immediately. Old stains can be treated by soaking in a solution of Hypo (sodium thiosulphate), 3 ml to 100 ml (½ teaspoon to 4 fl oz) warm water.

Iron mould

On linens or handkerchiefs soak stains in lemon juice and press under a piece of damp fabric. Repeat until stain disappears. Use oxalic acid – 3 ml to 250 ml (½ tsp to ½ pint) hot water on cotton or linen. If coloured, test first. (Caution: oxalic acid is poisonous.) On silk and wool, use the appropriate Stain Devil remover, then rinse well and wash. A proprietary rust remover, such as Movol, may be used on white fabrics. Test on a scrap first. Wash immediately. Lemon juice has a gentler action and is advised for very fragile, old fabrics.

Jam

Fresh stains usually wash out. Soak old stains in borax paste made up as per the packet instructions or heavy-duty detergent solution. If some stains remain, try hydrogen peroxide. Launder. For fabrics which cannot be washed, scrape off as much as possible, and try sponging with cloth moistened with solution of dishwashing liquid. Follow with a clean cloth well wrung out in clear water.

Lipstick (see Grease)

Make-up (see also Lipstick, Mascara)

Applies to foundation cream, moisturizer, base, etc. Wipe fresh stains. Soak for 5 minutes in a weak ammonia solution: 5 ml to 500 ml water (1 standard medicine spoon to 1 pint). Rinse well. Launder in a solvent detergent solution at highest temperature for the fibre type.

Dried stains may be softened with glycerine before washing in a solvent detergent.

For fabrics which cannot be washed, wipe up wet deposit or brush dried one. Apply a grease solvent – preferably an aerosol such as Shout or Frend. Allow to dry and brush lightly.

Mascara

Treat as above with aerosol spray, followed by diluted ammonia (mixed as above). Alternatively, soak overnight if necessary in a strong solution of solvent detergent, and then wash.

Meat juices (see Blood)

Metal polish

Blot residue and dab area with white spirit. When dry brush off powdery deposit. Launder in heavy-duty detergent (if washable) according to fibre type.

Mildew

While growth is fresh, laundering in heavy-duty detergent usually removes it. Chlorine bleach (1 part to 10 parts water) plus 1 tablespoon vinegar, may be used on whites, but not on crease-resistant, drip-dry or embossed fabrics. Soak other white fabrics – except nylon – in one part hydrogen peroxide to four parts water.

On coloured fabrics, rub dampened areas with hard soap and dry in the sun. Follow with repeated laundering to reduce marks.

For fabrics which cannot be washed, spray with Mystox (5% in a solution with white spirit). Smell should disappear after a few days. (See Directory for distributors.)

Milk (see Blood)

Nail varnish

Applies also to Hair lacquer. Wipe immediately with tissues or cotton wool with absorbent pad under stain. For all fabrics use amyl acetate, but test a small area first. Be particularly careful with acetates. Dab remaining colour with methylated spirit followed by careful laundering in heavy-duty detergent.

Oils (see Grease)

Paints

Prompt treatment is most important. Some paints, such as Dulux Silthane Silk, can be washed out in mild detergent or by sponging carefully when stain is fresh. Seek professional advice for napped fabrics, such as corduroy or velvet.

Oil-based paint. Dab fresh stains with white spirit or Polyclens Plus and sponge with cold water. Launder if possible. Dried stains on fabrics require drycleaning: tell drycleaner the nature of the stain.

Emulsion paint. Sponge fresh stains with cold water, then launder. If ignored, a plastic film will develop which cannot later be removed.

Paraffin

Remove surplus immediately as oil can penetrate fibres rapidly. Apply an aerosol dry spray, such as Frend or Shout, repeat if necessary. If washable, launder in solvent detergent.

Perfume

Rinse immediately. Lubricate a dried stain with glycerine solution before laundering.

For fabrics unsuitable for washing, lubricate with glycerine, then wipe lightly with cloth wrung out in warm water. Blot.

Perspiration

Sponge fresh stain with a weak solution of ammonia, i.e. 5 ml to 500 ml water (1 standard medicine spoon to 1 pint), then rinse. If colour is affected, sponge with vinegar, then rinse. Bleach white cotton in solution of hydrogen peroxide or soak in detergent solution. For fabrics unsuitable for washing, dab with white vinegar solution 5 ml of vinegar to 250 ml (one standard medicine spoon to ½ pint) of warm water to deodorize area. Garments with acetate linings should be professionally drycleaned. Spray with Mystox solution if odour is still persistent, then dryclean.

Rust

Treat as for iron mould and use oxalic acid 3 ml to 250 ml (½ tsp to ½ pint) hot water on cotton or linen. Use oxalic acid with care as it is poisonous. On silk, wool and nylon, use the appropriate Stain Devil remover, then rinse well and wash.

Scorch marks

Rub light marks immediately under cold running water, and then soak in warm borax solution made up as per the packet instructions. Rinse well and launder if possible. On whites careful bleaching with hydrogen peroxide (one part to four parts of water) is a last remedy. If fibres are damaged, there is no remedy.

Shoe polish (see Grease)

Spirits (see Alcohol)

Tar (see Creosote)

Tea (see Coffee)

Urine

Cold rinse, then launder in heavy-duty detergent. Soak dried marks in detergent solution according to fibre type.

Vomit

Remove surface deposit, rinse well under running cold water. Soak and launder in heavy-duty detergent solution according to fibre type. For fabrics which cannot be washed, remove deposit and sponge with warm water with a few drops of ammonia added. Blot.

Wax polish (see Grease)

Wine (see Alcohol)

———6———
Be Your Own Valet

General clothes care

I once shared a flat with a girl who got up at the crack of dawn every day to press her trousers. She obviously hadn't heard about Keep-a-Krease, a drycleaning service that guarantees knife-edged trouser creases for six months.

The trouble with clothes care is that it takes time and organization. Even new clothes, unless they're properly looked after, will soon look tacky and secondhand if buttons are falling off and pleats are falling out. Hanging hems, clinging dog's hairs and snagged fabrics all spoil the smartest outfits. Conspicuous Thrift clothes care means working at it whether it's a sleek, well-groomed Sloane Ranger look or a carefully contrived sporty impression you're after. So avoid the temptation at the end of the day to sling your clothes into a heap, as there they will crease up more because of body warmth. Change into something else if you want to relax but keep your workclothes smart. Fold sweaters neatly. Check your wardrobe is doing an efficient storage job – clothes shouldn't be crammed together; make periodic checks and wrap those things you're not wearing in acid-free tissue-paper (this prevents fibre damage) before storing away in cardboard boxes, or give them to charity shops if you've really gone off them. Rows of hooks fixed to the inside of your wardrobe door for hanging up belts by the buckles are also useful to organize ribbons, scarves, and ties so that you can see them at a glance. Fix some small plastic bins, from DIY shops, to a wardrobe interior for socks and underwear. See-through plastic or wire mesh drawers can take sweaters and knitted items as these should not be hung up. Neither should antique clothes: costume conservators store dresses flat in acid-free tissue in an architect's plan-chest as hanging puts undue strain on the shoulders.

Be careful with clothes-hangers. I have seen horrible damage done to clothes at antique costume sales of all places: where thin wire ones were poking out and ripping the sleeves of Twenties chiffon dresses. By the end of the afternoon they'd slipped off the hangers and been replaced so many times that the shoulders were in shreds. Invest in some padded coat-hangers or shaped wooden or plastic ones, even though they are more expensive. Shoulders on tailored garments are much better for it, as wire ones can permanently distort shoulderlines if clothes are left hanging too long. Proper trouser- and skirt-hangers keep items secure and stop them slipping off. Zip-up dust-cover bags prevent dust forming on the shoulders as do cotton fabric shoulder-covers. Use a piece of sticky-tape to remove dust rather than a clothes-brush as it is less likely to damage fibres. It's a good idea to air your clothes regularly: take them out of protective bags and hang them outside. Moths and grubs dislike airings and sunlight. Metal buttons and copper studs look better for a shine-up with the appropriate metal polish. To avoid staining the fabric cut out protective cardboard collars. Antique buttons and those in fragile or delicate materials should be covered in foil before sending to the drycleaners.

When it comes to fragile clothes it's best to dryclean and store them flat whether old or new. This goes for anything likely to pull out of shape, such as knitwear and jersey fabrics. Some fabrics develop a shine from rubbing caused by wear – on the seats of suits, skirts and trousers, for example. The remedy is to brush the area lightly to remove dust and then sponge with a solution of one teaspoon of ammonia to 500 ml (1 pint) of water. Afterwards, sponge with clean water. When the fabric is thoroughly dry, press using a damp cloth, lifting the iron up and down for each part of the garment; do not iron in strokes. Baggy knees and seats can be corrected by pressing with a very damp cloth and applying pressure again, in an up-and-down movement; the steam should shrink the fabric back into place.

Ironing (See ironing symbols, page 37.)

First of all check your iron. Some have worn-out thermostat controls which means you could ruin something when pressing it. If the thermostat is no longer accurate, get an electrical shop to repair it. It is worth investing in two irons, the ordinary and steam variety.

Steam irons are marvellous for today's cottons and linens, particularly if used in conjunction with spray-on starches, but their action may be too vigorous for old, fragile clothes. And while steam irons are invaluable for professional results, on newish clothes, check that the steam holes are not furred up; Sunbeam do a special cleaner. Sole plates may become sticky, too, after using adhesive webbing, so clean with Dabitoff sole plate cleaner. Additional ironing aids such as a sleeveboard are helpful with blouses and shirts. If you plan to do tailoring alterations, there are a number of other useful aids.

Most embroidered fabrics, such as Chinese silk blouses and Indian cottons, should be ironed from the back. Certain fabrics, such as starched cottons and Tricel, benefit from ironing on the front. To prevent a shine on woollens and viscose, use a damp pressing cloth. Avoid ironing buttons, zips, elastic and elasticated cuffs and panels. Don't iron on the right side over seams and hems as they will leave a mark. Turn clothes inside out and press up to seams and hem stitchlines from the wrong side, using a damp pressing cloth over another thicker one. Finally a word about pressing cloths. Some sewing experts maintain that the special ones as sold in haberdashery shops are unnecessary for professional results: all that's needed is a well dampened piece of clean muslin. This is a matter of personal choice. Much more important is to know the difference between pressing and ironing. Ironing is the application of swift strokes along the fabric applying some pressure. Pressing is the holding of the iron on the same spot and applying heavy pressure before lifting the iron up and repeating the process. Ironing when pressing is indicated, may mean a fabric is stretched irretrievably out of shape. On the other hand, iron-on webbings will not adhere properly to a fabric unless pressed very firmly with a hot iron and a damp cloth.

As with every craft, ironing has a method. This is how to iron a shirt: lay the collar flat and iron first on the wrong side and then the right side; this keeps it in good shape. Iron one side of the yoke and then repeat with the second side of the yoke. Iron the back; if the shirt can be opened out flat this is simplest, otherwise thread the shirt over the ironing-board. If ironing on a table you may find it easier to 'fold' the shirt by threading one sleeve through the other sleeve if you cannot open out the shirt quite flat; this enables you to iron right up to the neckband or collar. Iron the first cuff on the wrong side, and then the right side. Iron the sleeve on one side, then the other. Repeat with the second cuff and sleeve, make quite sure the first sleeve is arranged so it does not become creased.

Arrange the shirt so that the front of the centre opening is quite flat; iron the front of the shirt. Many people prefer to put shirts on a hanger; correct folding, however, is all part of the craft.

To fold a shirt. Button up the shirt if you intend to fold it.

Lay the shirt on the ironing board or table with the front downwards. Take one side and sleeve and bring this so the sleeve is hanging down the centre back. Lift the cuff and place this just below the collar, making a neat fold. Repeat with the second sleeve; you now have a neat shape. Bring up the tail part of the shirt about one third of the length. Bring down the front of the shirt and lightly finish this with the iron.

Drycleaners' alterations and valeting

Many drycleaners now employ a highly skilled tailor who can transform shapeless, ill-fitting clothes into instant fashion. Almost anything is possible from completely relining and remodelling coats, suits and dresses to adding new pockets, making jacket vents and replacing missing fabric belts. Biggest boon of all is making tailored buttonholes – homemade ones can mar a garment. Drycleaners usually expect clothes altered on their premises to include cleaning, although they don't always insist on it, but pressing is recommended. The following will help you make the most of services on offer.

1   Check that your cleaner is a member of the Association of British Launderers and Cleaners (ABLC). If you have any complaints, laundering or drycleaning queries, or wish to know of local firms undertaking expert cleaning of suede or antique clothes, or to locate specialist dyeing firms contact them at the Customer Advisory Bureau, Association of British Launderers and Cleaners (see Directory for address).

2   For a really successful tailored fit women should wear the bra, belt and shoes they intend wearing when clothes are finished. According to one Sketchley tailor, many of her customers turn up without bra and belt and wearing flat shoes only to find that finished hems, seams and darts need further adjusting. If you or the tailor cannot manage fitting appointments – pin the fabric where you want adjustments

made, then write out a list of your measurements and what you want done. Not the most satisfactory way of achieving a good fit, but the tailor will do his or her best.

3   Avoid taking secondhand clothes in for alteration when dry-cleaners are busiest: lunchtimes, early mornings, late evenings and bank-holiday Saturdays are not the best times for stating problems in detail. Give yourself time to explain exactly what you want and write a note of these points. In the case of major alterations be prepared to wait at least a fortnight. Always ask the tailor for an estimate of any alterations beforehand.

4   Expect to pay for any extra service on top of the drycleaning bill. These vary a good deal depending on cleaners and the area, so shop around. Knife-pleating in kilts and circular sunray skirts, for instance, can be costly, so be wary about secondhand pleated skirts bargains unless you are prepared to tack in pleats and press them yourself after cleaning. Alternatively, you can ask a cleaner to wrap a pleated skirt in a net bag before cleaning; it helps the pleats stay put. Delicate silk blouses and evening dresses may also need careful ironing – known as 'hand-finishing'. Charges vary according to style and fabric. Invisible mending and re-weaving is very pricey, usually being sent out to experts. Charges tend to be calculated by the inch of the repair. Patterned rather than plain fabrics usually give better results. Expert patching is half the price of invisible mending, but whether or not it's worth the saving depends on whether clothes are casual or smart and whether the patch will look too obvious.

Storage

Dust protectors

1   Use old shirts to cover the shoulders of clothes, or make cotton cover bags from old sheeting. Cotton covers are better for storing clothes than polythene bags from the drycleaners or nylon ready-made ones as both types tend to attract static electricity. Cotton bags open at the top and closed at the base are the best for long-term clothes storage.

2   Check that your wardrobe doors, bedroom windows and floor coverings fit well and that there are no dust traps.

3   Check that your clothes-brushes are clean. Bristle ones have to be cleaned with heated bran (use a baking tin in the oven for twenty minutes) rubbed well into the bristles. After an hour remove the bran by shaking, combing and rubbing with a clean cloth. Washable clothes-brushes should be cleaned several times weekly.

Coat-hangers

1   Never use wire hangers or the shoulders of your clothes will go out of shape. You can make your own padded hangers by covering wooden ones with Terylene wadding and covering with washed calico or gingham. For dresses with heavy skirts and delicate and antique clothes, attach long tapes from the inside tops of the skirts to the hangers to prevent strain on the bodice.

2   Investigate skirt- and trouser-hangers – some designs offer considerable space-saving advantages for tiny wardrobes.

3   Dirndl and circular skirts should never be hung up, even if waist loops are provided, or else hemlines will quickly fall out of shape. Fold in quarters between sheets of acid-free tissue-paper and store flat in a chest-of-drawers.

Acid-free tissue

This is the paper most suited to storing all kinds of clothing. Use it to line chests of drawers, to pad out puffed sleeves and bodices, to roll around any extra long hems of small garments like christening dresses. Where possible, roll delicate silk scarves and shawls around a cardboard roll first covered in acid-free tissue, as this prevents any harmful chemical reaction on the fibres. Rolling fabrics rather than folding prevents shattering the fibre. Acid-free tissue is also essential for wrapping around lamé fabrics to prevent tarnishing.

Fabric treatments

Mothproofing and dirt-resisting preventatives can be helpful short-term solutions, but they should not be used on antique clothes. There can be a reaction causing colour changes and fibre damage. Checking clothes regularly, good ventilation and careful cleaning will prevent most damage. Avoid storing starched clothes for any length of time – folding old starched garments such as christening robes, can damage fibres and attract grubs.

Long-term storage

Lastly, if garments are not going to be worn for some time it is worth tacking pockets of overcoats and mackintoshes flat, and tacking the hems of pleated skirts. Keep knitted and accordion-pleated skirts neat by cutting off the foot of an old stocking, and storing skirts in these. Check that the stocking covers the whole skirt length. For preventing hemlines showing on children's dresses, unpick the hems, then wash and press before putting away. When needed again they will be easier to lengthen and show practically no mark.

Sewing repairs

All Conspicuous Thrifters need to know how to carry out at least minor repairs and to have a basic sewing kit (see Chapter 2). Both time and expense can be spared by doing these things yourself – and it is much more rewarding.

Buttonholes

Frayed ones look tacky – on overcoats especially. You can catch loose threads with fray-preventative or clear nail polish. Bound buttonhole repairs can be achieved with iron-on double-sided adhesive webbing. Cut a piece to fit the damaged area and slide it underneath the fabric before pressing into position as instructed. If carried out properly this repair should withstand drycleaning.

Collars

Detachable collars.   Sew tabs of Velcro 6 mm (¼ in) long, rough side up at back and two at the collar front 3 mm (⅛ in) long on either side of the shirt opening. Self-adhesive Velcro 'Spot-ons' also work well.

Instant collars.   If you want to change an existing collared shirt to a collarless one, simply unpick the original collar stitching at the neckband using a seam ripper. Cut a strip of double-sided adhesive webbing the size of the neckband, and slip it inside. Press the collar band with a hot iron and damp cloth.

Cuffs

Detachable cuffs.   Sew 3 mm (⅛ in) tabs of Velcro either side of each cuff opening. Fixing self-adhesive Velcro 'Spot-ons' also works well.

Worn cuffs. These can be trimmed off altogether, hemmed and threaded with elastic. Alternatively, instead of conventional folded-up cuffs, turn them inside out and stitch down.

Darning

Whatever method you choose to repair holes, gashes and three-cornered tears, you must know your fabric's fibre so that the thread matches as near as possible to the warp threads running lengthways. Before patching, see whether the damage can be repaired by darning a few threads taken from the seam or hem. If only short threads are available use a long needle, thread it and pull it through. Wind the next row of stitches around the needle, rethread through the loops and pull through. Repeat if possible until the same scrap of thread is used up.

Machine darning.   This produces an efficient but somewhat noticeable repair. It is perfectly acceptable for overalls and jeans, but less so for dresses and blouses in fine fabrics. Machine darning stitches are very hard to unpick and feel hard to the touch. To do the best job by machine you need an embroidery hoop to prevent puckers. Fit the straight-stitch needle-plate and remove presser foot. Set stitch length at 0, the pressure control at 0 and lower the feed dogs. Stretch the fabric to be darned into a hoop and place under the needle. Lower the presser foot lever even though presser foot is not fitted. Then holding the top thread in your left hand, turn the wheel towards you one full circle. Pull the top thread to draw the bobbin thread through to the surface of the fabric. Check the threads are out of the way and start sewing, all the while moving the hoop from side to side, or backwards and forwards, until the hole has been repaired. If you want long darning stitches move the hoop slowly; for longer stitches, move it quickly.

Woven darns.   Darns on socks should be smooth and stitches should be neat and unobtrusive. Use threads or yarns that match, and if necessary separate the strands so that you're not using more than three at a time. A darning mushroom is useful as it prevents the threads puckering. Place stitching lengthways over the hole, then weave threads across, picking up every other thread. As your thread turns to go back with each row you will have some stitches that are left outside the woven area, and these should be made as neat as possible.

Hems

It's the eleventh hour and someone you know has decided they're going to wear *those* trousers or *that* dress or skirt, and the hem length is not right. Or perhaps you've put on your glad rags only to discover that half the hem is down. The instant solution is usually to use an iron-on adhesive webbing for hems. Simply follow the manufacturer's instructions, making sure that the pressing-cloth is damp and the iron hot enough to fix the webbing effectively. If you wish to remove it at a later date to make a proper hem, soak the webbing until it lifts away.

Patching

As with darning (see above), it is essential to know your fabric's fibre and to understand its construction. Some fabrics are light and delicate, others are heavy and bulky; some unravel easily and are loosely woven, while others are so tightly woven it is hard to find a thread. Some fabrics drape, gather or hold a pleat better than others, and certain patching jobs cannot be successful unless this is understood. Similarly, adding fabric, or making new panel insets, means the fabric weight has to be considered. The grain, or direction, of fabric is very important in patching. During the manufacture a loom is threaded for weaving with warp or lengthways threads. The crossways threads of weft (or woof) threads are woven by the shuttle under and over the warp threads. Where the weft threads turn results in finished edges called selvedges; these are slightly tighter than the rest of the fabric. The warp and weft in the patching fabric should line up with the warp and weft threads of the area to be repaired or the patch will bag and not 'sit' properly on a garment. Ready-made patches resolve this problem to some extent but obviously offer less camouflage as fabrics are rarely identical.

Camouflage patching. You can achieve quick, near-invisible, repairs to cigarette holes and hopeless stains in the following way. Cut a piece of Bondaweb iron-on webbing slightly larger than the hole, then iron on a piece of matching fabric cut from a seam or hem. Remove paper backing and place adhesive-coated patching fabric on the piece to be retained before pressing with a hot iron and damp cloth. Remember, it is important to check that the pressing-cloth is damp enough and the iron hot. On delicate fabrics, just the point of the iron is enough to secure this kind of repair.

Corduroy and velvet patches. These differ slightly from other patching jobs as they not only have to be cut on the straight grain of fabric but also with the nap going in the right direction or repairs will show. Corduroy also has the added complication that the 'grooves' of the corduroy have to be matched exactly. To repair a corduroy hole or tear, cut a square or rectangle from the item to be mended, with two of the edges coming between the corduroy ridges. Clip the corners diagonally and turn in the raw edges. Place the patch under the hole and match the ridges before cutting. Tack the patch in position. Next, working on the wrong side of the fabric stitch the patch to the turned-in edges. Finish by pressing the seams open and trimming excess corner fabric. Oversew edges to prevent corners unravelling.

Reinforcing

Many secondhand dresses and blouses may need reinforcing under the arms, or on the elbows, to prolong life. Reinforcing fabrics should have some 'give'; silk net or chiffon is good on fine wools and silk. Place some white card or paper against the worn part and you'll be able to see how thin it is and how much reinforcement fabric is needed. Always start repairs like this with three running stitches, never a knot as this wears and can rub. Tack the reinforcement fabric in position and then sew tiny running stitches in rows around 3 to 8 mm long on the wrong side of the fabric; rows should be 3 to 8 mm apart. Stitch rows lengthways along the fabric until secure; to avoid puckers, check stitches are not too tight. Trim any frayed edges and press reinforced area from right side of the fabric with a pressing-cloth.

For heavier reinforcement jobs, such as the knees and seats of jeans, the fabric is placed on the right side over the damaged area, tacked and machine-stitched decoratively in position (see Chapter 11). Reinforcing men's tailored trouser seats is not advisable as extra fabric may look odd. If the seats wear through quickly the answer is to wear trousers of tougher quality, such as a mix of wool and polyester rather than pure wool.

Torn pockets. This is an irritating blemish on otherwise perfect bargain jackets or coats. Patch pockets are particularly prone and unless repaired as soon as stitches come undone, they can also tear supporting fabric. When this happens, you will need to reinforce with cotton or a piece of iron-on mending tape. Cut a strip long enough to cover the tear and place it on the wrong side of the fabric. Tack this in position. Using matching thread, darn, using very small stitches across the frayed area. Alternatively, treat the slit with fray preventative and sew a firm bar of stitches either side of the pocket to finish and to prevent further tearing.

Trousers

If hems have frayed along the fold edge coat with fray preventative, or iron on reinforcement tapes (see also Chapter 10.) To maintain pristine creases in jeans fold carefully in the original lines and before each wearing turn inside out and spray the inside of the crease with starch. Turn back again and iron on the wrong side of the fabric, pressing with a damp cloth. Baggy knees on jeans can be prevented by ironing adhesive webbing (Vilene) on the wrong side when the jeans are new. Baggy, shiny seats usually appear when fibres have been subjected to constant wear – serge trousers are particularly prone (see General Clothes Care above).

Waistbands

Saggy waistbands usually mean new stiffening is required. The easiest way is to unpick along the inside edge, cut out the old interfacing and replace with new. If your waist is still the same size and the waistband doesn't need completely replacing, simply press the existing waistband flat with a damp cloth, and then cut a piece of skirt-band iron-on adhesive webbing to the required size. Place this with the rough adhesive side down on the fabric. Press with a hot dry iron and damp cloth. Leave to cool. Finally, fold the waistband along the slotted centre line and press again. Re-stitch the waistband fabric. This kind of repair makes a skirt feel new to wear again – very morale-boosting.

Zips

You're just about to knock everyone off their feet with that new dress bargain or designer jeans bought for 10p when the zip goes. If you haven't time to replace it and can inch your way out of the garment with the zip open no further than the broken bit, a quick rescue job is possible. Fix a safety-pin through the fabric edge to one side of the zip across the zip's front teeth and then again through the fabric edging on the opposite end. When the safety pin is closed it makes a small, barely noticeable bar and prevents the zip opening beyond it.

Special fabrics

Chamois leather

Secondhand garments are usually pretty grubby but unlined items wash well in a special shampoo. A teaspoon of olive oil in the final rinse helps soften the leather, and all trace of soap must be removed or stiffening results. Garments should be gently eased into shape while drying.

Furs

Repairing and altering old or secondhand fur coats are specialized tasks best undertaken by professionals. I have tried quick repair methods such as iron-on tape to reinforce fur that has worn away, but it is not a lasting repair. If you do find a secondhand bargain fur coat, and the lining and condition are fairly clean, treat it to heated bran or silver sand depending on type and colour, this will probably work (see Glossary). If you think it worthwhile, it's probably best to have furs professionally cleaned. If you attempt your own cleaning, then work on one skin panel at a time and stick to the same cleaning method throughout.

Leather

If the leather is washable, then use a good leather shampoo and handle according to the instructions. If the label is missing, it's better not to risk DIY cleaning, because if there's a lining there could be problems with shrinkage. Jackets should be professionally cleaned about every three to four months, depending on how much they are worn. A pair of leather shorts or trousers should really be cleaned after every three wearings.

Antique leather is fashionable these days: if you want to give your old bomber jacket an authentic 'Biggles' patina, simply sandpaper the surface lightly with finest quality abrasive paper. Professional leather curers use a cross between a blow-lamp and a drill to get the current coveted 'pitted look of ages'.

Leatherette and vinyl

One secondhand clothes-shop owner I know achieves good results on soiled white leatherette sleeves by rubbing them with white spirit. Several spray-on cleaners exist specially for leatherettes and vinyls. Car-accessory shops are a good hunting-ground.

Mackintoshes

Severe stain removal is generally best undertaken by a drycleaner as many fabrics are proofed. DIY spot removal and home washing tends to remove this proofing which then has to be replaced. Fabric proofers for making mackintoshes water-repellent also make closely woven fabrics darker and slightly stiffer. They are available from haberdashery departments and camping stores. Many of the raincoats that turn up in charity shops, for example, will have stains, hem-line marks, and belts and buttons missing. It is probably worth having a completely professional overhaul job done on an otherwise good mack, particularly if it only cost a couple of pounds in the first place. Rubberized riding mackintoshes soil easily, but don't try to remove bad grease marks yourself.

For other stains, or a general sprucing up, a coating of dry french chalk may be rubbed in and left overnight before brushing out; alternatively, sponge over with sudsy water. Brush ingrained dirt off cuffs with a nail-brush. Rinse thoroughly and hang up to dry, straightening out any creases. Never press or iron rubberized mackintoshes. Tears can be mended on the wrong side of the fabric with a patch stuck down with rubber solution – the kind sold in bicycle-puncture repair-kits. Pack-flat macks and bags of nylon ciré or parachute nylon can be washed. Rinsing in fabric conditioner prevents creasing; finish with a cool iron.

Suede

Secondhand suede bargains may prove difficult to clean, the main snag being that colours are usually unfast and you get patchy results. Professional leather cleaners re-oil and tint, and that means taking out the lining and then resewing it. If cleaners seem reluctant to accept responsibility for bright colours, you can try leaving on fuller's earth or french chalk for five minutes and then shaking and brushing out. Always use a rubber suede brush, never a wire one, and avoid spot removers. Steaming and brushing with a rubber brush can do wonders to perk up tired suede. Suede garments worn regularly should be treated every three to four weeks.

Swimwear

Always rinse after wearing whether it was an all-day sea-bathing session or a ten-minute swimming-pool dip. Salt and chlorine can affect elastics and colours. Home dyeing is not recommended as dyes will not be permanent. Never roll up wet swimwear, put out to dry on a towel before taking home. Hang up to dry away from strong sunlight.

7
Changing the Colour

Colour, more than anything else, can transform a wardrobe. Basic fashion styles may stay more or less fixed through several seasons but colours don't. Certain colour combinations scream 'Last Year' more than anything else, yet changing the colour of clothes costs a fraction of replacements. Picking up charity-shop bargains may very well mean buying clothes in hard-to-wear luminous oranges or pinks. I once scooped, for 40p, a bilious green Indian silk shirt that had never been worn; after treating with Dygon it became a wearable cream which didn't even need re-dyeing.

You don't need a washing-machine for home dyeing – although it takes much of the toil out of dyeing large articles and heavy wash loads. Just the stove and a preserving pan – or large saucepan, washing-up bowl or plastic dustbin will do. All you have to know is what fabric you are dyeing (see Chapter 3) and follow the dyeing instructions to the letter. Never be tempted to economize on dyes. Craft shops sell several differing ranges of fabric dyes, but I use the Dylon method, as these dyes are the most widely available and simplest to use.

Professional firms can dye garments requiring special handling (see Directory). This is not cheap, however, but it is worth it if you have, say, a couture dress in an unsatisfactory colour, but nevertheless superbly cut and styled. Professional dyeing may result in slight shrinkage of the fabrics owing to hot temperatures, and trimmings may not react in the same way as the main fabric. Therefore, jobs are usually undertaken at your own risk.

Hot-water dyeing

A washing-machine is undoubtedly the most painless way to dye larger articles; if it is a single or twin-tub you can use it either for hot- or cold-water dyeing, for large loads of colour, stripping and stain removal with Dygon or for whitening with Dylon Superwhite. If it's an automatic, you can use Dylon Liquid or Wash 'n Dye – or polyester dyes or Colourfast (currently only suitable for use in automatic washing-machines). Some automatics are also suitable for cold-water dyeing but check with Dylon first (see Directory). Twin-tub top-loading machine lids must be lined with kitchen foil to prevent staining and the process must be supervised throughout – it is not like ordinary washing. Keep a particularly watchful eye for spills and seepage and wipe these off immediately, or dye may stain the enamel. Clean out the machine afterwards by running with very hot water and a cup of bleach for the full cycle.

Don't overload the machine or the dye will not take evenly. For washing-machines with a 4 kg (9 lb) loading the average maximum dye load is 2 kg (4½ lb). Single or twin-tub machines should first be filled with very hot water before adding liquid dye or Wash 'n Dye powder and agitating to mix. Wet the articles first, then immerse and run the machine for a further five minutes. Rinse and dry as usual. For fully automatic machines follow the warm wash cycle. Rich, deep colours in hot-water dyes can only be obtained by simmering, but this is not suitable for woollens which may felt or shrink. The temperature in a twin-tub can be raised and maintained at a higher level, so a strong colour can be obtained, but in fully automatic machines operating on the hottest cycle, the final dye shade may be lighter than that shown on the dye container.

For those without washing-machines very good dye results can be obtained simply by using a large heat-resistant pan on the kitchen stove. Most of my dye successes have been achieved with an aluminium preserving pan – it's difficult to dye in anything much smaller. The secret with the stove method is to keep stirring all the time and to check, when necessary, that the dye solution is thoroughly mixed with salt – so avoid home-dyeing sessions on a day when children are playing under your feet and friends are calling round. Dyeing requires all your concentration. Keep your eye on the clock and time everything exactly.

Cold-water dyeing

A plastic bucket, bowl or baby bath is ideal for cold dyeing of small articles. If you haven't a washing-machine, use a plastic dustbin, the bath or the kitchen sink for large items. If you can use the sink or the bath, check that plugs fit tightly. Items have to soak for at least an hour, and the movement of a heavy wet load has a suction effect on loose plugs; before you know it, all the dye will be down the plughole. Most stainless steel, enamel or porcelain sinks are suitable for cold-water dyeing purposes – but remember, if they are cracked or chipped then the dye will penetrate the cracks leaving 'veins'. Clean enamel and porcelain sinks with all-purpose sink cream and a little diluted bleach; clean stainless steel with detergent.

Equipment

In addition to a washing-machine or containers for dyeing, you will also need the following equipment:

Clock (or watch)

When dyeing, items have to be timed accurately.

Dyes

Make a collection of basic primary colours, i.e. bright red, deep yellow, cobalt, fuchsia pink, kingfisher and a black, in hot-water multi-purpose dyes, and the equivalent in cold-water dyes, with charcoal instead of black. Start with small tins, then as you become more expert change to large economy sizes.

Dye tins

As these are made of soft metal, can-openers are not necessary. The ideal gadget for opening is the tip of a potato peeler, but check all the dye powder is thoroughly cleaned off after use. I keep an old one aside solely for this job. Do ensure that all dye powder is removed from a tin; it's easy to leave a bit behind which could considerably affect the final dye colour. Thus, rinse out tins with hot water.

Foil

Used for lining the lids of top-loading machines, and for covering your preserving pan to prevent heat loss when boiling up water for dyeing.

Kitchen scales

These are essential for weighing articles before dyeing as dyes are formulated according to the dry weight of the material.

Measuring jug (or milk bottle)

Used for mixing correct ratio of water to dye small items.

Protective clothing

Rubber gloves should be worn to protect from dye stains. An overall or PVC apron is also useful for protection against accidental splashes.

Salt

Economize by buying large packs. Cold-water dyes need substantial amounts for colour fixing.

Stirrer

This should be made in a material that won't catch or snag clothes, such as an old heat-proof melamine spoon. I use old wooden chopsticks – these get stained with dye, so I keep a separate one for each colour as previous dye colour may affect subsequent new colours.

Thermometer

For gauging exact water temperature, this is useful when dyeing woollens.

Vinegar

For fixing woollen colours when dyeing with cold-water dyes, and when using tins of multi-purpose dyes. It is not necessary when using liquid dyes on woollens.

Washing soda (or Dylon Cold Fix)

Used for fixing cold-water dyes, except on wool. A large pack is the most economical size.

Testing your fabric

If you've studied the Fabric Guide in Chapter 3 and are still not sure after making tests, then be careful. Take a test snippet from the seam or hem of a garment so when you're next dyeing something you can throw the scrap in. I keep dye samples for testing in a polythene bag. It's a good idea to measure the exact size of any fabric test pieces first of all so you can see after ironing whether there has been any shrinkage – old fabrics and some woollens can be affected by the high temperatures of hot-water dyes and may need a cold-water treatment instead. If in doubt send Dylon (see Directory) your fabric sample.

What to dye

All the natural fibres, i.e. cotton, linen, silk and wool, together with manmades, such as nylon, viscose and Lycra dye well. Dylon's range of polyester dyes will also dye previously hard-to-dye manmades like Terylene, Crimplene, Dacron, Tergal, Terlenka and Tricel, to rich pastel colours.

Fabrics that do not take kindly to the dyebath are all the acrylics – Acrilan, Dralon, Courtelle, Orlon and Neospun – also, pleated Tricel and anything with special flame-, moth- and water-proofed finishes which may mean nightwear, woollens and raincoats. Don't home-dye pure cashmere, angora or mohair unless you're very experienced because these fabrics tend to felt. (See Dyeing Old and Problem Fabrics later in chapter.) Other unsuitable materials are fur, felt and glass-fibre fabric, or any garment with a bonded foam interlining or foam plastic backing, e.g. some jersey fabrics and trimmings such as a dress belt. All new fabrics to be dyed must be washed first to remove any dressing.

Hot-water dyes can dye a surprising number of things, including satin shoes, feathers, wooden beads and buttons, raffia, tights, nylon-pile tape (Velcro), and ethnic lurex fabrics – all dye (tint) prettily. Elastic, ribbons, fringing and woollen yarns also dye well.

Trimmings

Trimmings may well be in a completely different fabric from the main garment, for instance, nylon lace on a cotton skirt. In this case the colours will blend but don't expect an exact match when dyed. For special advice on colour matching write to Dylon (see Directory) sending a fabric cutting. Buttons on clothes will sometimes take dye depending on the material: mother-of-pearl and unvarnished wooden ones tint, as do certain types of plastic; but metal and leather buttons

77

cannot be dyed. The same applies to metal fastenings and zips – also bra clips and polyester stitching on clothes made of a different material. It's worth replacing zips in the correct colour if featuring somewhere prominent, i.e. the trouser fly, or down the back of a skirt or dress. Coloured bra clips are more difficult to replace, so I would avoid dyeing as the original clips may look tacky on bright colours. If there are any sewing alterations to be done in the way of moving buttons, letting out seams, darts and hems, then complete these beforehand – new dye colour does not always penetrate through stitching, and some of the original colour may show.

Feathers can be dyed using Dylon Multi-purpose Dye. The contents of one tin should be thoroughly dissolved in ½ litre (1 pint) of boiling water and added to the dyebath which contains 4.5 litres (1 gallon) of warm water. Add ½ litre (1 pint) of white vinegar. These proportions relate to 225 g (8 oz) dry weight feathers. The feathers should be washed in a good soapy solution, rinsed thoroughly and then immersed in the dyebath soaking wet. Raise the temperature of the dyebath to 90°C (180°F) and maintain at this temperature for ten minutes only, moving feathers constantly. Rinse the feathers until water runs clear; dry in normal way. Feathers are very fragile and should be treated with care throughout the entire process.

Dyeing patterned fabric

Sometimes patterns on otherwise attractive clothes can be just a little bit overpowering. Dyeing usually won't make a pattern disappear entirely unless it's something very pale. For example, pastel-coloured polka dots on a white background might be dyed out using a bright primary colour or navy, aubergine or black. I've had considerable success dyeing many a strident pattern into something more muted and wearable. A loud Viyella paisley printed blouse of mine over-dyed a subtle smoky blue, and it went beautifully with a skirt, sweater and trousers in the same colour. Thus, home-dyeing is certainly a cheap way of co-ordinating an outfit.

For best results on fairly strong colours or patterned fabrics over-dye to a darker version or related shade. For example, pale blue to stronger blues; orange to tans or browns or deep reds; lavender to violets, blues or aubergine. Beiges, creams and pale grey will dye almost any darker colour, but with a slightly smoky, dulled-down tinge. So, unless your fabric is white or has a white background to start with, the original colour will always affect final colour results. Only if you strip off the original colour with Dygon (which does not strip fast colours) can strong or dark colours be changed into light ones. Dyeing everything black is not a solution to deal with existing streaks, patchiness and stains, as home-dyed black will invariably be of different shades and is lighter than professional, vat-dyed black – particularly on cotton fabrics. Indeed, any dye-colour results will vary according to the fabric – two different kinds of white silk can pick up entirely different hues of the same dye.

Dyeing old and problem fabrics

Full instructions for dyeing come with each dye pack, but it is generally assumed by dye manufacturers that clothes to be treated will probably be reasonably new. If clothes are old or antique ones there may be problems. Not only must you check that the fabric is suitable and tough enough to withstand high temperatures, but also old stains embedded in old fabrics need to be treated. The use of Dygon at high temperatures, and chemicals used in stain removal treatments before immersing in hot-water dyes, may result in a general weakening of the fibres. Hidden stains may often come to light after dyeing, particularly underarm perspiration stains which may dye darker than the rest of a shirt or a blouse.

Having said this, however, doesn't mean that you should avoid dyeing anything secondhand or old; it just means exercising more care. I have successfully dyed several Forties blouses in silk crêpe de chine and chiffon, but they were in good condition and were completely colour-stripped with Dygon first. Dygon is also very useful for colour-stripping embroidered fabrics where colours have irretrievably bled or run. I have treated an embroidered pink crêpe de chine kimono, but found that even when stripped back to the cream embroidery, colour streakings were still visible. My solution was to over-dye in rust, though any strong to dark colour would have worked equally well. Of course, you lose the embroidery colour at the expense of camouflaging the stains. Small areas of faded silk embroidery thread can sometimes be tinted back with a diluted Dylon Color-fun fabric paint (see page 81); and irremovable old stains can either be camouflaged with fabric paints, or embroidered over. Old velvet is another fabric that can be dyed with considerable success. I once over-dyed a child's rather garish bright red velvet dress a rich aubergine, using dark-brown dye – the tucked-bib, front trimmings went coffee and the ribbon a wine shade. The ombré effect (see Special Effects later in chapter) is an excellent method of disguising patchiness. Old lace can be treated in a similar way and made up into a tiered skirt, starting with darkest colour at the hem and working through to light at the waist. Cream to coffee also looks good, as would the more unusual shades of grey.

Sometimes over-dyeing a particularly luminous colour can cause problems as it may not be possible to use Dygon. A case in point was a Chinese brocade cocktail suit of mine in a cotton/viscose mix of fluorescent orange, with black bindings and fastenings on the jacket's mandarin collar and sleeve cuffs. These could not be unpicked and colour-stripping the orange would have faded the black edging. After fabric tests, Dylon (see Directory) advised me to dye it in a mix of Midnight Blue and Cherry Flame to achieve the aubergine I wanted. Simply trying to over-dye aubergine would have resulted in a gingery brown.

Dyeing some fabrics such as cashmere, angora and mohair is a risky business for the amateur home-dyer and not recommended by Dylon, although I have had some success with Chinese beaded cardigans and jumpers (these are often a mix of nylon, angora, cashmere and lambswool). The secret is not to let the temperature reach simmering point, and not to leave the garment in the dye container for longer than ten minutes – any more and the wool may start to felt. The effects are very rewarding because the pearls tint along with the rest of the wool. When dyeing ordinary woollens, always treat them gently, manipulating by hand. To keep fluffiness use hot water with Dylon cold-water dyes and add 1½ cups of white vinegar for each tin of dye instead of salt, Dylon Cold Fix or washing soda. For deeper colours use multi-purpose dye at below simmering point. Pure cashmere, however, which is so expensive, may be better colour-changed by experts (see Directory).

Colour and colour mixing

If you are starting from white, then the colour spectrum is the limit, with forty-seven colours in Dylon's hot-water dyes; twenty-four in the cold and six in the polyester dyes. And dyes from the same range can be mixed together just like paint. As a useful guide, remember school painting rules:

blue   + yellow = green
red   + blue = purple
yellow + red = orange

When you are starting from a secondary colour (purple, green, or orange) or from a pastel, the results can be very exciting.

yellow   + pink   = coral
pale green + yellow   = lime
light brown + medium red = rust
pale blue   + pink   = lilac
yellow   + brown   = golden brown
dark brown + light red   = reddish brown

BASIC DYE COLOUR CHART

Original colour of fabric	+ Dye colour	= Result
Red	Yellow	Orange/red
Red	Blue	Purple
Yellow	Pink	Coral
Yellow	Brown	Golden brown
Blue	Yellow	Green
Pink	Pale blue	Lilac
Green	Yellow	Lime
Green	Red	Brown
Light brown	Medium red	Rust
Dark brown	Light red	Reddish brown

You can have a lot of fun experimenting with off-beat fashion shades which may require a *soupçon* of another colour. My favourite is khaki which is not currently available in the Dylon range. For each 225 g (½ lb) dry weight of white cotton fabric you need a tin of Olive Green: a tin of Havana Brown – you can change around the amounts, or add, say, half a tin of Old Gold instead of Havana Brown, or reduce the amount of Olive Green by a quarter or a half – whatever your particular khaki preference. Dygon, which is really used for colour-stripping and stain-removing can also be used to create interesting effects for those prepared to experiment. A 'stonewashed', or faded denim, look can be achieved on some types of denim without harming the fabric fibres if left in Dygon solution; the time varies according to shade desired. You can hurry up the whole process by treating denim as for ordinary colour-stripping, but turn off the heat as soon as the denim begins to fade to white (around twenty-two minutes). A somewhat tricky timing operation perhaps, but worth the effort. Test various pieces of denim first until you get the shade you want. (This method is not suitable for indigo-dyed denims or colour-fast denim.) Always rinse and wash fabric thoroughly after treatment, three to five times if necessary.

Colour points

Cold-water dyes are gentler on delicate fabrics, such as silk and wool, and also on older fabrics because multi-purpose Wash 'n Dyes involve high temperatures. Cold-water dyes give lighter shades on wool than hot-water types. Colour-tinting is effective and over-dyeing an existing colour gives colour depth without resorting to colour stripping. Although cold-water dyes and colour-fast dyes for washing-machines are fast, I prefer to wash my home-dyed articles separately.

Note. If fabrics aren't colour-fast to start with, re-dyeing can cause problems: the original dye may come out faster than new dye goes in! So always strip colour from non-fast fabrics with Dygon before dyeing.

Special effects

The ombré effect – where fabric is shaded light to dark – mainly in pink, blue, green or brown, is a firm favourite for summer dresses, skirts and tops. It not only looks extremely attractive, but can also be incredibly slimming. Dylon's Multi-purpose dyes, used in very hot water, are suitable for a wide range of natural and synthetic fabrics, but natural fabrics, particularly cotton, can also be dyed with Dylon's cold-water dyes. To achieve this subtle shaded effect, thoroughly wet the garment and immerse it in the dye, then pull it out slowly, a little at a time with a gentle bouncing movement to avoid hard lines. Colours start pale, growing darker the longer the fabric is left in the dye. After shading, rinse or wash the garment to remove any excess dye.

Many dark-coloured clothes can also be shaded by using Dygon, colour and stain remover. Immerse the wet garment in the Dygon solution and gradually pull it out. The longer the fabric is left in Dygon, the paler it will be. After shading, wash the garment to remove Dygon residue.

Over-dyeing jeans gives an interesting 'shot denim' effect. Turquoise, rust and Indian pink give the most exciting results.

Useful quantities and tips

It is important that items should move freely in the dyebath. The weight and quantities given below are approximate.

1 *Bucket* The average bucket holds 9 litres (2 gallons) of water, enough to cold-water dye one wool cardigan around 7 oz in weight.
2 *Milkbottle* This makes an alternative to a 1 pint measuring-jug. One pint of multi-purpose hot-water dye is useful for dyeing wooden beads and strings of pearls, mother-of-pearl buttons, etc. Leave soaking for ten minutes.
3 *Preserving pan* This holds approximately 7 litres (1¾ gallons) of water, enough to hot-water dye a cotton grandad shirt and a pair of cotton ankle socks or nylon tights.
4 *Sink* The average sink holds approximately 13 litres (3 gallons) of water, enough to cold-dye a cotton towelling bathrobe.
5 *Washing-machine* One with a 4 kg (9 lb) loading can take 2 kg (4½ lb) of clothing at one time. See weight guide below:

Woman's jersey wool suit	Lightweight	500/750 g	(1–1½ lb)
Wool sweater	Lightweight	200/250 g	(6–8 oz)
Man's thick wool sweater		750g/1 kg	(1½-2 lb)
Jeans or trousers	Cotton	250/320 g	(8–10 oz)
	Wool	420/500 g	(13–16 oz)
Cotton dress	Short-sleeved	320/500 g	(10–16 oz)
Skirt		420/500 g	(13–16 oz)
Overall/Jumpsuit	Cotton	500/750 g	(1–1½ lb)
Blouse		155/200 g	(5–6 oz)
Shirt		200/250 g	(6–8 oz)

Once a hot-water dye powder is diluted with water and you then decide to delay your dyeing spree, you can still use the dye at a later date, provided you boil it up again. You can also delay any used cold-water dyes if they are mixed with Dylon Cold Water Fix or washing soda provided the salt has not been added.

However, dye which has been mixed with water and 'used' should not be strained for further use as, although the water is coloured, the main strength of the colouring chemicals will have been exhausted.

Use double quantities of dye powder and allow double time for simmering if you want deep, dark colours. This is only suitable for tough, newish cotton fabric – not old fabrics or woollens.

The main reasons for disappointing dye results are overloading the container, insufficient stirring and economizing on dye amounts.

8
Lingerie, Nightwear and Baby Clothes

What to collect

Lingerie and underwear

Victorian petticoats
Nightdresses
Camisoles
Pantaloons
Thirties and Forties crêpe de chine
Silk and satin lace-trimmed camisoles
Camisole tops and cami-knickers
Anything in lacy knitting
Old ladies' undies: vests and bloomers; boned basques
Any 'naughty' underwear, such as suspenders, garters
Men's longjohns and matching vests in cotton or wool
String vests from army surplus shops

Nightwear

Men's silk and wool dressing-gowns
Men's silk pyjamas
Women's housecoats from Thirties to Sixties, and kimonos
Nighties
Négligées
Lounge pyjamas

Babywear

Christening gowns (Victorian onwards)
Bonnets

Shawls
Smocked cotton and Viyella dresses
All-in-one romper suits
Coats
Knitted layettes

Tracking down intact, undamaged lingerie examples of the Barbara Stanwyck and Myrna Loy type is not easy. Understandably, if they're glamorous bits of perfect nonsense people will hang on to them; and if it's lingerie that has been worn for any length of time, then the chances are it will need repairing. It is still possible, however, to discover someone's unworn honeymoon trousseau that has never seen daylight. These turn up in the better-class antique clothes shops and antique costume sales (see Chapter 1); or you may inherit examples. My mother donated four sets of practically unworn Thirties peach camisole tops and knickers to me saying, 'They were too hot to wear in India.' She had kept them carefully for forty years wrapped in tissue paper – and, apart from the odd iron mould spot and some fraying at the seams, most of the Valenciennes lace trimming was intact and only noticeably weak in a few places. I successfully dyed the chiffon camisole top and cami-knickers black with Dylon Multi-purpose dyes, but I wouldn't recommend dyeing satin or silk – or indeed any other old fabric – without testing the fabric first (see Chapter 7). Replacing authentic rouleau straps is fairly simple although narrow 3 mm (⅛ in) satin/polyester ribbon makes an excellent substitute, and can be an improvement on the original Thirties adjustable straps which tend to look heavy.

Blood, iron mould and rust stains from metal fastenings are the worst problem for an antique clothes dealer friend of mine, who specializes in Victorian christening gowns, petticoats, bloomers and nighties. She buys job lots costing between £400 and £600 a time at country sales. Many of the containers and trunks haven't been opened for fifty years, so it's a pretty musty business. The first thing she does is to soak the whole lot in a biological detergent which deals to some extent with any blood and perspiration stains before treating iron mould spots with a solution of oxalic acid (see Chapter 5). The stronger cottons can take a bleaching with diluted household bleach; finer, more fragile stained cottons are treated with Dygon before being hand- or machine-washed. She expects to run her washing-machine for at least three cycles before achieving dazzling results and usually uses brand whiteners such as Dylon Super White and Acdo Glo-white. All this, plus the action of today's detergents with their added fluorescents will usually do the trick. Sometimes aids like Reckitt's Blue or blue bag helps whiten, and a final starching helps the garments to regain former crispness. Missing buttons are replaced with authentic cloth-covered ones (see Directory) or mother-of-pearl, but she never uses antique glass buttons as they're liable to break and are not safe on children's clothes anyway, where they may be chewed. She dyes stubbornly dingy cottons pastel colours with Dylon Wash 'n Dye (see Chapter 7), while anything delicate and antique in lace or silk goes to a specialized drycleaner or hand launderer for treatment.

Don't forget old lace probably never was sparkling white but cream verging to almost coffee; it may need tinting back (see Chapter 7). For this reason replacing ribbon trimmings in traditional baby pinks and blues may not look quite right against old lace – it's better to pick warmer shades of peach, apricot, cinnamon and cream.

Handmade laces often took their names from places of origin: Honiton, Chantilly, Cluny, Valenciennes, etc. Machine copies of Valenciennes lace are still made in Buckinghamshire and Bedfordshire. Earliest lace was probably needle point – a development of cut-and-drawn embroidery·– where the lace was built up by using buttonhole stitches and twisted linen threads. Bobbin lace possibly evolved from macramé techniques and it consisted of twisting and plaiting numerous threads around pins and sticks. Lace makers worked from a parchment pattern pinned to a pillow on which designs were printed or drawn. But most oldish lace pieces around today's homes will probably be Victorian machine-made examples. You can identify these by the way designs repeat so exactly, on very even backgrounds. Other typical heirloom laces, namely the Edwardian chemical ones, are designs which were machine-embroidered onto the fabric before immersing in a chemical bath to remove the unworked areas. Crochet laces and machine-made copies of filet lace probably evolved from the French knotting techniques traditionally used to make fishing nets.

Men's secondhand silk dressing-gowns and pyjamas are also a worthwhile investment. Dressing-gown bargains, however, may have twisted interlinings on collars and cuffs caused by careless washing. They should always be drycleaned as interlinings tend to be unwashable. As with men's ties, once the interlining shrinks and creases up very little can be done save undoing the seams and replacing with washable interfacings, using the original as the pattern. Alternatively, you can take the opportunity to replace the complete collar and cuffs – these may be frayed and worn anyway – with a quilted satin wadding, again using the original fabric as a pattern. Missing belts and belt pulls are easily replaced; traditional silk-look dressing-gown cords and tassels are still obtainable at most haberdashery counters. More exciting are tasselled cords sold in Indian fashion shops: these come in lovely colours often with elaborate beadwork and gold threadwork, but are not washable (tassel heads have a cardboard base). Don't treat old stains on dressing-gowns and housecoats yourself – they may have been washed in. Contact a specialist drycleaner (see Directory) or embroider a suitable motif over the top.

Secondhand baby clothes often present cleaning problems (see Chapter 5 for details on stain removal and drycleaning). When washing any secondhand babywear, it's advisable to pre-soak in a sterilizing agent such as Milton or a biological detergent.

Your fashion identity

Don't just wear camisole tops with predictably pretty Victorian petticoats. Go for the contrast of fragile, lacy tops with tough leather jackets and trousers, army surplus, or with a man's dinner jacket and trousers for the evening. Wear a camisole top instead of a bikini bra on the beach – under a blouse or a dress unbuttoned down the front to show off the lace. Lace-trimmed camisoles and cami-knickers double as summer outerwear: if the crotch is too low, stitching several rows of shirring elastic (in the same colour as the fabric) at waist level; cinching-in with a stretchy belt also makes them look a lot sexier. Victorian nighties can be treated as shirtwaister dresses, using a beaded belt; or wear them yokel-smock style over lots of white petticoats teamed with brightly coloured cowboy boots and fishnet tights. Victorian pantaloons look great with striped T-shirts or collarless grandad shirts; men's longjohns and vests can be dyed bright colours as can string vests. Forties and Thirties nightdresses and slips can double as slinky evening dresses if they're dyed less obvious lingerie colours, i.e. from peach to black. Dyeing black may also camouflage any irremovable stains, but check that the fabric is tough enough to withstand high temperatures. Men's dressing-gowns can lead a double life – as evening wear belted with a cummerbund.

Pyjama jackets, particularly silk and striped winceyette, can double as loose unstructured summer jackets; pyjama trousers also adapt to casual beach and day-wear.

Clothes renovation kit checklist (see Essential Sewing Kit, Chapter 2)

Bra-repair fastenings.

Buttons and poppers.   Mother-of-pearl in small sizes, also linen-covered buttons. Clear poppers.

Cottons and thread.   White embroidery cottons, and silk thread in peach and white.

Elastic.   Baby elastic and pastel-coloured shirring elastics, as well as black and white.

Eyelet embroidery (broderie anglaise).   For trimming.

Fraying preventative.   For treating damaged seams.

Lace oddments.   For trimming.

Nylon and silk net.   For backing fragile lace areas when patching.

Pins and needles.   Lace pins for pinning out pieces when washing, etc. Fine (no. 9) needles for hand stitching silk, chiffon, organdie. Ballpoint sewing-machine needles nos 9 to 11, and nos 11 to 14 for lace and fine fabrics.

Ribbon.   Extra-narrow, 3 mm (⅛ in) satin/polyester ribbon for trimming Victorian undies, and babywear. Also for repairing camisole and slip shoulder straps.

Rouleau turner.   For rolling hems on delicate garments.

Washing, drycleaning and stain removal (see Chapters 3, 4 and 5)

Sewing repairs

Lace

When hand sewing lace, always use a fine needle and thread to match the colour of the lace. Tack the lace to the fabric before sewing to avoid puckering. To sew lace to fabric, place pieces right sides together, trim fabric allowance to 6 mm (¼ in), roll the fabric over the lace edge and whip-stitch together. Turn lace back and press lightly over a cloth.

Narrow lace can be attached to a very narrow hem or false hem by oversewing on the wrong side. Wider lace, often made to a shaped design, is usually laid flat on the material and satin or blanket stitch worked finely and closely over the edge. The material is then cut away at the back to within about 3 mm (⅛ in) of the stitching. The raw edge is then overcast or blanket stitched.

For slips that have given way under the arms or at the front where clips or brooches have been pinned, appliqué lace over the frayed parts. Do this very neatly, and then cut away the ragged parts underneath. It is possible to appliqué lace so well that it looks as though it is part of the design. Repairing an undergarment with lace makes your garment look new rather than mended.

Applying lace by machine.   Place lace right side up on the right side of the fabric and stitch with fine thread, turn and stitch back. Trim away surplus fabric from seam edge.

Lace appliqué.   All-over lace fabric, used in slip tops, lace blouses and dresses, should be appliquéd at the seams rather than stitched which creates too much bulk and detracts from the beauty of the pattern. Allow enough fabric to overlap at the seams so that you can cut around each motif. Tack the edges to tissue paper and whip-stitch the seams around each motif so that the joining is invisible. Excess fabric in darts and tucks should also be cut away and appliquéd in this way. If a lace motif has a heavy outline thread, it can be imitated by placing a similarly heavy thread around the edge of the cut-out design and overcasting.

Patching.   Tack a lace patch on the wrong side, hem all round the hole with stab-stitch on the right side, then cut away the ragged edges underneath. If you cannot get a match or nearly matching pattern, use plain net of a similar colour and mesh and embroider a pattern on it to match.

Repairing lace edging.   Where lace edging is badly torn, place a new matching lace piece over the damaged area, taking care to line up the design carefully, and whip-stitch it down around the motif. The torn section may then be carefully cut away.

Torn lace.   Cut away all torn lace, edgings and motifs from the lingerie. Rolled hems can replace a former lace edging, as can binding in a contrasting colour and satin ribbon. Or use appliqué shapes cut from scraps of satin or crêpe de chine left over from other garments to cover the holes left when motifs are removed or fabric is weak. Alternatively, reinforce weak areas by patching with net using trammelling stitches.

To insert lace into a slip, which has worn at the seams, open out the side seams and insert strips of lace. In this way it is possible to add as much as 100 to 150 mm (4 to 6 in) to the all-round size of the slip. To insert lace or ribbon, pin the garment seam edges to pieces of tissue paper and tack the insertion strips in position. Then stitch through both fabric and paper. This will make the seams perfectly straight and the stitching line even and smooth (the paper pulls away easily after the stitching is complete); ballpoint needles may be used for delicate silk slips where seams have pulled out or frayed in wearing. In this case stitch ribbon or lace insertion over the seams, cutting the old frayed seams away.

When a slip is trimmed at the top and hemmed with worn lace or net but the fabric part is still quite good, you can simply replace with new lace. Or, better still, use old, matching lace from a similar garment that you don't need. If you want to add length to the slip, buy your trimming band wider than that which trimmed the garment originally. Stitch the lace on from the right side, using the machine edge-stitcher, which allows you to stitch directly on the edge. Always stitch lace on top of paper so that the lace will not tighten under the machine needle.

Victorian undies and nightdresses

Flat covered buttons.   These are not used a great deal today but they can be useful on garments which are frequently laundered, when pearl buttons would be crushed, or on babies' wear when hard buttons would be uncomfortable. Can cause rust stains if clothes are stored damp for any length of time.

Underlaid patch.   For holes in knitted underwear and elastic foundation garments a round underlaid patch, herringbone-stitched in place, gives the maximum stretch. Cut away the worn part to make a hole which is either round or oval. Cut the patch piece about 25 mm (1 in) bigger in diameter than the hole. Tack the patch under the hole with the ribs of the patch and garment parallel. Herringbone stitch the edge of the hole to the patch, using small stitches and a strong thread – buttonhole twist, or mercerized cotton. Then, on the wrong side, herringbone stitch the edge of the patch to the fabric of the garment.

Victorian camisoles and pantaloons

Ribbon casings.   Narrow satin/polyester ribbon makes an easy, attractive casing for drawstrings or elastic. Press the top edge of the casing to the right side on the seam line. Trim to 6 mm (¼ in). Topstitch the ribbon – it should be at least 15 mm (⅝ in) wide – to the right side of fabric, covering the raw edge. Fold in the ribbon edges for the casing opening. Run narrow ribbon through casing on a safety-pin or bodkin. Cut ribbon ends off diagonally to prevent fraying.

Lace and broderie eyelets.   Narrow ribbon slips easily through lace and broderie eyelets. Use ribbon-trimmed eyelet lace for baby clothes, for little girls' dresses, for an exquisite lingerie trim, for fragile-looking blouses. Use bands of eyelets with several strands of ribbon threaded through to trim Victorian petticoats.

Baby clothes

Narrow ribbon.   This has many uses. It threads easily through lacy and openwork stitches to add colour contrast, to highlight a stitch, or to point up a design detail. In baby layettes, narrow satin ribbons can be added to pretty dresses, bonnets, bootees and as a threaded-edging on shawls. Very narrow 3 mm (⅛ in) (bébé) ribbon is also ideal for drawstrings on baby clothes. Use bright coloured narrow ribbon also for embroidery on knitted and crocheted underwear.

Tips for working with ribbons.   Use polyester sewing thread in your sewing machine and a needle suitable for the ground fabric. If the ribbon puckers, try a larger stitch or loosen the top tension a little. If you prefer to hand sew, use prick stitch or tiny hemstitching.

Smocking.   Secondhand baby dresses may have bits of smocking missing. Here's how to go about mending the honeycomb or waffle pattern. Unlike most other smocking stitches, it is worked from right to left. For reversed over-stitch pattern, work from left to right. Take up two folds, bring the needle out on the second, fold a little below the point where it entered the material. The next stitch will take up the third fold at the same level, coming out a little higher up.

Useful machine stitches

Blind hem.   A blind hem produces a very neat, invisible decorative shell hem on lingerie, or decorative tucks on blouses and dresses made of fine soft fabrics and saves long hours of careful hand sewing. *Note* Use the zig-zag needle-plate and the presser foot stated under each use.

Diamond stitch.   A decorative stitch which can be sewn in parallel rows with a twin needle, or combined with other decorative stitches. *Note* Use the zig-zag needle-plate and the zig-zag presser foot.

Lingerie stitch.   Used for seaming and overcasting sheer, soft fabrics in one operation. It also produces a delicate shell hem on lingerie and other fine garments. *Note* Use the zig-zag needle-plate and the zig-zag presser foot. If sewing stretch nylon, fit the stretch-stitch foot.

Seam and overcast in one.   Set the stitch length at ½–1 and the stitch width at 3–4. Place the right sides of the fabric together and position under the presser foot so that the zig-zag part of the stitch sews just over the raw edge.

Shell hem (see also under Hand Sewing below).   Turn the raw edge under 12 mm (½ in) and press. Set the stitch length at 1½–2 and the stitch width at 2–4. Place the fabric right side up so that the zig-zag part of the stitch sews just over the folded edge, pulling the fabric in to form a shell hem. Trim away excess fabric close to the stitching line.

Hand sewing

Shell hemming.   One of the quickest and most decorative edgings. It is not really satisfactory on an edge cut on the warp or weft; it is at its best on the true cross of the fabric. Thin materials are best, as found in Thirties slips and cami-knickers, etc. Turn down a hem about 3 mm (⅛ in) wide, with a deep first turn, on the right side. Tack and mark faintly dots 3 mm (⅛ in) apart. (Experienced stitchers won't need dot marks.) Start at the right-hand end of the material. Use fine thread to match the fabric. Each shell is fixed with a buttonhole stitch and the thread is slipped along inside hem to the next stitch.

Sewing on shoulder straps. The strap is not sewn on the embroidery, but set on the edge of the material from the wrong side with a reversed seam. In dainty lingerie, made of chiffon, for instance, the straps should be sewn on at the base of the hem. Stitch carefully so that the outside of the garment looks smooth. For extra strength, the straps can be fastened at the upper edge as well with feather-stitch.

Attaching flat elastic

Three-step zig-zag can be used to attach flat elastic to cuffs, waists of dresses, waistbands of underwear, etc. Set the stitch length at 1½–2½ and the stitch width at 4. Turn over the raw edge the required amount and press, pin or tack into place. Mark both the elastic and the garment into quarters to ensure that the elastic is evenly distributed.

To attach flat elastic to lingerie, set the stitch length to 3–4 and the stitch width at 3–4. Mark the elastic into quarters and match these to the centre front, centre back and side seams. Place the middle of the elastic under the centre of the presser foot and stitch into place, making sure the elastic is evenly distributed.

9
Dresses, Blouses and Skirts, and Light Tailoring Alterations

What to collect

'Retro' dresses

Anything in crêpe-de-chine, lace, chiffon, silk
Printed cottons and velvets from the Thirties to Fifties
Fifties and Sixties cotton sundresses in witty prints, with ruched and
    boned tops
'Little Black Dresses' – any period from Thirties onwards
Shirtwaisters in silk and wool
Indian pleated-look crêpe cotton dresses; also Fortuny-inspired
    pleated styles (see also ethnic dresses)
Wedding and evening dresses (see Chapter 13)
Vintage designer names to look out for include: Mary Quant; Biba;
    Ossie Clark; Hardy Amies; Hartnell

Blouses and shirts

Anything embroidered or smocked from China, Mexico, Hungary,
    etc. (see also ethnic)
Anything in broderie anglaise, silk, chiffon, lace and satin
Marks & Spencer viscose/rayon blouses (circa 1950)
Men's shirts in needlecord and Viyella
Grandad shirts in plain white and striped cotton
Evening dress shirts with dicky fronts
Indian cotton in frilly Victorian styles
Madras checked shirts
American baseball and Hawaii shirts

Skirts

Kilts
Culottes
Dirndl skirts
Rock-and-roll skirts in felt, taffeta and moiré
Shot silk and appliqué, sunray pleated, gipsy Spanish flamenco, fish-tail long crêpe evening skirts
Long velvet skirts
Indian embroidered and crêpe cotton skirts

Finding bargains in 'Retro' secondhand dresses is not difficult, provided you are prepared to undertake a few sewing repairs. Dresses that have survived the Second World War usually lack belt, zips and buttons, and probably suffer from 'hem-line droop', damaged underarms and fraying seams. Discouraging news for those who want instant fashion perhaps, but dresses like these are well worth patient renovation – their fabrics and cut have a miraculous way of flattering almost any figure type, and look stylish year after year. Even when long past repairs, 'Retro' dress fabrics and buttons may be worth saving – either to recycle or renovate something else.

Some 'Retro' dresses may need a lot of work to make them wearable. A typical example is a black crêpe dress (circa 1940) which I bought for £1.50 in 1973 from a market stall. It sported a guipure lace yoke and cuffs lined with grubby, pink chiffon. Having replaced the pink chiffon with an infinitely more flattering black, I then found myself having to remove a very ugly back-fastened brass zip – more suited to a holdall than a dress! After closing the gap and taking in the whole back seam about an inch, I then inserted a new, unobtrusive zip at the side and pulled in the enormous waist with a sash made from left-over hem fabric (the dress was shortened two inches). The whole operation took an entire afternoon, but I am still wearing a dress that would cost at least £80 today.

Dresses made from lush and expensive fabrics, either with damaged necklines, or those cut in rather matronly styles, frequently find their way into charity shops and jumble sales. The important thing here is not to be put off by the size. Large measurements can always be reduced, whereas letting-out alterations are almost impossible unless you're a professional seamstress. I recently paid a pound for an outsize dress at a War on Want shop. It was in navy Swiss lace

96

(currently costing around £40 a metre) and lined in a stiff nylon – the kind used in men's jackets. After cutting this out, a navy silk chiffon lining was revealed that instantly gave the dress today's unstructured look. Worn with a body stocking, and cinched in tightly at the waist with a satin cummerbund, its character was transformed.

Remember, too, dyeing can change and co-ordinate unwearable colours, and dyeing black may usefully camouflage an irremovable stain, as can strategically placed embroidery or lace motifs, (see Sewing Repairs, Chapter 8). Painting over blemishes with fabric paints is also worth considering. I have successfully camouflaged cream paint marks from the black background of a 'Retro' floral-printed crêpe-de-chine with black fabric paint.

The very sight of stained and ruined underarms on otherwise pretty 'Retro' blouses and dresses is discouraging. Where underarm discoloration has occurred, do remember that this will be impossible to recolour. In fact, it's best to regard all damaged underarms as an inset patching job (see page 103). Do remember that such dresses are likely to be going for pence rather than pounds, and that the repairs may not always be as time-consuming as they look.

More often, repairs to 'Retro' dresses may simply mean replacing a missing belt or loop carriers, or re-stitching broken or frayed seams (see Sewing Repairs in this chapter). Drooping, uneven hem lines – particularly those of dirndl skirts – can be adjusted with a hem leveller. Hems that are too long can be shortened easily enough; those that are too short may need a false one which is easily achieved by sewing a carefully matched strip to the let-down edge of the original hem, on the wrong side, and the new piece of fabric turned up along this seam. Or insert a band of similar weight fabric using a machine zig-zag stitch. Attaching a flounce or frill to an underslip of jap silk is also a neat hem-lengthening device (see Sewing in this chapter).

Wearing some kind of protective underslip is also a good idea when dress fabrics are fragile and better not worn in direct contact with the skin. I wear thin cotton T-shirts with sleeves and V-necks in colours that match the dress or blouse in case the fabric colour runs. The T-shirt must be fairly close-fitting, and have enough of a sleeve to protect underarms. An Indian sari blouse in thin silk also makes a good alternative – particularly on dresses with scooped necklines. Lace collars made from old handkerchiefs can conveniently cover up damaged V-shaped necklines: sew lace to a nylon net backing (rather

97

more delicate than bias binding) and whip-stitch to blouse or dress neck. Missing covered buttons and belts can be professionally re-covered in 'Retro' styles by a few firms (see Directory). For outsize waistlines, several rows of shirring elastic can reduce a size 18 to a mere size 10. Wide elasticated belts are also useful here. Drooping shoulders are greatly improved with new shoulder pads (see Sewing Repairs in this chapter).

When it comes to men's secondhand shirts, expect to repair collars and cuffs – most bargains will need turning or reinforcing. Collar points may also be in outdated styles, and collar shapers are useful for re-shaping to a more fashionable line. Removing collars and cuffs can sometimes improve, as can letting out darts in slimfit styles.

Your fashion identity

No hard-and-fast rules exist for wearing 'Retro' dresses. It's fun studying vintage films to see how Joan Crawford, Lauren Bacall and Ginger Rogers actually wore them. Wearing Eighties 'Retro' however, doesn't mean being a Forties fashion clone because today's hairstyles, makeup, underwear and accessories are very different. Grandad shirt bargains have infinite variations, whether worn as belted mini dresses or casual tops. Outsize lace frocks can be worn cinched in with elastic belts and teamed with coloured body stockings and tights, or worn over frilly petticoats. Fifties sundresses look a lot more interesting worn over primary-coloured net tu-tus – buy them from ballet shops, and accessorize with matching home-dyed fishnet tights and painted pumps. Long velvet evening skirts and kilts can verge towards 'Eighties Ethnic' with great swatches of matching fabric pinned and draped over the shoulders. Tops with these skirts don't always have to be Daz-white and lacy – experiment with deep-dyed jewel colours, or tie-dye a leopard print shirt (see Special Effects, Chapter 14), or wear with Russian-style side-fastened shirts and military-looking leather belts.

Clothes renovation kit checklist (see Essential Sewing Kit, Chapter 2)

Adhesive webbing.   For quick hems and repairing frayed buttonholes.
Collar shapers.
Belt puncher.   Useful when making covered belts.

Boning. For repairing bodices.

Buttons. In sets of eight (shirt size), mother-of-pearl and glass.

Dress shields. In various sizes and styles to suit different armholes.

Elastic. Shirring elastic in different colours to suit dress fabrics. Use it to pull in large waists and for decorative gathering on large, loose sleeves and shoulders.

Fabric remnants. For trimming and patching, and adding covered buttons, belts, inserts to false hems, etc. Pick them in Liberty-style floral and abstract patterned crêpe-de-chines, Tana lawns, vicuna wool and Viyella. Useful trimmings: velvet and tartan ribbons, pieces of old lace, suede, beads and sequins for hiding holes and stains, ready-made pie-crust frilling and ruffles in black and cream for lengthening hems, filling necklines, etc.

Fraying preventative. For fabric and seams.

French chalk. For marking alterations.

Grommet puncher kit. Provides larger rings for lace-up fastenings on bodices.

Hem leveller.

Hooks and eyes.

Pinking shears. Useful for neatening untidy seams.

Pressing-cloth. Essential for sewing alterations.

Press studs. Clear type.

Seam ripper. For undoing old seams, removing old zips, shirt collars and cuffs, etc.

Shoulder pads. Ready-made ones in nylon-covered foam. Or make your own.

Sleeveboard. For the proper ironing of sleeves.

Tailor's dummy. These are expensive, but essential for serious clothes alterations. The most flexible types are adjustable and a wise investment if you've a whole family's clothes to alter. You may find a secondhand tailor's dummy in your exact size – a size or two smaller is also fine.

Thread. Embroidery thread for embroidering over stains and making belt carriers on dresses.

Velcro (nylon pile tape). Tabs of this make shoulder pads and dress shields detachable. Also for detachable collars and cuffs (see Sewing Repairs, Chapter 6).

Wrist pincushion.

Zips. Various sizes and lengths for skirts and dresses. Black and white are the most useful spare colours.

Washing, drycleaning and stain removal (see Chapters 3, 4 and 5)

Sewing repairs

Fastenings

Before inserting any replacement zip check whether these can be repositioned to improve the line. I always try and avoid back-fastening zips as these look more obtrusive than side-fastening ones. Other zip fixing points to watch for: always stretch new zips slightly before sewing in and match zip to function, i.e. skirts, trousers, anoraks, these zips all vary slightly in style and come in different strengths. Nylon zips tend to be more flexible than metal but are less strong. Try and match zip to the colour of your fabric and avoid using pins to position – double-sided adhesive is better – pinning causes a zip to 'snake'. Keep zip closed while sewing and always sew in the same direction, i.e. from base up. Sewing from the top down and all the way round in one go causes that unsightly 'zip bulge' as does stitching too near the teeth. When unpicking old zips always use a seam ripper, fabric can easily be damaged with sharp scissors. If original garment stitching is too small to unpick successfully, the old zip may have to be completely cut out. So check there is enough fabric for taking in at the seams.

Replacing a dress side-fastening. Examine the way the zip was put in and note the original stitch marks. The opening should be 12 mm (½ in) longer than the zip teeth. Close the dress opening on the seam line with temporary tacking stitches. Then press open and remove tacking. If the side seams are particularly fragile or less than 15 mm (⅝ in) you can add extra width to the front seam by stitching on seam tape in a colour to match fabric.

Working from the dress right-side out, position opening over the closed zip. Turn under back edges of the opening approximately 3 mm (⅛ in) outside the seam line; pin and tack close to the zip teeth easing the fabric to the tapes. Check fit by trying on garment and adjusting where necessary. Check that the front fold laps across the zip teeth correctly so that these and any back stitches are covered and that waistline seams match up. Tack across base and along the teeth, easing the fabric. Then using the machine zipper foot and working from base up, stitch the back edge, taking care to avoid stitching too near the zip teeth or the effect will look bulky and zip will wear out faster. Next stitch other edge again working from base up. Finish ends by neatening on wrong side with oversewing. A small bar tack can be worked for reinforcement.

Hooks, eyes, bars and worked bars. Buy hooks, and eyes in sizes 0, double 0 and triple 0 – the last being smallest. A card usually has both round and straight eyes, so that you can choose the type best suited to the opening. Utilitarian metal hooks and eyes are generally put on the inside of the closing so that they do not show; if they do, cover with matching coloured thread. Placing quite close together prevents unsightly gaps; keep the line by placing exactly opposite each other. Use a buttonhole stitch for extra strength. Attach the hook first, on the underside of the part of the garment which will be uppermost. The bend of the hook should come well in from the edge, i.e. at least the depth of the eye. The eyes and bars are also attached with buttonhole stitches. A handworked bar is less conspicuous than a metal one. Make several strands into a loop, and then work buttonhole stitches closely over the bar that is formed.

Snap fasteners. Measure the spacing and mark the position for these very carefully. Hold the fastener exactly in place and take several stitches through each hole to secure it. Never let stitches go all the way through the fabric. When the stitches for one hole are completed, slip along in the material to the position for working the stitches in the next hole. Clear plastic snap fasteners are very useful on dresses and blouses. Buttonhole stitch is the best for attaching. Remember that the half with the nipple has a flat back and should be placed on the uppermost layer of material so that when the garment is ironed on the right side the back of the fastener will not rub and wear through the fabric. The other section has a 'bumpy' back which, when ironed, easily wears through material.

Tapes to hold shoulder straps. Haberdashery counters stock ready-made tapes. To make your own, use 3 mm (⅛ in) satin/polyester ribbon. Cut a 50 mm (2 in) length of ribbon, turn one end under and whip-stitch it to the shoulder seam at the place where the lingerie straps cross the shoulder. Turn the free end of the ribbon under and sew a small snap fastener there. Sew the other half of the snap to the seam.

Velcro (nylon pile tape) tabs are also a good idea here: sew (soft side up) 25 mm (1 in) pieces to the tops of the dress shoulder seams; then sew on corresponding 25 mm (1 in) strips (hooks side up).

Button pulled out.   When a button has pulled off, leaving a hole in the fabric, repair the hole by placing a piece of fabric or tape under it, and then stitch back and forth over it (iron-on webbing can also be used). This will fill the hole and make the spot strong enough for the button to be sewn on again.

Buttons.   Buttons are divided into two groups: (a) those with holes; (b) fabric-covered ones without holes. When a button is sewn on, it must be very secure and sufficient room must be left under the button for the other layer of material when the article is 'buttoned up'. In order to provide for this a shank needs to be formed.

For buttons with holes, place a pin on top of the button when it is in position. Stab-stitch through both buttonholes, and the fabric, until there are enough stitches to hold the button securely in place. The stitches over the button should also pass over the pin. Then release the pin and wind the cotton round the strands of cotton between the button and the material until a firm stem is formed. Fasten off securely on the wrong side. Where the fabric is very thick, use a rug needle or match instead of a pin. If the button is going to be subjected to great strain, it is advisable to put another small button under the material and take all the stitches through this button as well. This avoids pull on the material and a subsequent tear.

Covered buttons may be made professionally by haberdashers from scraps of your own fabric. Or you can cover wooden, or composition moulds, yourself. If a shank pulls out of a machine-made button, use a scrap of the same fabric and re-cover it yourself. If you have none of the material, cut a circle of fabric as similar as possible, and slightly larger than the tin or composition backing, turn in the edge, and blind-stitch or whip it underneath, catching it at the extreme edge of the top covering. This may not be very strong because it has no shank, but another, less strategically placed one, may be moved and replaced by the repaired button.

Link buttons (for shirt and shirt-waister cuffs).   Sew a double thread through two buttons; then work over these threads with blanket stitch. An effective linking device can be made using narrow 3 mm (⅛ in) ribbon or cord and sewing a button to each of the ends.

Other sewing repairs

Shoulder pads. These should match the sleeve cut. You may need more or less padding depending on whether your shoulders are square or sloping. If you have 'hollows' in the upper chest, pads extending down the front help disguise them. *Ready-made pads* come in many types and shapes. Make these detachable in washable dresses and blouses by sewing a 75 mm (3 in) strip of Velcro (nylon pile tape) smooth side up to the shoulder seam, and a corresponding strip, rough side up, to the inside top of the shoulder pad. Suit and coat pads often come uncovered so check that they are drycleanable.

Shield reinforcement. When the underarm parts of blouses, dresses, shirts, etc. have worn thin, they can be reinforced. Cut out both sides of the shield pieces to match the straight of the fabric and fit to the underarm. Put the two halves together and stitch into the underarm seam. Then attach edges to the garment with running stitch. Incidentally, avoid using machine-stitching for patching blouses and dresses. No matter how good zig-zag and darning stitches are, they look too obtrusive on delicate fabrics.

Underarm patch. To avoid a bulky patch where seams cross, such as underarms, unpick the seams with a seam ripper and cut away all the ragged and thinning material. Cut a patch, using the pieces as of the original garment pattern. Hem all round. Snip up from each corner of the hole on the right side, and trim away any ragged edges. Turn in 3 mm (⅛ in) and hem all round. Normally patches must always be set in to match a straight thread and corners must be worked absolutely cleanly so that in certain weaves the seam is not visible at all. However, this is not always possible. A good tip for blouses and dresses which are worn under the arms is to set a section of material in such a way as to make it appear to be an intentional part of the original design. Damaged underarms on lace blouses can have a gusset patch of lace appliquéd on (see Chapter 8). This repair also worked for silk blouses, too; matching lace can be appliquéd onto the collar so that repair gusset looks part of the design. This kind of repair gusset is also useful when armholes are too tight.

103

Broken stitches in seams. This is usually caused by the fabric having more elasticity than the stitching. The machine tension may have been too tight, or the fabric was not stretched enough in stitching to give a sufficiently long stitching line. Stitching the fabric over tissue paper helps, because this stretches the seam slightly and avoids breaking threads when the seam is opened. If your machine is electric use a zig-zag stitch.

If you have a puckered seam and need to restitch it, pull the seam just a little as you stitch. Then, when you press it, shrink up all the stretch you have put in. Avoid stitching broken seams twice, or they will be just as tight as they were originally and when pressed will break again.

Try to avoid making too long or too short stitches. Stitches that are too long do not hold the fabric securely enough, and very short ones hold the fabric too tightly. For chiffon, sixteen stitches to 25 mm (1 in) is right; for lightweight woollens, ten to twelve is ideal; and for cottons it is best to have nine to eleven stitches.

Pulled seams. When a garment is tight, or when the fabric is loosely woven, fabric threads sometimes separate along the seams. If the garment is already too tight, this cannot be repaired by taking a deeper seam. So, turn to the wrong side, and stitch along the seam side of the pulled-out part. Then with your needle point flick the worn fabric threads back towards the seam. Open the seam and catch the original stitch down over the frayed part with uneven tacking stitches in matching thread. Press the seam from the wrong side. Treat any frayed edges with fray preventative. When much more ease is required in the seams, let them out and cover the pulled part with a band of fabric, braid, ribbon or bias binding. This repair can be made to look as if it is a decorative feature of the garment.

Pulled pleats. Pleats generally pull out where they are stitched down. If the skirt has plenty of room, the pleats can simply be set over 6 mm (¼ in) to cover the pulled part, and restitched. However, the usual reason they pull is that the skirt is on the tight side and there is no room to spare for such a repair. In this case, unpick the original stitching for some distance from the base. Working on the wrong side, pin and tack a piece of seam binding along the pulled part, then restitch the seams from the right side.

Arrowhead. For extra strength at the end of the stitching on the pleats, an arrowhead can be worked. To make this, begin by drawing a triangle (using french chalk) of the size desired and taking stitches, with silk or cotton thread according to dress or skirt fabric. Take a straight stitch across the point of the triangle. Continue until the triangle is filled in.

Let-out seams. When a seam has been let out so far that the edge is very close to the seam, bind each edge to prevent further pulling.

Covered belts. These can be made from double strips of fabric stitched together right sides facing and turned inside out. If the fabric is fairly thick, only a light iron-on interlining is needed, except perhaps in the case of very wide belts which may need extra stiffening. For thin fabrics an interlining must be inserted to prevent the belt from folding over or becoming wrinkled when worn. A light interlining of iron-on Vilene, half the width of the belt strip, may be tacked onto the fold line before the belt is stitched together. This keeps the upper edge of the interlining in place, the lower edge being held by the seam. The edge of the interlining must be trimmed away close to the seam, but the fabric turnings, about 12 mm (½ in) wide, remain. The belt is then turned inside out and must be pressed flat with the seam in the fold. Belts' seams should always lie in the fold, whether or not any interlining is being used. If the belt is to be very stiff, buckram can be used. The outer fabric may be tacked over the interlining, its edges catch-stitched, and the inner fabric then tacked on with its edges slightly set back. The inner fabric is stitched on with slip-stitch and the belt pressed flat. It can be stitched through or left plain. Some drycleaners and haberdashery shops offer a belt and button recovering service (see Directory).

For a professional look trim with genuine 'Retro' buckles; for other more modern styles, recycle buckles from other garments.

Belt carriers and belt buckles. Try on the belt to see where the carriers should be placed. If the bodice and skirt are joined together, the belt must cover the waist seam and therefore the belt carriers should be fastened above and below the seam. The carriers may be made of buttonhole thread to match the colour of the dress; two or three threads should be stretched and worked over with close buttonhole stitching. If material is to be used for the carriers, the strips should be cut about 6 mm (¼ in) wide and should be long enough for their ends to be turned in and over when sewing them to the garment.

To attach belt buckles, the pin is run through about 25 mm (1 in) behind the end of the belt; the end is folded over to the inside and stitched down. A few eyelets should be punched into the other end of the belt, so that it can be adjusted as necessary.

Sewing

Make your own frills

Used on skirts and sleeves to give a full, fluffy effect. They may be cut straight, on the cross or shaped. Narrow frills are better cut on the straight or cross. If straight they should be cut horizontally across from selvedge to selvedge of the fabric. Frills must hang gracefully; if cut the wrong way of the fabric they will poke out and look stiff. Allow 1½ to 2 times the length required for the finished frill when cutting.

The base of a frill may be finished either with a very narrow stitched hem, or joined with an embroidered edge. The joins in the frills should be made with a single seam. Here are some methods for successful frilling.

(a) Mark the half and quarter points along the top of the frill and place onto the skirt to which frill is to be attached. Gather each quarter of the frill separately. Place the quarter points of frill and skirt together with the frill upside down and the right sides touching, and tack into place before machine-stitching.

(b) Tiny pleated frills look best when they are 25 mm (1 in) to 38 mm (1½ in) wide. First cut strips of perfectly straight material to the depth required, and 3 to 3½ times the finished size. Make and machine-stitch a very narrow hem along the bottom edge. You can also buy ready-made frills of this type in various colours and styles from larger haberdashery shops, but the fabric is normally manmade, such as nylon.

Flounces

These are similar to frills only much deeper. Prepare and finish bottom edge as for narrow frills.

Shaped flounces look best when made of fine cotton, silk or crêpe de chine. These fit without bulk at the top edge, and are full and very frilly at the hem base. Flounces mounted onto a foundation petticoat may number as many as six or even more; sew them in tiers as fashion decrees. To apply a shaped flounce to a skirt, make a narrow turning along the top edge of a flounce, then tack to the skirt and machine-stitch by the edge.

Make your own ruches and ruffles. Ruches may be set on or used as an edging – or to decorate knitwear. The easiest to make are ribbon rouches as the edges need not be neatened. If some other material is used, cut it into straight or bias strips, taking care not to cut them so wide that the ruche will droop. Edges can be neatened by hemming, machine-hemming, zig-zag edging or overcast edging. Gathering may be done by hand, in the case of delicate fabrics, or by machine, but check the thread tension is slackened. Two rows of gathering will make it easier to mount the ruche, which may be sewn on by hand or by machine, according to the fabric. If sewing by hand, use a running-stitch and a backstitch alternately. Ruches and frills need about double their finished length of material or less if cut on the bias. Gathered frills may also be stitched on reversed, pressed over, and then the seam edges neatened from the inside by overcasting, or by turning them in against each other.

Rose ruches. Rose ruches are made of taffeta bias strips, pinked at the edges. The upper double pleats should be stitched together in the centre, thus producing a very full ruche.

To make a rose ruche, the pleats should be caught together in the centre, just below the edge. Rose ruches are sewn on by hand, before the folds are caught together.

Net ruffles. For net ruffles, either a double- or three-fold strip should be used, or the pleats can be folded double, so as to ensure a very full ruffle edge.

Hems
Faced (false) hems. These involve letting the original hem down to its fullest extent. The raw edge is then trimmed and checked to see that it is straight before pressing and adding a faced hem in as similar colour and weight to the original garments as possible. Wide-width bias binding or tape can also be used. Cut the facing fabric to the required length approximately between 50 mm (2 in) and 100 mm

107

(4 in) wide. (If possible, a facing hem's selvedge threads should run in the same direction as the selvedge edges in the garment.) Next, place the right sides of the fabrics together checking the edges are even. Tack and then machine-stitch. Press seam open and fold the facing hem to the wrong side making the join approximately 6 mm (¼ in) from the lower edge of the garment on the inside. The raw edge of the dress turning should come to the lower edge fold in the inside of the hem. Tack in place before turning in the other raw edge of facing hem, approximately 6 mm (¼ in); tack this in place too, before finally slip-hemming in position. Remove the tacking stitches before pressing on the wrong side.

Bridging stitch. For those with electric machines, a bridging stitch is a very useful means of lengthening a hem when fabric is scarce. It is mainly used to join together two pieces of fabric with folded edges, at the same time producing a decorative effect as the stitch shows on the right side of the fabric. It can also be used for a lay join where a decorative gap is left between the two pieces of fabric; and is suitable for patchwork, attaching straight-edged lace and inserting lace or braid.

To join the two pieces of fabric by machine use the zig-zag needle-plate and the zig-zag presser foot. Set the stitch length at ½–1 and the stitch width at 4. Turn under a seam allowance on the two pieces of fabric and press. Place the fabrics right side up, butting together the two folded edges under the centre of the presser foot. Keep the two edges closely butted while sewing. Trim away excess fabric close to the stitching line.

Turning a new hem. Nothing gives new life to an old skirt more readily than a new hem line. Look at yourself in the mirror; if your bargain skirt sags, get someone to help you to turn up a new hem. First, pin the hem at the new even length. This can be done by measuring from the floor with a metal rule and putting a row of pins around where the new hem is to be. Or you can use a piece of french chalk to mark round the hips and then measure an even distance down from this line to the hem line. Or you can stand before a mirror and pin the points that sag until you have a perfectly true line. Using a hem leveller helps when you're working on your own. Review all your hems in your full-length mirror. Make sure both dresses and slips are the correct length and that the hem lines are even. In tailored skirts or narrow skirts, even a slight sag will be conspicuous as there is no fullness to hide it.

Curved hems. Sometimes it's necessary to turn hems on circular skirts. These can be finished off by binding with bias tape, leaving a superfluous fullness at the edge of the turning which can be reduced by pressing if the curve is slight. If the fullness is too much, then make tiny pleats in the turning. Pressing should be done carefully, from the edge inwards, and a damp pressing-cloth should be used.

Stitched-edge hem (see also decorative stitched edge below). This provides a neat finish for edges which cannot be rolled. Turn the edge and stitch; turn again and hem invisibly by hand.

Narrow machine-turned hem. This is useful for when a tiny hem is needed. Some hemming-foot sewing-machine attachments can turn your fabric edge twice and stitch in one operation.

Decorative stitched edge. It is often used on very circular hems, and wherever a decorative finish is wanted. Pink the edge of your fabric, turn the hem and press. Make as many rows of machine-stitching as desired.

10

Suits, Overcoats and Jackets, and Heavy Tailoring Alterations

What to collect

Suits

Anything pin-striped for the 'Al Capone' look
'Retro' Forties tweed padded shouldered styles
Fifties and Sixties fitted costumes with pencil pleated or dirndl skirts
  and 'shortie' box jackets
Beatle suits
Chanel-style suits
Men's evening suits with waistcoats and pegtop trousers
Morning dress
Cocktail suits in brocade, lace and velvet
Fifties 'Elvis' Teddy-boy suits in flecked and bird's eye tweeds

Overcoats

Men's herringbone tweed
Harris and Donegal tweed men's overcoats in single- or double-
  breasted trench styles, i.e. Ulsters
Men's gabardine raincoats in fawns and greys
Cashmere, mohair and camel overcoats
Crombies and Chesterfields with velvet collars/cuffs
'Retro' coats with padded shoulders
Wrapover styles
Evening coats in brocade, velvet, satin, etc.
Fifties and Sixties duster coats – real Garden Party numbers
Loden, suede and sheepskin coats – if not too damaged and dirty,
  and in the style you want

Jackets

Reefer and pea type, also duffle coats
Beatle (collarless) jackets
Navy blazers
Donkey-type jackets
Men's linen and seersucker jackets – the kind seen at vicarage fêtes
Men's Norfolk jackets
Dinner jackets
Riding/hacking jackets in tweeds and Bedford cord
Miscellaneous suit jackets (where the skirt is missing) in needlecord,
    wool-crêpe, velvet, etc.
Also, men's waistcoats, including white pique cotton evening dress
    waistcoats

Good makes and designer names to look out for

Hardy Amies
Pierre Cardin
Jaeger
Simpson
Aquascutum

'I buy suits very seldom because it is an experience I dread. Nothing seems to fit exactly, and the business of trying things on is dispiriting, for one is brought face to face with one's own deficiencies. This time I thought I might try to give myself a slightly brighter, more outgoing look by getting something that wasn't dark grey. But the attempt failed. If clothes say anything about their wearer, I shudder to think what they say about me.'

Alexander Chancellor, *Spectator*, June 1982.

The trouble with 'the suit', and its appeal to conspicuous consumption, is that it tends only to look good and to fit superbly when it is bespoke and could cost in the region of, say, £500.

One answer for those forced to attend formal or family functions, or for those in jobs where 'the suit' is obligatory wear, is to renovate secondhand ones. Walk into almost any charity shop and you'll find racks of practically unworn men's suits hanging up forlornly, most costing from £2.50 upwards. With very little alteration these can pass for much more expensive off-the-peg numbers. Small details date a suit – the width and style of lapels, slimness/closeness of jacket fit – but probably the biggest style giveaway is the shape of the trouser leg. Ill-fitting crotches and too short or too long sleeve lengths can apply to new suits as well. And, lapels apart, I would say most of these alterations are not beyond basic sewing skills. However, resetting tailored shoulders requires considerable tailoring expertise (see Directory).

When it comes to most simple tailoring alterations 'big really is beautiful'. With today's clothes being worn several sizes too large the chances are that, if necessary, suits two or three sizes too large can be altered to fit. Even when things are slightly on the small side, or too short in the sleeves and legs, alterations can be made. Just check the seams and hems – good quality tailoring usually has fabric to spare. I once scooped a Pierre Cardin man's tweed suit for £5 at a Save the Children jumble sale. The impoverished recipient had the crotch shortened and the trousers and sleeves lengthened for around £15 at his local drycleaners. All this, plus cleaning and pressing, brought his total outlay to somewhere around twenty pounds. An equivalent new suit would have cost several hundred.

Fortunately, tailoring Eighties-style favours the loose, baggy Chaplinesque fit as opposed to Norman Wisdom tightness. Pegtops are purposefully worn several sizes too big; braces pull up trouser crotches, and by the time a belt or cummerbund has clinched in the waist, there may be no further need to alter. The same applies to raglan-sleeved overcoats and gabardine mackintoshes. The Eighties way to wear these is 'big', with sleeves rolled up and waists belted tightly in. Men's dinner jackets are another good buy. They give the Trilby look on the cheap, and are often made from top quality materials, are well tailored and, even better, appear hardly worn. I picked up one in a jumble sale for 20p, and a few days later I found a full evening dress kit of jacket, waistcoat and pegtops for £2 on a Portobello Market stall. But the accolade in clothes trouvées must surely go to a photographer friend who came across an antique Burberry mack early one morning on the way to work. It had been stuffed ignominiously into the dustbin! She promptly sent it to the cleaners and now wears a much admired coat.

Bargains in women's costume suit jackets are also fairly thick on the ground, the passage of time having somehow separated them from the original skirt. An art student colleague of mine used to wear an aunt's Forties Dior suit jacket. Its Harlequin fabric was made up from hand-stitched tweed off-cuts – there was no seaming, the fit being achieved by the diamonds diminishing in the right places. Bargains in 'Retro' women's overcoats also abound, but these tend to be in the larger sizes, and may need considerable taking in on the shoulders and side seams to make them fit. Shoulders can be pleated or tacked (see page 120), but if coat revers are particularly fussy, this kind of alteration may not look right – it really is best suited to coats or jackets with uncomplicated shawl collars. If you do suspect your 'Retro' coat, or something else, is a good example of period style or even haute couture, consider carefully before you alter. Costume museums place high value on authenticity; original seams and stitching are just as important as the fabric. Any altering could damage permanently, as well as devalue.

Finally, unless they are perfect, it is best to avoid damaged or dirty leather, suede and fur coats. Altering and cleaning these successfully is really a job for experts, and usually costs far outweigh advantages. The quality of fur coats available at charity shops and jumble sales varies, but most of the ones I've encountered seem well beyond repair, although they could possibly be recycled for trimmings, muffs and hats etc. However, Christie's costume sales often include sales of secondhand furs where quality and prices are correspondingly higher (see Directory for address).

Generally speaking, any major tailoring alteration requires sewing expertise way beyond the skills of most amateurs. But if saving money and learning a craft is your aim, then it is worth going to evening classes to learn how to set a sleeve properly. There are, of course, the tailoring alternatives of your local drycleaners, but the less ambitious tailoring jobs are worth attempting for yourself. Relining a coat or jacket is something that can be tackled with impunity. Indeed, a new lining, using a printed fabric, can make a tremendous difference to an old coat, and it can be made detachable.

Your fashion identity

As with everything in secondhand clothes, it's what you put with them. Accessories are the way to score on dressing up dull, neutral-coloured bargain coats and macks, and these can be new or second-hand (see Chapter 15). For those whose coat bargain comes without a matching belt, make one up from material in the hem. If there isn't enough fabric, then clinch the waist in with a belt made in a contrasting material. Providing this is done with intention and flair, it can lift something boring immediately into the designer class. An old military-style Sam Browne belt in leather and brass looks great on almost everything, especially a man's Fifties Harris tweed coat or a gabardine mack; a punky black studded leather cartridge-holder belt would also look just as stunning. Dinner jackets take on a new lease of life worn with, say, heavily embroidered ethnic skirts in bright primary colours, or with sunray pleated skirts in metallic glittery colours, with black ski-pants or skin-tight straight trousers in black grosgrain or satin to match the dinner jacket lapels. You could cover buttons in black satin to match lapels for authentic detailing and extra style. Dinner jackets also look good worn with delicate lacy camisole tops, boob tubes and leopard print T-shirts. Wear an 'Elvis' suit with authentic Fifties accessories – right down to 'Brothel Creepers' and 'Slim Jim' ties; female Elvis fans may prefer winkle-picker stilettos. Morning-dress coats can either be cut down to make a boxy jacket or worn long with satin boxer shorts, fishnet tights and a topper, à la Liza Minelli in *Cabaret*. A man's pinstriped suit, which looks even better on a woman, can be worn either on the big side or altered to fit. Keep one as a classic wardrobe standby for formal family gatherings, job interviews, or wear it with a (man's) panama hat, black patent pumps, black tights and a plain white silk T-shirt underneath (or even gangster-style with black shirt and white satin kipper tie). Fifties cocktail suit jackets (without skirt) look good with jeans, Zouave pants and gypsy flounced skirts of 'Retro' crêpe. Wear Forties and Fifties costume jackets, with padded shoulders in the authentic Joan Crawford mode, i.e., without anything underneath. But don't forget to sew in, or wear, the appropriate dress shields, and swop original hard shoulder pads for softer substitutes (see Chapter 9).

Clothes renovation kit checklist (see Essential Sewing Kit, Chapter 2)

Collar board.   Useful for pressing together thick edges of fabric.
Dress (curtain) weights.   For weighting hems in coats and jackets.
Lining fabrics.   For lining coats and skirts.
Long mirror.   It is essential to see what you are doing!
Needleboard.   This is an expensive, but important, item if you're going to repair garments with napped materials such as velvet and fur

fabric. The board which is literally a bed of needles, prevents matting and shrinkage. The pile falls between the needles which are angled to prevent matting, as the seams are pressed down. Lift the iron up and down when pressing, rather than sliding it along. Velvet should be pressed on the wrong side along the grain line, parallel to the selvedge, never on the cross which could stretch it out of shape. A cheaper alternative is to cover your ironing board with terry towelling and place fabric right side down on that.

Needles. Use fur and leather needles for sewing on trimmings to coat collars, hems and cuffs.

Petersham ribbon. Used for edging jackets, etc.

Pressing-cloths. Have a heavy and lightweight one handy for different fabrics.

Punched leather trimming. Used for edging jackets, etc.

Seam ripper. For ripping seams and stitches with minimum damage.

Seam roll. A large firm sausage used for pressing seams open on delicate fabrics. Seams are pressed together first of all, then pressed again with the seam roll placed underneath to prevent seam marks showing through on a fabric's right side. To save money, it can be made from an off-cut of dowelling rod, approximately 50 mm (2 in) diameter, or use an old rolling-pin. Wrap the rod in two or three layers of white flannel, check the closing seam is neatly tucked underneath, and overstitch to close.

Sleeveboard. For the proper ironing of sleeves.

Stiletto. For use if you plan to do your own tailored buttonholes.

Tailor's chalk. For marking alterations clearly.

Tailor's dummy. (See Chapter 9)

Tailor's ham. A ham-shaped cushion for pressing large, curved areas. Professional tailors usually make their own. All you need are two oval pieces of fabric, approximately 20 cm (8 in) by 30 cm (12 in), that will not shed fibres all over your tailoring operations. White linen, cotton, or an old piece of blanket will do – having a different fabric either side of your ham makes it more versatile. Machine-stitch edges together, leaving an opening; then turn inside out and fill with washable Terylene wadding. Overstitch edges to close.

Tailor's press mit or cushion. For shaping collars and cuffs.

Tailor's wooden clapper. Useful for hammering seams flat and making them easier to sew, e.g. at the crotch intersection on trousers.

Thread. Linen variety.

Velvet. For edging jackets, etc.

Washing, drycleaning and stain removal (see Chapters 3, 4 and 5)

Tailoring

Making it fit

Where a slim well-tailored fit is essential then, obviously, rules exist for how to go about the work. Classic tailoring, particularly when it comes to a man's suit, is very traditional and conservative over detailing. Repairs and alterations have to be undertaken with precision so that nothing looks obvious. Threads must match fabric exactly; stitching must be true and preferably of the same size as the garment's original. Always pin and try on as you go, carefully noting measurements. And, remember, tailored suits and jackets are hardly the place for experimentation.

1 *Jackets and coats.* Always take in equal amounts from both side seams. This applies to all garments, whether coat, jacket, skirt, trousers or a dress. Then, if more has to be done, the back seam, then the front. If a coat or jacket needs still more adjustment a little more can be lost, around 38 mm (1½ in), by adjusting the front buttons. Finally, alter the front seams above the pockets and then the darts. For sleeves take in the front seam only.

2 *Trousers.* To take in, pin the side and inside leg seams first. Then pin the crotch and the back seam from the waist. Remember that waistbands will have to be removed if you are taking in over 50 mm (2 in). If the trousers are too tight in the crotch, a gusset can be sewn in. This is quite a tailoring feat, and best left to the drycleaners.

3 *Skirts.* Taking in skirts depends on the style required, but taking in side seams invariably means removing and replacing side-fastening zips or else the hip line will be spoilt. Further taking in can be done on the centre back and then front seams as necessary. I have also experimented with turning skirts around, preferring the back pleats in the front, and have then taken in the side seams and re-inserted the zips to the correct side. Darts are sometimes too long and therefore may need adjusting. *Note.* Professional tailors work to conventional style rules; double-breasted jackets have no back vents; straight skirts

116

with back plackets tend to have none in front, but there may be various in-fashion styles when this convention cannot be so rigidly enforced.

Coat linings

The following method should be used:

1 Try on the coat inside out. Then, using a seam ripper, very carefully unpick the old lining, making notes as you go of how it was originally sewn in, and checking whether there are any pockets, extra fullness, tucks and so on. Suitable replacement lining fabrics are Dycel or a good quality dress satin. Men's tailoring suppliers have the correct conventional lining fabrics for tailored clothes. But not all coat linings have to be of conventional fabrics, some casual styles may cry out for something more experimental. As a rule, lining fabric should not be thicker than the garment fabric. Stretch nylon jersey lining fabric is a useful all-purpose one that suits most garments and is practical for cleaning and sewing – though you may dislike the feel. The important thing to remember is that coat sleeve linings should always be of a slippery fabric, so if your coat or jacket is to have some thick novelty fur fabric, then be sure to line the sleeves in something thinner, or leave them unlined. Cuffs and turnings can always be covered in something to match the main lining. Other lining fabrics worth considering are printed furnishing chintz, silk in eye-catching patterns such as leopard skin, ikat woven cottons, quilted satin Liberty Prints. Again the decorative qualities can be emphasized by binding worn coat edges and covering buttons to match.

2 Remove the old lining and press pieces flat. Cut out the new lining, using the original as a pattern, and check you leave enough fabric for the shoulder pleats at centre of shoulder. Check also that the original pattern pieces have allowed enough ease. If more is needed, allow 3 mm (⅛ in) extra outside all edges. Tack underarm seams, and seams in the back section if it is a fitted style. Next, tack along the centre back line. Then turn the coat or jacket inside out and put it on a tailor's dummy. (If you do not have one, place it on the table.) With french chalk, mark the centre-back line of the coat and neckline.

Frayed sleeve lining. When the edges have frayed at the base, a piece

117

of tape or grosgrain ribbon can be pinned over the worn areas and whip-stitched in place. Turn the end of the ribbon under and finish off, keeping it in line with the seam of the sleeve. This same repair can be applied to frayed lining edges or the worn backs of trouser hems.

Worn neckline. If a coat lining is worn only at the neckline, use a piece of similar fabric to patch it. Cut the patch piece to fit along the seams at this section, turn the edges under and whip-stitch in place.

Underarm shields These provide a camouflage for otherwise good linings. Cut two pieces of lining fabric in shield or half-moon shape, making one end of the moon higher than the other (or use ready-made underarm shields). This end goes towards the front of the armhole. Seam the pieces together along the outer curve and turn to the right side. Clip notches along the inner curve. Unpick the original sleeve lining at the underarm and insert the shield. Sew it in place with running-stitches. Then whip-stitch the sleeve lining back into place.

Skirt linings

Back lining for a straight skirt. This lining is used to prevent the back of a skirt from seating. It should be of a firm fabric such as nylon acetate. Cut out the lining like skirt back, but make it 15 cm (6 in) shorter. Make darts; then stitch, seam and press. Afterwards pink the lower edge. Pin the lining to the skirt, wrong sides together. Sew the lining to the front side seams. On the placket side, clip the lining seam at the base of opening. Turn the seam allowance under, and sew to the back edge of zip tape. Line both front and back of knitted or jersey skirts, using a nylon jersey knitted fabric and zig-zag stitch.

Lining a full skirt. For thin fabrics needing extra body use organdie, taffeta, or stiffened net as lining material. For thick fabrics, such as tweed, use jap silk or manmade equivalent of similar weight. Cut the lining piece to matching skirt section. Tack and stitch together. Let the lining hang before taking up the hem.

Jetted pockets

These can be useful and practical additions to otherwise pocketless coats and skirts. You can make your own pocket bags from a spare piece of cotton fabric in a colour that matches the garment or buy ready-made pocket bags from haberdashery counters. These usually come in calico or a nylon jersey, some have a piece of iron-on adhesive webbing already attached for easy fixing.

Always try on garments first before marking out and pinning the exact position of a pocket before finally sewing. For a comfortably fitting pocket bag measure the size of your hand and allow 2–4 cm (¾ in to 1½ in) all round. Next working from the wrong side of garment open up a side seam using a seam ripper. Pin and tack on pocket bag, then stitch in place. Press on right side of garment with a damp cloth and hot iron.

Zips

Most professionals I have talked to never seem to use the standard zipper-foot attachment for sewing in zips – or electric sewing machines come to that. One drycleaning tailoress, who does hundreds of zips a week, swears by the following method. Tack the seam opening first, then stitch the closed zip in place over the seam. Remove the tacking stitches. Press the zip over a tailor's ham to keep the curve of the side seam, taking care to avoid direct contact with nylon zips.

Conventional zip insertion.   For skirts use the following method:

1 The placket on the left side should be 25 mm (1 in) longer than the zipper chain.
2 Close the placket opening on the seam line with temporary tacking stitches. Press open and remove tacking.
3 If the seam is less than 15 mm (⅝ in) wide, extend the width of the front seam by stitching seam tape to it.
4 With the skirt right side out, place the opening over the closed zip with the tab 18 mm (¾ in) from the top edge. Turn under the back edge of the opening 3 mm (¼ in) from the seam line; pin and tack from the base up, close to the zip chain, easing the fabric to take tape.
5 Lap the front fold over the zip so that the chain and the back edge stitching are covered. Tack across the bottom and along the chain,

119

easing the fabric. Using the zip foot, stitch the back edge; then stitch across the bottom and up the placket, keeping the stitching even.

Inserting simple zips. Use the following method:

1 Set the stitch length on your machine at 1½–3. Fit the straight-stitch needle-plate and then the zipper foot, which is adjustable to allow you to sew to the left or right of the zip.
2 To sew down the right side, release the screw at the back of the zipper foot and position the foot to the right of the needle so that the needle passes through the opening on the left side of the foot. Tighten the screw.
3 To sew down the left side, position the foot to the left of the needle.

Shoulder pleats

This alteration reduces enormous shoulders on dinner jackets and coats without having to reset sleeves in armholes which is a major tailoring job.

1 Measure width you want the finished shoulders to be, use french chalk to mark the position of the pleats.
2 Remove existing shoulder pads.
3 Try coat on, pleating and pinning fabric on right side. If necessary make two small shoulder pleats, approximately 25 mm (1 in) wide on each shoulder rather than one large pleat. Check that outside fold of pleat laps armhole seam by approximately 20 mm (¾ in).
4 Try on coat again, readjusting pleats if necessary. Tack in position.
5 Press with a damp cloth over a tailor's ham before machining topstitching in place along inside edge of pleat.
6 Stitch original shoulder padding back in place.

Neatening seams

The simplest seam finish is to overcast by hand using short stitches. Quicker but less professional is to trim edges with pinking shears.

Buttonhole-stitch. This gives a very secure and hardwearing seam finish. Sew with sewing silk to match the fabric colour. Stitches should be as close together as possible. Linen thread or cotton are not suitable here as little knots in the stitches would be too hard and tend to press through, especially in the case of thin materials.

Blanket-stitch. This is also used as an alternative to buttonhole-stitch. When working, hold the seam edge down (for the buttonhole-stitch the seam edge should be held up), and for every stitch, loop the thread round the needle.

Folded seams. The neatest-looking seams are those in which the seam edges have been folded back. Various stitches may be used to secure folded edges. In the case of hard fabrics, cover the folded cut edge with a very closely worked herringbone-stitch. Alternatively, seam edges may be hemmed down narrowly, or machine-stitched.

Saddle stitching

When done well this can give tailored garments instant Savile Row style, adding interest to otherwise dull or over-severe lapels. Use small, neat even stitches in a thread that matches the fabric.

Work your saddle stitches approximately 3 mm (⅛ in) from the outside edge of the lapels. Make the line of stitches taking a short backstitch on the outside (right side of fabric) and a longer stitch on the wrong side.

Covered weights

If the hem of your jacket, coat or dress needs weighting to keep the line, simply cover some dress weights with cotton fabric and sew these to the seams at the upper edge of a hem.

Tailored worked buttonholes

These make a great difference to any tailored item. If you have to repair damaged buttonholes of this kind be sure to match thread exactly using buttonhole thread. If you have to make an extra button-hole, practise first on spare scraps of fabric until you feel reasonably confident. Drycleaners offer an expert service in tailored buttonholes and this may be well worth using, as a badly made one instantly looks shoddy.

Fabrics: some sewing reminders

Suede and leather

The common problems with suede and leather alterations are associated with cutting out, seaming and finishing replacement leather.

Preparation and cutting.   You will need to add about 15 per cent extra to allow for wastage when cutting; look out for any grain in the suede and make sure you cut it as a nap fabric. To begin with, place the pattern on the leather and hold it down with weights while you draw round the material on the wrong side. Always cut through a single layer, reversing patterns for right and left sections. And cut areas which will get the hardest wear (collars, cuffs) from the thickest part of the leather. Use tailor's chalk for transferring markings, and remember that unpicking causes unsightly marks. Never pin suede or leather – use clothes pegs.

Sewing.   Most domestic machines will sew thin leather. Place a layer of thin cotton tape over the seam line and stitch through it to prevent the leather being stretched out of shape. Seams are usually opened out and stuck down with fabric adhesive. Don't use iron-on webbings as leather tends to shrink when heated. Hems can be stuck in place and topstitched.

Finishing.   Don't ever iron suede or leather. Badly crumpled suede garments will straighten out if hung on hangers in a steamy bathroom for a short time.

Velvet

One of the problems of working with velvet is not being able to get the nap to run the same way throughout the garment. As a result, one side looks lighter than the other. Also, if you make a mistake with velvet and have to unpick a seam, you'll be left with a permanent mark.

Preparation and cutting.   Make sure you follow the correct layout for nap fabric on your pattern, and remember to buy extra alteration fabric, too. Use long fine pins when placing the pattern pieces on the fabric. To transfer markings, use a tracing wheel on the wrong side of the fabric. Make small accurate tacking-stitches as velvet, particu-larly the nylon variety, tends to be slippery.

Sewing.   Always sew in the direction of the pile. Loosen the tension slightly on your machine to avoid puckering, and use a larger stitch than usual. Never topstitch as this flattens the pile.

Finishing. To press, a needleboard is useful but an alternative is to place layers of a towel or another piece of velvet, piles facing, on to the fabric and press lightly. For seams, stand the iron upright on the board and pull the wrong side of fabric lightly over sole of iron, or simply hold it in front of a steam iron. For a really professional press send the garment to a drycleaners.

Fur fabric

Fur fabric is similar to velvet in that there can be problems in getting the nap to run the same way throughout the garment. Don't attempt anything with intricate seaming; and don't cut with scissors.

Preparation and cutting. Place pattern pieces on back of fabric and mark where you need to cut. Use a razor or sharp knife to cut the backing and gently pull the two pieces apart.

Sewing. Sew with the nap as in velvet. Pull out hairs caught in seams with a pin and then brush. This makes the seams practically invisible.

Finishing. As for velvet. Or press gently with a warm iron on the wrong side.

Jersey

Jersey fabric stretches during cutting or sewing, and seam stitches tend to break when the jersey is stretched. Some jerseys have a definite 'one-way' (the knitted ones especially) and should be treated as napped fabric. Finer jersey should be lined to prevent seating.

Preparation and cutting. Don't let the fabric hang over the edge of a table when cutting, and make sure the 'stretch' grain goes around the body and not up and down.

Sewing. If the edges roll up after you've cut out your pattern pieces, machine-stitch 6 mm (¼ in) from the edge before sewing. Alternatively, if you know you won't have to trim a seam, zig-zag stitch the edges – this will keep them flat and neaten your seam at the same time. Use a zig-zag stitch to sew all seams; if you have a straight-stitch machine, adjust the tension. (As a test, try sewing two pieces of jersey together. You'll probably find normal tension is too tight.)

Interface those areas which should not stretch, e.g., buttonholes, necklines, etc. Fine viscose and nylon jerseys can ladder easily, so finish seams with edge-stitching.

Finishing. Press seams only across, not up and down, being careful not to pull them out of shape.

———11———
Children's, Teens and Sports Clothes

What to collect

Dresses

Anything smocked or embroidered
Anything in velvet, broderie anglaise, organdie, etc.

Coats

Velvet-collared tweed classic fitted styles
Duffles
Anoraks
Riding jackets
Blazers
American campus jackets
Velvet cloaks for parties

Skirts

Kilts
Corduroy and denim pinafores
Divided skirts
Old-fashioned gymslips

Knitwear

Anything non-felted
Fair Isle and Arran sweaters and cardigans
Berets, gloves and scarves
Lacy knits
Polo necks

Any Shetland sweaters in good condition
Woollen tights in fancy knits

Trousers

Velvet, corduroy and denim jeans
Dungarees

Shirts

Anything Aertex, Viyella or Clydella in checks or plains
Striped rugger shirts
Chinese cotton embroidered blouses
USA baseball and bowling shirts

Sportswear

Anything in cricket sweaters
Mini skirts for skating, tennis, etc
Track suits
Jodhpurs
Shorts
Fifties and Sixties sunbathing suits, with ruched tops and flounced
   or bloomer skirts

Today, children's clothing seems to cost as much as, or more than, their adult equivalent. And to justify this feat, manufacturers and retailers argue that children's clothes involve comparable, if not more, finishing than adults. Rising costs in sewing patterns, materials and new fabric also mean that home sewing children's clothes is hardly cheaper, particularly if personal time is taken into consideration. However, making children's clothes can give tremendous satisfaction, and when made of fabrics recycled from adult clothing they can cost very little. This improvisation was certainly expected during the Second World War; and DIY dressmaking may also be the only way around dressing children with awkward, problem figures.

When it comes to providing children's clothes on the cheap, charity-shop organizers, notably MIND and War on Want, claim they're also setting new social trends and providing a therapeutic service. Despite some criticism of certain charities' distribution network, financial organization and political aims, depressed, stay-at-home mothers on tight family incomes do, indeed, find relief meeting others in the same predicament. There is nothing quite like a charity-shop bargain for bringing people together. And when children grow out of clothes so quickly, buying secondhand makes sense. Several mothers I know have actually trained offspring to hunt out their own charity-shop wardrobes: some girls and boys as young as five seem quite capable of deciding what is good value for money. Older children soon develop an eye for quality fabrics, and immediately discern whether something's hand- or machine-embroidered. And it's less strain all round when a child's secondhand Arran sweater at 20p gets ruined – rather than a new one costing £20.

Many high-street cleaners recognize that more secondhand school uniforms are being bought as compared with two decades ago. Parents seem very particular over let-down hem-line marks showing, and will point them out. The main snags, however, with children's clothes are stains. Lollipop colours can be difficult to remove, as can other sugar-based stains. Often these marks are invisible on a garment until it is drycleaned; then they appear as hard brown irremovable stains, having caramelized in the heat. If you're washing secondhand children's bargains, always check any pockets are empty. Other points to check are whether zips work on sportswear, anoraks and trousers. Also check signs of wear and tear on trouser knees, seats and hems. Sweater neck openings on otherwise perfect sweaters may be too tight, but this can be remedied quite easily (see page 133). Safety is another thing to watch for. Worn fabrics may be highly flammable, so avoid any nightwear unless it is labelled flame resistant. The same goes for footwear.

Generally, children's clothes in charity shops tend to have minor things wrong. Quite a few specialist secondhand outlets exist, however, to deal in expensive velvet-collared tweed coats and smocked dresses. Clothes sold in these places will undoubtedly be more expensive, but will probably be in perfect condition.

Your fashion identity

Traditionally, British children have been discouraged from showing too much interest in fashionable clothes, unlike their foreign contemporaries. School uniform, whether new or secondhand, is a considerable drain on the family budget, and few teenagers have a special clothes allowance to keep up with the latest fashions. Dressing up boring regulation mackintoshes and skirts to make them wearable after school hours does take some imagination, but it is worth doing.

A single glittery Indian woven scarf, for example, can do a lot for institutional navy blue and bottle green. Indifferent flared or pleated skirts can lead a double life clinched in at the waist with a bright elastic belt, especially if worn with leotard tops and footless tights – or a tie-dyed leopard print T-shirt (see Special effects, Chapter 14).

Boys, too, can box clever when obliged to dress up. A secondhand suit can be altered as required. A pair of dark cord, or velvet, jeans can be teamed with a white school shirt sporting detachable broderie anglaise ruffles. Secondhand collarless grandad striped shirts, with traditional starched wing collars, get a new lease of life when worn with a new or secondhand bow-tie. Add to this a fancy waistcoat and cowboy boots for an instant Clint Eastwood image.

Clothes renovation kit checklist (see Essential Sewing Kit, Chapter 2)

Adhesive webbing. For putting up hems quickly, and for fast patching jobs.

American initials. These are sports letters for sewing on cardigans and baseball jackets, etc.

Anorak cuffs and jacket welts. Made of stretch nylon or jersey, they are useful renovators for secondhand and old anoraks.

Beads. For decorating old sweaters.

Buttons. Have sets of novelty ones available for cardigans, blouses and dresses. 'Fruity' and animal buttons can encourage young children to dress themselves. Check that these have no sharp edges. Glass ones are unsuitable as they can break when sucked by young children.

Patching pieces. Keep a supply for mending and reinforcing trouser knees and seats. Denim, corduroy, etc., can be dyed to match.

Punched leather trimming. Available by the metre, it is useful for edging cuffs, trouser hems, edges of pockets, etc. Elbow and shoulder patches in quilted cottons or needlecord are easier to wash than conventional leather elbow patches.

Safety ribbon. This shines at night, and is useful for sewing on cyclists' jackets etc.

Sequins. For decorating old sweaters.

Studs. Hammer-type studs for dressing up old leather and jean jackets.

Suspender braces. For dungarees.

Thread. Jeans thread.

Velcro (nylon pile tape). Self-adhesive 'spot-ons'. For fastenings on children's sweaters.

Zips. A supply of jean zips is always useful – these have extra tough metal teeth. Ordinary nylon trouser zips are not suitable.

Washing, drycleaning and stain removal (see Chapters 3, 4 and 5)

Sewing repairs

Dresses

To add length to a smocked or party dress, make or buy a secondhand white cotton petticoat and sew on a deep 12 cm (5 in) flounce of white broderie anglaise. On a young child a petticoat can be made more secure if small cotton tape loops are sewn to the elasticated waistline; corresponding buttons are then sewn to the inside waistband of the dress.

Patches

Paratroop patches. Are good for sports, play or work clothes when they are made to reinforce points of greatest wear. They are usually cut in ovals or rectangles, either from the same material as the garment, from cotton mesh dyed to match a fabric or sometimes from leather, and are stitched on the right side. Boys' and men's sports jackets can be successfully reinforced at the elbow with neat patches made of small pieces of leather or suede.

Unfortunately, one disadvantage of using real leather is that it does not wash well. So for reinforcing jeans or a child's sweater cut an oval piece of cotton or needlecord quilting, bind the raw edges with bias binding and apply a patch to each elbow, or alternatively sew on using a zig-zag stitch on your machine.

Crotch patches. For trouser and jean crotches, unpick the middle seam and the inner leg seam as far as necessary, and mark the outline of the part to be mended with tacking thread. Then cut out sections of material to the shape of the marking, in the same grain and with ample turnings. Pin them in and tack them on from the right side.

129

Then cut away the worn parts and stitch and thoroughly press the seams. Finally, close the leg seams and then the middle seam.

Appliqué patches. Sew the edges of the area to be appliquéd by hand or machine and trace on paper the size of the patch needed to cover it. Cut out a silhouette of, say, flowers, fruit or an animal, which must be large enough to cover the mend. Turn in the patch edges and secure to the garment by machine or by hand. Use slip-stitch, whip-stitch, running-stitch, blanket-stitch, long-and-short-stitch, or any type of feather-stitch. Bondaweb double-sided adhesive webbing can also be useful instant patching on jeans. Use more than one appliqué piece if necessary, and make the whole effect appear planned.

-12-
Knits

What to collect

Anything in Fair Isle, moss and chevron lacy knits – e.g. sweaters, cardigans, scarves, shawls, hats and gloves
Summer knits in silks and cottons
Aran knits
Ethnic knits from Afghanistan, Mexico, Norway
Chinese beaded and sequinned knitwear
Any good, hand-knitted sweaters
Anything cashmere, mohair, angora in plains and floral prints; also leopard print
Intarsia sweaters (traditional diamond patterned) Fair Isles etc.
'Retro' knits in good condition if possible
Designer labels and makes to look out for: Jaeger, Lyle & Scott, Pringle, Marks & Spencer (Shetlands)
Men's V-necked sleeveless pullovers in lambswool, etc.
Chunky knit jackets and coats
Sweater dresses
Cricketing sweaters with V-necks and cable-stitching
Twinsets

At the age of nine, I remember being greatly impressed on reading about a man who'd taken a whole year to knit his daughter's wedding dress – complete with matching full-length lacy veil. Admittedly, this male knitting champion had been in the navy where, thanks to a legacy of crocheting and darning sails and fishnets, these skills are still counted as acceptably masculine. There doesn't seem to be anything particularly 'feminine' about darning and knitting, despite the sewing manuals of the Thirties and Forties continually exhorting women to darn their menfolk's socks. One such manual noted: 'More husbands have become aware of their wives' disinterest in them through permanently missing buttons and ragged socks than any other way. A happy home must have no frayed edges – nerves are easily jangled by such things. Ugly words can be heard through stocking holes and sheet rents . . .'

Judging from the piles of sweaters, sporting undarned elbows, that end up in British charity shops – not to mention the half-finished DIY knitting efforts – a good many homes must be resounding with 'ugly words'. Sweater elbows seem the most vulnerable wear area; the biggest 'worn elbow' culprits undoubtedly being architects and draughtsmen whose drawing-board activities literally seem to 'etch out' elbows. But if sweater bargains are top quality lambswool or cashmere, it may be worth resuscitating them with new knitted elbow patches (see Knitting Repairs later in this chapter). And traditional elbow patches of ready-made leather, or cotton quilting in contrasting or matching colours, can make an attractive alternative. Prudent clothes watchers will, of course, reinforce unworn sweater elbows before any damage occurs.

Always avoid anything felted when it comes to woollens being sold cheaply. Nothing can be done to reverse matters, because high temperatures have actually changed the yarn to a fabric closely resembling felt. A drycleaning process exists for softening sweaters that have been badly washed and feel gritty (see Directory). I have managed to improve slightly felted garments simply by washing in a special wool detergent and then rinsing in a solution of dilute acetic acid and distilled water.

Shapeless lacy knits can sometimes be resuscitated after careful washing by pressing out excess moisture between towels and then pinning them flat over a piece of insulation board (available from DIY shops) covered with clean towelling. Covetable knits such as Chinese beaded cardigans, Fair Isles, Arrans, cashmeres, mohair and angora all need extra careful washing, handling and storage if they're to last. If these do turn up in jumble sales and charity shops you can expect to find small things wrong. But holes can be camouflaged, and in the case of a bargain hand-knitted Fair Isle I would even go as far as home-dyeing a particular yarn to achieve an exact darning match. You don't have to be a knitter to make alterations. There are all kinds of ways to effectively camouflage holes in a plain Shetland or lambswool sweater. And simply threading fine, or shirring, elastic around loose welts and cuffs can do wonders for the look and fit of a garment. Also, shoulder pads considerably perk up drooping cardigan shoulders.

Knits in garish colours but of otherwise handsome stitch and style often go for a song so consider home-dyeing these (see Chapter 7). Remember Dylon cold-water dyes (safest for wool) will 'quieten down' Day-glo pinks, oranges and greens, and will subdue loud patterns. Hot-water dyes can effectively brighten up drab colours, while a black dye will always cover too strident a pattern. Tight necks on children's sweaters can be opened up and altered by stitching Velcro tabs (in a colour to match the yarn) the length of opening. Alternatively make a crocheted edging in either a matching or contrasting yarn; then use button-through loops to close the gap. Frayed sweater necklines and cuffs can be darned or bound with jap silk, and bedjacket-styles in open loose-weave knits can be threaded with narrow 3 mm (⅛ in) polyester/satin ribbon. Do this with a bodkin; then tie tiny bows at about 6 mm (¼ in) intervals and stay-stitch in position. Satin ribbon ruching and lace can effectively brighten up boring Professor Higgins-style cardigans; a chunky cardigan or sweater can be lengthened into a coat or dress with inset bands of similar weight fabric, such as heavyweight linen, jersey or leather. Embroidery, weaving and appliqué techniques incorporating lurex thread, tassels, pompoms, beads, pearls, sequins and toy-shop ephemera – or using recycled tapestry panels, fringing and patchwork appliqué – turn recycled knits into something approaching art works. Repairs on this scale really need a sewing machine with a zig-zag stitch, as this has enough give and is strong enough to hold the seams. Other recycling ideas for old knits include making old sleeves on sweaters and cardigans into leg warmers; and déclassé Sixties U-necked tank tops can be transformed into waistcoats.

Your fashion identity

So much depends on the style of the knit and on how much you're prepared to improvise. Cotton jersey T-shirts look good sleeveless these days, with exposed raw edges. Doctor Who-style black lambswool, or botany wool polo necks as worn by punk aficionados, or classic primrose as favoured by the horsey set, can be quite difficult to wear with anything else. Mohair jacket cardigans of the Sixties look stylish worn with authentic Sixties stretch ski-pants, white socks and winkle-pickers, or with a printed Fifties dirndl skirt. Sequinned and beaded Chinese woollens, often of cashmere and angora, look fine worn with jeans or as evening tops; sleeveless ones can look stunning worn with long evening gloves and an evening skirt.

Clothes renovation kit checklist (see Essential Sewing Kit, Chapter 2)

Bodkin.   For weaving ribbons, shirring elastic, etc.
Crochet hook.   For working edges.
Darning mushroom.
Darning wools.   In assorted colours.
Depiller.   For removing unsightly pilling.
Elbow patches.   In leather or suede (ready-punched), and quilted cottons.
Embroidery frame.   For working embroidery on knits – it prevents puckering.
Liquid detergents.   Special ones for washing wool, e.g. Woolite and Soft Touch.
Needles.   Darning needles for embroidery and sewing on sequins, beads, etc; knitting needles (nos 9 and 12 are the most useful for alterations); tapestry needles.
Net bags.   For washing delicate woollens in. Can be made from nylon net curtaining.
Ribbons.   In assorted colours.
Spare wool, and ribbons and silk.   For embroidery, appliqué work and binding raw edges.
Thread.   Clear nylon thread for beading.
Wadding.   For shoulder pads, and for padding out embroidery for three-dimensional effects.

Washing, drycleaning and stain removal (see Chapters 3, 4 and 5)

Recycling wool

Don't expect wool that is unpicked and washed to knit into the same size sweater. It will also be thinner, e.g. 4-ply will resemble 3-ply, and so on. Use old wool to knit smaller items such as scarves, hats, etc.

Useful wool weights

1 1¾ oz of 3-ply or 3 oz of 4-ply makes a back or front of a jumper. (1 oz is about 25 g.)
2 1 oz of 3-ply or 1½ oz of 4-ply makes a pair of short sleeves.
3 3 oz of 3-ply or 4 oz of 4-ply makes a pair of long sleeves.

Preparing old yarn

The following method applies to unravelling old yarn and making it fit to use again:

1 Wash and dry the woollen garment.
2 Pull a strand of wool and wind it round a chair-back, or bend a wire coat-hanger into a square shape.
3 Make skeins by tying the yarn ends together and knotting loosely in several places to prevent the skein itself becoming a great loopy mess. When the skeins are complete, wet each one in warm water; then squeeze out the excess water in a towel.
4 Hang up the skeins to dry, tying weights to the base to straighten out the kinks. Alternatively, if a wire coat-hanger has been used, you can leave the skeins on it and steam them over a pan of boiling water until kinks are straightened.
5 When sufficiently straight, loop the skeins into a figure-of-eight to prevent tangling, and then dry away from direct heat before winding into balls.

Dyeing

The Russell Dye system available from specialist yarn and weaving shops, (see Directory), is useful for home-dyeing small quantities of woollen yarns and is therefore useful in creating exact matching wools for repairs. Vegetable dyes made from onion skins, beetroot, etc., also work well, but they need special mordants for fixing and making them washable.

Sewing repairs

Darning

Chain-stitch darn.   This, done on ribbed knitting with matching yarn and a little care, can be almost invisible. Begin by securing the yarn with a few stitches through the existing stitch loops. Then weave your needle in and out of the loops across one edge of the hole, being sure to catch each loop. When one row is caught, turn the garment round and go across again. Catch each single loop in each row. Repeat until you have laid threads across the entire hole.

Don't cut off the yarn, but bring the needle out at the corner of the hole, and begin making a series of chain-stitches, using threads previously placed across the hole as a stitch foundation. When reaching the end of a row, bring the needle out in the next row of loops. Working the needle over and under the threads, go up to the top of the darn and begin the next row of chain-stitches. Continue until the hole is covered.

Swiss darning.   This is a useful decorative embroidery stitch that looks as though it is knitted in as part of the garment. Swiss darning is only suitable for stocking-stitch; each stitch is covered with the yarn so double thickness is created. You can use silk or cotton, but motifs look more integrated if the same yarn is used. The basic principle is to embroider over knitted stitches, placing your needle precisely through the stocking-stitch 'holes'.

Begin at the back by inserting your needle at the base of the stitch to be embroidered. Pull the yarn through to the front.

Starting one row above, take the needle from left to right under two loops of the same stitch, bringing the yarn through to the front.

Remove the original stitch by pushing the needle into the base and continue working. Keep the stitches at the same tension as the knitting or puckering will develop.

Push the needle into the base of the last stitch at the end of each row. Work up through the centre of the same stitch, pushing needle from left to right under two loops of this stitch on the row above. Continue this along the row.

Stocking patch

This is a good method for repairing very large holes in the heels of men's and children's woollen socks, as it gives so much elasticity.

1 Cut away round the worn part to get a round or oval hole.
2 Cut a patch piece of suitable jersey, or knit a square to fit into the hole with the rib running the same way in patch as in sock.
3 Tack some paper under the hole and join the edges with blanket stitch seam.
4 Remove the tacking stitches and paper when the patch is completed.

Snags and pills

Don't cut off snags or loose pieces of wool from garments, because the rest of the wool will start to unravel. Take a blunt needle and push the loop or strand through to wrong side and knot, taking care to see that the yarn stitch on right side doesn't pull out of shape.

Use a special wool depiller for removing unsightly pills caused by friction. Knitted skirts may pill on the inside if worn directly next to tights – wearing a thin silk petticoat can prevent this. Silk linings complement knits very well and are useful for preventing coarse Afghan and oriental beaded knits from scratching.

Changing over sleeves

If the sleeves of a pullover begin to wear on the underside and elbow, it is a good plan to change them over to the opposite arms. This levels up the area of wear. It is advisable to damp-press first to eliminate elbow-bag.

Knitting repairs

Frayed edges

Knitted or woven woollen garments, especially children's wear, can be lengthened, repaired, tightened or strengthened, by knitting bands on to the edges of the worn parts. Choose the size of the needles, and the colour and thickness of the wool, according to the thickness of the wool in the garment you are renovating. Pyjamas, jerseys, jumpers and similar garments can sometimes be made to look very attractive by using wool of a contrasting colour.

To cast on directly to the fabric, thread a piece of wool into a darning needle and make small vertical stitches, not more than 3 mm (⅛ in) apart, through the material just above where the hem ribbing joins on. Knit off each stitch as it is made; this is easier than waiting until the row is completed. Knit as long a hem as you want. Trim the frayed hem and catch lightly, but firmly, to the inside of the new ribbing. Press on the wrong side.

Using this method you can make cuffs, waistbands, collars, wristbands and ankle bands on all kinds of garments – whatever their material.

Lengthening woollens

To lengthen knitted jumpers, pullovers, etc., unpick the side seams and pull out a thread of the knitting where the garment has to be lengthened, about 50 mm (2 in) above the waistband. This separates the garment into two pieces. Pick up the stitches on one side, knit in the amount required for lengthening, then graft the two pieces together again. Sleeves can be lengthened in the same way. Use contrasting wool or a striped pattern if you fancy it, especially if you are knitting with oddments of wool.

General pattern instructions

All the patterns given in the following pages have been worked out in 4-ply yarn. The yarn has either been used singly, knitted on a size 2¾ mm (no 12) needle, or doubled to knit with two strands of yarn, on a size 3¾ mm (no 9) needle. A 2-ply Shetland, which is a 4-ply equivalent, is particularly useful for knitting repairs. It is pure wool and comes in a good colour range that blends in well with many of the old pure wool yarns. Thus, matching up old colours is less of a problem. When working on secondhand knits, it is advisable to find a yarn that matches the wool weight which the garments were originally knitted in. Coarse and fine versions have been given for many of the patterns to make renovating easier.

Abbreviations. The following abbreviations have been used in the knitting patterns: k., knit; p., purl; st., stitch; tog., together; sl., slip; inc., increase (by working twice into same st.); dec., decrease (by working 2 sts. tog.); y.r.n., yarn round needle; p.s.s.o., pass slip stitch over; m., main colour; c., contrast colour; in, inches; mm, millimetres; cm, centimetre; oz, ounce. Garter stitch is knit on every row.

Tension points. The patterns have been worked to the following tension:

On two strands of 4-ply yarn, 10 sts. and 21 rows measure 5 cm (2 in) square, working in garter stitch (knit every row).

On single 4-ply yarn, 13 sts. and 31 rows measure 5 cm (2 in) square, working in garter stitch.

If your tension comes out either too large or too small, use a larger or smaller needle accordingly.

If the tension of the yarn you use does not match the tension given in each pattern, experiment with tension squares on different size needles until you get one which is close to the tension given at the top of each pattern.

Generally speaking, the nature of the patterns given (belts, bobbles, shoulder pads, elbow patches, etc.) means that pieces will still be perfectly wearable and usable even if the tension is approximate and not exact. For instance, if an elbow pad is made up at a tighter tension than indicated, the pad will be slightly smaller.

Elbow patches

The first place sweaters and cardigans usually wear out is at the elbows. Knitted elbow pads can look effective, particularly if knitted in a stripe, picking up colours from a Fair Isle yoke. On a traditional blue sweater, with a Fair Isle yoke of blue, turquoise and red on a cream background elbow pads, belt and underarm pads could be made in cream with a narrow blue stripe. A garter stitch looks good here (knit every row) but rib (k.1, p.1; repeat from* to end of row) or moss stitch (k.1, p.1; repeat from* to end of row, but on return row p. instead of k., and k. instead of p.) may equally well be substituted into the pattern.

Yarn amount. You will need two 25 g (1 oz) balls of 4-ply yarn in the main colour, and one 25 g (1 oz) ball in the contrast colour, or 5–6 balls of one colour.

Tension. Using two strands of 4-ply yarn, and size 3¾ mm (no 9) needles, 10 sts. and 21 rows should measure 50 mm (2 in) square.

Working. The patching may be worked in either all one colour, or in a stripe pattern, to match the existing pattern. This is an 8 row repeat: *knit 6 rows in the main colour, 2 rows in the contrast colour; repeat from* ending with 6 rows in the main colour.

1 Using yarn and needles as above, cast on 12 sts.

2 Working in garter stitch and the 8 row repeat colour sequence, work 1 row straight, then inc. 1 st. at each end of the next row and the 5 following alternate rows (24 sts.).
3 Continue in the stripe pattern for a further 46 rows, then dec. 1 st. at each end of the next row and the 5 following alternate rows (12 sts.).
4 Work 1 more row, then cast off the remaining sts.

To work a finer elbow patch, use the following pattern:

Tension. Using one strand of 4-ply yarn, and size 2¾ mm (no 12) needles, 13 sts. and 31 rows should measure 50 mm (2 in) square.

Working
1 Using yarn and needles as above, cast on 14 sts.
2 Working in garter stitch and the 8 row repeat colour sequence, work 1 row straight, then inc. 1 st. at each end of the next row and the 6 following alternate rows (28 sts.).
3 Continue in the stripe pattern for a further 66 rows, then dec. 1 st. at each end of the next row and the following 6 alternate rows (14 sts.).
4 Work 1 more row, then cast off the remaining sts.

Note. The elbow patch worked in double yarn will be stronger. Oversew patches neatly into position. If you wish to decorate a striped elbow patch further use the contrast coloured yarn and work two rows of double crochet around the edge of the patch before sewing into position.

Underarm patches
To disguise worn-out underarms:

Yarn amount. About an ounce should be enough for two patches.

Tension. Using two strands of 4-ply yarn, and size 3¾ mm (no 9) needles, 10 sts. and 21 rows should measure 50 mm (2 in) square, working in garter stitch.

Working. The patch may be worked in either all one colour, or in a stripe pattern, to match the Fair Isle yoke. This is an 8 row repeat: *

knit 6 rows in the main colour, 2 rows in the contrast colour; repeat from ending with 6 rows in the main colour.

1 Using yarn and needles as above, cast on 5 sts.
2 Working in garter stitch and the particular garment's colour sequence, inc. 1 st. at each end of every 3rd row until there are 23 sts. (27 rows).
3 Continue in stripe pattern for a further 16 rows, then dec. 1 st. at each end of the next row, and every following 3rd row until 5 sts. remain.
4 Work 1 more row, then cast off the remaining 5 sts.

To work a finer underarm patch, use the following pattern:

Tension. Using one strand of 4-ply yarn, and size 2¾ mm (no 12) needles, 13 sts. and 31 rows measure 5 cm (2 in) square.

Working
1 Using yarn and needles as above, cast on 6 sts.
2 Working in garter stitch and the 8 row repeat colour sequence, inc. 1 st. at each end of every 3rd row until there are 30 sts. (36 rows).
3 Continue in stripe pattern for a further 24 rows, then dec. 1 st. at each end of the next row and every following 3rd row until 6 sts. remain.
4 Work 1 more row, then cast off the remaining 6 sts.

Note. The underarm patch worked in double yarn will be stronger. Oversew patches neatly into position. If you wish to decorate a striped underarm patch further, use the contrast coloured yarn and work two rows of double crochet around the edge of the patch before sewing into position.

Shoulder pads

New shoulder pads considerably improve sad shoulderlines. You will need 6 × 25 g (1 oz) balls of 4-ply yarn. Ready-made shoulder pads or terylene wadding for filling.

Tension. Using two strand of 4-ply yarn, and size 3¾ mm (no 9) needles, 10 sts. and 21 rows should measure 50 mm (2 in) square.

Working. Using yarn and needles as above cast on 30 sts., and work in garter stitch for 65 rows or until the pad is square.

To work finer shoulder pads, use the following pattern:

Tension. Using one strand of 4-ply yarn, and size 2¾ (no 12) needles, 13 stitches and 31 rows should measure 50 mm (2 in) square.

Working. Using yarn and needles as above, cast on 39 sts. and work in garter stitch for 93 rows. Cast off.

To make up: fold knitted square in half to form a triangle, insert the shoulder pad (or wadding) to suit shoulderline, and stitch edges. Catch this down inside the sweater, so that the straight edge of the triangle runs along the head of the sleeve, and the top of the triangle lies flat going back towards the neck.

Bobbles

These are ideal disguises for lacy-knit sweaters. First, darn holes as discreetly as possible. Buy matching yarn in 2- or 3-ply, then make small bobbles to be sewn at the base of each chevron. The amount of yarn you need depends on the size and number of bobbles required.

Working. Using size 2¾ mm (no 12) needles, form a knot to make the first stitch. Then k.1, y.r.n., k.1., y.r.n., k.1 all into this st., turn, p.5, turn, k.5, turn, p.5, turn, k.2 tog., k.1, k.2 tog., turn, p.3 together. Draw thread through the remaining st.

Repeat this until there are enough bobbles for the whole sweater. Attach each one with a bodkin to the base of each chevron.

Stretched cuffs, neckbands and waistbands

For stretched cuffs, turn back the cuffs and sew a row of bobbles (see above) at even intervals just inside the edge, to hold them in place.

Where the neckband has come undone, fold it back on the inside and catch down, ensuring that when you sew it you catch the loose stitches into the thread. Sew on a row of bobbles (see above) to match the cuff.

Where the waistband has stretched, fold it back inside itself for 12 mm (½ in), and sew into position. Thread some narrow elastic through the casing that has been formed. This will create a fashionable bloused effect.

Improving your knitwear

Alterations to a 'Retro' cardigan

'Retro' hand-knit cardigans are frequently found in old clothes shops. They are often beautifully made, but some may lack proper button-holes. I bought one for 50p which had, in place of the normal ribbing, a patterned front band knitted in stocking-stitch and was backed with petersham ribbon which it would have been a shame to remove.

I first undid the sewing which held the two fronts together, then removed the non-functional buttons. I then crocheted a decorative edge, working first one row of double crochet, then a fancy stitch edge.

Materials. 2 × 25 gram (1 oz) balls of 4-ply yarn in main colour (1 for each shoulder pad), 2 × 25 gram (1 oz) balls of 4-ply yarn in contrast colour. One fairly fine crochet hook (size 2 mm). Seven 'Retro' style contrasting buttons. 3 mm (⅛ in) elastic (optional).

Working. Work along the first row of double crochet, double crochet 5 sts.,* work 4 chains, double crochet into next 5 sts.*; repeat from* to* until you have worked your way around the edges of the garment, ending where you started off, then work 4 chains, place hook through first stitch worked and draw the yarn through this and the stitch on the needles thus forming a knot. Darn in the end.

Work this edge all the way around the jacket (front bands, neck and bottom edge) and around the base of both sleeves. Attach new buttons to front, and use the loops in the crochet as buttonholes. (This edging is also useful for a child's sweater neck that has to be opened up.)

Shaping-up a shawl

This is a suggestion for lace stitch shawls with garter-stitch borders that have gone badly out of shape.

Working. Pin out the shawl into a stretched square, placing the pins fairly close together, at 25 mm (1 in) to 38 mm (1½ in) intervals. Do this on a carpet covered with an old sheet or towel if your ironing board is not large enough. Steam press, either with a steam iron, or with a dry iron under a damp cloth. Leave for at least half an hour. The shape should be considerably improved.

For really shapeless shawls, handwash in a liquid detergent. Do not spin. Pin out when still damp, then steam. Leave in the pinned position until it is dry.

Adding fringe and beads to a shawl. This treatment weighs down the edges slightly, making the shawl hang better.

Materials. Three to four (1 oz) balls of yarn, though this will depend on the size of the shawl and the length of the fringing; a quantity of beads to match the colour of the shawl; a sheet of card about 14 cm (5½ in) by about 10 cm (4 in); a medium-sized crochet hook; a beading needle; a further needle fine enough to go through the centre of the bead, yet with an eye coarse enough to thread the fringing yarn through; colourless nylon thread.

Fringing. Cut the yarn into strands about 28 cm (11 in) long – this will make quite a long fringe. The easiest method is to wind the yarn around the length of the card. When the layers become quite thick, cut at one end only.

Taking four strands of yarn at a time, and using the crochet hook, pick up the shawl with the wrong side facing you. Fold the strands in half, push the crochet hook through the edge of the shawl (away from you), pick up yarn strands through the loop (previously formed by folding in half), and pull this loop back through. Pull fringe ends through this loop, then tighten the knot which has been formed. Continue working at even intervals around the shawl edge. Fringing knots work out approximately 18 mm (¾ in) and 25 mm (1 in) apart.

Beading. Take the needle which is thin enough for the beads to fit through, yet has a thick enough eye for threading yarn. Thread the needle and, taking the fringing one strand at a time, thread a few beads on to each strand. Fix the beads in position with a large knot.

To enhance the beaded effect, bead areas of the shawl as well as the fringing. To sew on the beads, use a finer beading needle threaded with colourless nylon thread, or fringing yarn if the colour is subtle enough. Work on the shawl's wrong side bringing the needle through to the position needed for the bead. Thread the bead on to needle, then push the needle through to shawl's wrong side again, fixing the bead in place. Check that it is the bead's decorative side which shows, and that the hole isn't showing. Continue beading in this way, checking that threads on the wrong side aren't too tight (causes puckering) or too slack (the beads may droop or fall off).

Beads may be evenly distributed over the surface of the shawl, or they may be applied more densely in some areas, leaving other areas of the shawl unbeaded.

Dress up a sweater

This is a suggestion for cheering up botany wool or lambswool plain sweaters that are in fairly good condition. Use bright-coloured sequins and beads which always look good on a black background; and bobbles worked in contrasting balls of brightly coloured mohair also update a jersey. It is a good idea to look for yarn oddments at sales time for alterations like this.

To make large mohair bobbles. Using size 3¾ mm (no 9) needles and one strand of mohair, make 1 st. then k.1, y.r.n., k.1, y.r.n., k.1, y.r.n., k.1 into this st., turn, p.7, turn, k.7, turn, p.7, turn, k.7, turn, p.7, turn, k.7, turn, p.2 tog., p.3 tog., p.2 tog., turn, k.3 tog., draw thread through remaining st. to make knot. Attach the bobble to the garment by this thread and the starting thread.

Make several bobbles in each different colour, and attach at regular intervals to the sweater.

Recycled knits

Leg warmers

These can be made from sweaters or cardigans with unworn sleeves, but check beforehand that the sleeves are wide enough to fit over your calves.

Cut the sleeves off (if it's a set-in sleeve rather than a raglan), then undo the sleeve seam until the knitting opens out enough to fit on a pair of 20 cm (8 in) knitting needles. Cut again very carefully, following the straight line of stitching across the widest point, i.e. at the underarms. Pull out the loose pieces of wool, then place stitches that you have left on a knitting needle. (You will have to try to judge the size needle to use by the wool thickness the sleeve was originally knitted in and the size of the stitches.) As a rough guide, a 4-ply yarn takes a size 2¾ mm–3 mm (nos 11–12) needle; a double-knit yarn takes a size 3¾ mm–4 mm (nos 8–9) needle; a chunky yarn takes a size 4½ mm (no 7) needle or larger.

Work in k.1, p.1 rib for about 20 cm (8 in) to form a cuff, although the cuff length may vary depending on how long you want your leg warmers. Use your own leg for measurements and remember to allow for turnings at top and base.

Leg warmers may also be adapted from old three-quarter length socks by cutting off the foot and working an ankle cuff in its place.

Sleeveless waistcoat

This can either match the legwarmers above, or be made from another knitted cardigan or sweater.

Take the rest of the sweater or cardigan from which sleeves were cut. For set-in sleeves, use the same size needles as for leg warmer cuffs. Cast on 10 sts. and work in k.1, p.1 rib until the strip is long enough to fit around the armhole when the rib band is slightly stretched. Cast off, then secure into place by sewing flat with a flat seam. Work another similar band for the second armhole. For raglan sleeves, cut the armhole to the required shape, then machine around the armhole edge with a zig-zag stitch. Alternatively oversew around the edge using one thickness of yarn and a bodkin. Check that you catch every knitted stitch with the thread. You can also bind the raw edges by hand sewing petersham ribbon 1 cm (¼ in) wide.

Knitted extras

Knitted belt (with buckle)

First buy a buckle. The pattern has been worked out to fit 75 mm (3 in) buckle, but any size may be used. *See method for adjustment to width of belt.*

Yarn amount. Approximately 6 × 25 g balls 4-ply – extra yarn may be needed for a large belt.

Tension. Using two strands of 4-ply yarn, and size 3¾ mm (no 9) needles, 10 sts. and 21 rows should measure 50 mm (2 in) square.

Working. The belt may be worked in either all one colour, or in the 8 row pattern repeat for a striped effect: *knit 6 rows in the main colour, 2 rows in the contrast colour; repeat from* ending with 6 rows in the main colour.

1 Using yarn and needles as above, cast on 3 sts.
2 Working in garter stitch inc. 1 st. at each end of every row, until the belt is the required width. For a 75 mm (3 in) buckle the belt will be 15 sts.; for a 63 mm (2½ in) buckle there will be 13 sts.; for a 50 mm (2 in) buckle there will be 11 sts.
3 Work in garter stitch until the belt is the required length, then cast off. As a rough guide, the belt should be about 25–30 cm (10–12 in) longer than wearer's measurements.

To work a finer belt, use the following pattern:

Tension.   Using one strand of 4-ply yarn, and size 2¾ mm (no 12) needles, 13 sts. and 31 rows measure 50 mm (2 in) square.

Working
1 Using yarn and needles as above, cast on 3 sts.
2 Working in garter stitch and the 8 row repeat colour sequence, inc. 1 st. at each end of every row until the belt is the required width. For a 75 mm (3 in) buckle there will be 21 sts.; for a 63 mm (2½ in) buckle there will be 17 sts.; for a 50 mm (2 in) buckle there will be 13 sts.
3 Work in garter stitch until the belt is required length, then cast off.

To finish belt.   Fold the straight end of the belt through the buckle's centre bar (the prong should poke through the centre). Catch into place on wrong side and pass the slot-shaped end of belt through buckle.

Collar and cuffs

Knitted collars and cuffs make attractive additions to an existing sweater. To begin with, measure the distance all the way around neck, and the distance around each cuff. Make a note of them.

Yarn amount.   Approximately 4 × 25 g 4-ply yarn. More wool is needed if working double.

Collar.   Using either a size 2¾ mm (no 12) needle if working in fine

147

yarn, or a size 3¾ mm (no 9) needle if working in heavier yarn, cast on 17 sts.

1st row:	All k.
2nd row:	K.1,* y.r.n., sl.1, k.1, p.s.s.o.; repeat from* to end of row.
3rd row:	All p.
Repeat rows	2 and 3 six times more (15 rows have been worked).
Row 16:	All p.
Row 17:	P.1,* y.r.n., p.2 tog.; repeat from* to end of row.
Row 18:	All k.
Repeat rows	17 and 18, six times more (30 rows have been worked).

These 30 rows form the pattern. Repeat them until the collar measures a little more than the measurement of the neck, ending with row 30. Cast off.

As a guide, when the stitches are on the needle and the right side of the work faces you, it is the left-hand edge which is the edge that is attached to the neck. Join the cast-on edge of the knitting to the cast-off edge, with a neat stitch. Now attach the neck edge of the collar to the neck of the sweater, easing it in slightly. Work a row of double crochet around the edge of the collar to define the edge.

Cuffs. Work exactly as for collar, only with 11 sts. instead of 17 sts., repeating rows 1 to 30 until the work measures the distance measured around the cuff. Attach in the same way, working double crochet edging.

Crocheted corsage

This is a suggestion for sweaters and cardigans. Using a fairly fine crochet hook and coloured yarn, make a chain of 10 sts. Make* 8 chains, then join into a loop with a slip-stitch into the first of these chains. Repeat from* 3 times more, make 10 chains, then join to the foundation knot with a slip-stitch. Repeat the process until the corsage is the required thickness. Pull the yarn right through the stitch when working the very last slip-stitch, then attach to the garment with this thread.

Earmuffs

Buy a plastic Alice-band or hairband. Make two elbow patches (see Knitting repairs). Fold each patch in two and oversew the edges. Before sewing up the last 5 cm (2 in), stuff the pads with a little washable Terylene wadding. Then push the end of the Alice-band inside one of the pads, and overstitch to close, winding wool around the Alice-band a couple of times to catch it in place. Repeat for the other earmuff.

Patch pockets

To make garter-stitch patch pockets to match collar and front bands use size 2¾ mm (no 12) needles. Cast on 26 sts. and, using a yarn of the appropriate thickness, work in garter-stitch for 70 rows. Cast off, then catch into place by sewing around three sides. 3 × 25 g balls of 4-ply yarn are needed.

13
Fantasy and Special Occasion Clothes: 'You Shall Go to the Ball'

What to collect

Clothes

Chinese embroidered coats and jackets
Mandarin underskirts
Cheongsams (Chinese dresses)
Beaded tops
Indian saris
Matching Indian kurtas and pyjama sets
Mexican embroidered blouses and dresses
National dress from any country
Sequinned jackets; boleros and tops
Smoking jackets and hats
Any ballgowns from the Twenties to Sixties
Wedding dresses
Theatrical costumes
Uniforms and ceremonial dress

Fabrics

Anything in velvet, brocades, silks and lace
Any tapestry, beaded and embroidered panels
Fancy braids, fringes, trimmings, i.e. tassels and buttons

Accessories

Embroidered shawls, feather boas, fox furs, ermine tails, artificial
   flowers, fruit, feathers, fans
Brocade, satin, gold and silver kid evening shoes and bags from the
   Twenties to Sixties

Any long gloves in satin, kid or suede; also shortie gloves in lace and
satin
Diamanté/marcasite clips, belts and shoe buckles

Imagine you are crouching Cinderella-fashion on your bedroom floor
surveying your entire wardrobe dotted about in small heaps. On the
mantelpiece sits a gilt-edged invitation surrounded by assorted gas,
electricity and telephone bills. Every so often you pick up a dress
and walk to the mirror where you pin and adjust. 'It's no good,'
you sigh, 'everything looks wrong. I'll have to buy something new.'
Suddenly, out of the corner of your eye, you see the invitation and
the bills. It is only then you realize that to afford the sort of exciting
creation you want is probably going to mean no food for a year! For
one's expenditure doesn't stop at 'The Dress' – there are the matching
accessories to buy (bags, shoes, etc.) not to mention the facial and
hairdo. It's hardly surprising then, that many turn to hiring clothes
for gala occasions, but Conspicuous Thrifty types know how to glitter
and how to spend practically nothing achieving their glamorous look.

My answer is to radically re-think what constitute celebratory
clothes, and to think in terms of 'Rich Exotic Separates' and accessories instead. If a flying visit to your local charity shop and jumble
sale doesn't yield instant results don't be too disheartened. It may
well take several visits for the right bits and pieces to turn up, which
is where clever clothes hoarding scores. I once hung on to some
antique mandarin skirt panels for ten years before using them.

The silk and braids were fraying badly, but, after treating with
fray-preventative and sewing on a new narrow floral jacquard ribbon
which resembled the original, this skirt has been strong enough to
withstand many an evening frolic.

Fortunately, our current British lifestyle offers the opportunity to
'borrow' the national costume of other cultures for exotic effect. What
is more, they are readily obtainable – even if it does mean cheating
a bit and buying new. There's absolutely no reason why festive
embroidered saris cannot be worn traditionally by non-Asians.
Indeed, one Southall sari shop owner told me English girls were
buying saris for evening wear. Finding a new Afghan embroidered
waistcoat, Hungarian blouse, Magyar coat, Indian wedding coat, or
Japanese ceremonial kimono is not too difficult, and secondhand or
antique versions turn up regularly at costume sales and in specialized
antique clothing shops. Rich ethnic accessories, such as sequinned

and tasselled or beaded belts, usefully pull an evening outfit together, and never really go out of fashion. Traditional cheongsams, as worn by Chinese women, can present problems as the waists are cut very high and will probably need altering to fit European figures. However, it is worth doing, for Oriental clothes are invariably flattering: exposure is minimal, the Chinese having realized centuries ago that most arms and chests look more elegant covered up for formal evenings.

Evening dress seems to fall roughly into hundreds of variations on four classic looks. Firstly the *Oriental Princess,* which includes Chinese embroidered jackets, shawls, coats, mandarin underskirts and Japanese embroidered kimonos, Zouave pants, and side-fastening shirts. Then there's the *Neo-Classical* (Egyptian to Greek) look, with its Twenties and Thirties beaded chiffon long tunics; or long, slim evening skirts in shiny panne or plain velvets teamed with elaborate silk, chiffon beaded or lace tops and masses of ethnic-inspired jewellery. Thirdly, there's the *Edwardian Beauty,* whose hallmark is the lacy high collars, ruffled blouses and skirts with lots of frills and petticoats, in creams, white and black. And, finally, the *Fifties Debutante* look, with strapless boned bodices (or suntops) worn over masses of net petticoats and full skirts of moiré, taffeta, shot silk and lace, teamed with long evening gloves and high, strappy sandals.

The trick is to decide which look suits you, and to stick with variations of it until your age or shape decree you're ripe for a change. But depending on the colour and accessories, these four basic evening looks will carry you through a lifetime of grand occasions.

Your fashion identity

Think rich. Think bold. Remember the four basic evening looks and when you feel confident enough in one of them you can add according to the occasion or branch into the others if you feel adventurous. Rich, exotic, ethnic separates are a good investment and can lead a double life with impunity. You can dress down by topping a pair of jeans with pearly embroidered Chinese cardigans or embroidered jackets, and experiment with other evening tops. For instance, elaborate embroidered Afghan waistcoats in jewel-coloured velvets can be altered to fit as a tight bodice, and look stunning with a suntan, loads of fake ethnic jewellery and a long gathered skirt of chiffon or crêpe de chine in a contrasting or matching colour. Mix and match old bargains with new ethnic accessories: for example, the traditional Japanese obi, a kind of giant brocade bow that clips over a stiffened buckram cummerbund covered in silk or brocade, normally ties around a kimono waist but can also tie round the waist of an evening gown. Use embroidered Indian sari fabric lengths for making evening dresses. Chinese and Afghan silk embroidered and woven coats are 'natural' theatre and evening wear, and besides lasting for years, in common with other hand-crafted ethnic garments, they never really go out of fashion. Invest in a sequinned boob tube if your figure can take it. These can be made from a length of specially elasticated sequinned fabric to add instant evening glamour to any long skirt, as do sequinned jackets and boleros. These ethnic items never really go out of evening fashion and are classics in any sociable woman's wardrobe. Be prepared to pay around £50 as these items rarely go cheap, although specialist antique clothes shops have been known to knock down the price on less-than-perfect examples. Other alternative tops include body-stockings sewn with sequins and beads, or feathers and ribbons. Team these with evening skirts in suitably lush fabrics. Skirts can be recycled from unwanted dresses in plaid, taffeta, moiré and velvet. Make new ruches and ruffles and bright net petticoats from underneath to revive Fifties ballgowns and dance dresses. Lace jackets, peplums and shortie gloves all add glamour – remember Vivien Leigh's Scarlett O'Hara Southern Belle look? Full-length evening gloves are always eye-catchers: long black suede ones worn with a red strapless outfit look stunning, while dyeing grubby white satin ones brilliant kingfisher blue or Indian pink does wonders for a rather staid black or white ensemble.

Clothes renovation kit checklist (see Essential Sewing Kit, Chapter 2)

Acid-free tissue. For storage.

Beads and sequins. Collect old ones, and store them in a clear container (old typewriter ribbon boxes are useful).

Beading pad. This is useful when repairing large beaded areas, and the pad should be big enough to cover an ordinary ironing board. You can make one from a double layer of thickest quality Terylene wadding (20 cm by 30 cm). Cover this with cream or white ready-made cotton quilting. Lines of stitching (sewn from the back of any beaded fabric) between rows of beads prevents them from

153

slipping around when pressed. The pad protects delicate glass beads from breaking and also your ironing board surface.

Cotton-wool buds. Used with distilled water for cleaning tarnished metallic embroidery.

Embroidery frame. Essential for tackling embroidery additions and repairs.

Fraying preventative. This checks fraying seams and treats small areas of shattered silk to some extent.

Hammer. A small one is often used by professional beaders to hammer beaded seams flat when taking in.

Needles. Beading needles (sizes 9–12 are the most useful).

Nylon net. For patching and backing.

Thread. Metallic gold thread for repairing oriental embroidery, and other metallic thread, including silver, for repairing European embroidery; polyester thread for beading and sequin repairs; embroidery cottons and silks.

Ribbons (both old and new). Useful for providing camouflage.

Sable brush. For cleaning old and antique beading.

Silk cords and embroidered belts. Available from Indian shops, these are useful for replacing missing belts or sashes.

Tapestry wools and needles.

Trimmings and braids. Authentic antique ones can be bought at antique costume sales, as can *fringing and tassels*.

Washing, drycleaning and stain removal (see Chapters 3, 4 and 5)

Special cleaning tips

Lamé fabrics (any textile with a metallic yarn)

These can sometimes be cleaned with a paste made of carbon tetrachloride and powered magnesia. Brush off with a stiffish clothes-brush. Metallic embroidery on silk and satin evening dresses can be cleaned by brushing (use a child's soft toothbrush) with bicarbonate of soda, or cream of tartar, or powdered magnesia. Leave for a few minutes before brushing out with a clean clothes-brush. Never use silver cutlery or silverware cleaners to clean metallic threads. Always avoid touching threads with fingers and store lamé fabrics in acid-free tissue paper; test on a small inconspicuous area first, and if any discoloration takes place seek professional advice.

Silver lace braid

Silver lace braid, or cording on uniforms, can be cleaned with bicarbonate of soda, or magnesia if the tarnish is light. Work either of these into the trimmings with a stiffish brush and leave for an hour. Brush out afterwards with a fine toothbrush. French chalk and carbon tetrachloride mixed to a paste can also do the same tarnish-removal job. Again, the paste should be brushed off with a fine toothbrush.

Sewing repairs

Oriental embroidery, particularly old pieces, does tend to suffer from loose and damaged gold threads, making garments difficult to wear without incurring further damage. Trying to stick down loose threads with fabric adhesives is certainly no answer – the proper way is to replace the original couching threads. This is not as daunting as it first looks because tiny stitching-holes will have been left in the backing fabric and these form guidelines for the new stitches. The first step is to get the embroidery cleaned – either professionally or by using one of the methods suggested above. Next, chart the old pattern with the aid of pins (conservators use the long, rust-proof entomological type). Pin as near to the original design as possible, checking constantly to see that all the curly bits fit together. Replace the missing couching stitches using the original needle holes, working with a fine needle and a polyester thread. If gold thread needs replacing there are several kinds available. If the silk backgrounds on these embroideries have started to shatter, they should be backed on to net with trammelling couching stitches; small areas can be treated with a spray-on fraying preventative. When working with metallic embroidered fabrics keep a piece of acid-free tissue over the part you're handling, it prevents fingers tarnishing threads further. Oriental embroidered braids can be bought at costume sales in assorted lots, but I've also used new viscose jacquard ribbon in a floral design that looks very similar to some Chinese embroidered braids. Irremovable spots and faded areas on silk backgrounds may respond to painting out gently with fabric paints. Use these only very sparingly and mix paints with very little distilled water. Incidentally, you can clean metallic embroidery threads safely with distilled water

155

and cotton-wool buds. Work over areas very carefully, a square inch at a time. This is the safest method when all else fails, but take care with very precious fabric.

Oriental fastenings

Original frog fastenings are often missing, or are badly damaged, on secondhand Chinese clothes. It may not always be possible to replace elaborate styles, because these were often wired into shape. But a pretty one with (Turk's head) ball buttons can be made in the following way:

1 Machine-stitch a narrow strip 6 mm (¼ in) by 28 cm (11 in) of matching fabric cut from the hem of the garment. If there isn't enough spare fabric, substitute soutache (a silk-covered cotton braid) or narrow cording in a constrasting colour. The finished ball button measures approximately 12 mm (½ in) diameter, roughly shirt button size.
2 Lay the strip of fabric or cording on a flat surface and make a loop.*
3 Make a second loop and thread this over the first loop and under.*
4 Draw the cording up as if making a third loop, only this time weave in between the other pair of loops.*
5 Form the knot into a ball by pulling the ends up carefully and trimming off any rough bits. Leave enough shank to sew the button to the garment or to one loop of frog fastening, see 6.
6 Frogging can be made by machine-stitching two further fabric strips,* 6 mm (¼ in) by 70 cm (28 in) long, and rolling this around five times. Loop the cording or fabric strip*, approximately eleven times around this and stay-stitch in position. Leave one loop free on one half of the frogging for the ball button; and sew the ball button to the corresponding half.

Sequins and beadwork

Matching old beads and antique sequins is risky, but you may strike a lucky cache simply browsing round in junk shops. Couture and antique clothes had beads of finest crystal glass, but other materials also turn up, for example pearls, wood, metals and ceramic. It is difficult to say how each of these materials should be cleaned as the backing fabric will also be affected, so each piece of beadwork needs individual treatment. The same goes for sequins – particularly old ones which can dissolve in water – so seek expert drycleaning advice. The most common problem, however, is that the backing fabrics beads and sequins are sewn to may have shattered from their weight. If the damage is not too serious reinforcing at the back with a piece of soft, silk net might at least mean a garment is wearable for the odd grand occasion. Textile conservators suggest gentle preliminary brushing using an artist's sable paint brush. This will certainly do no harm.

The annoying thing about damaged and sequinned garments is their tendency to shed. If this happens, there is simply nothing for it but to painstakingly handsew each sequin back on individually to the backing fabric, taking care to follow the original pattern lines and the direction a sequin reflects the light. For sewing on beads, paillettes and sequins, you need a strong, fine thread (100 per cent polyester is ideal) and special beading needles that are long and fine (sizes 9–12 cover most dress repair jobs); a needle threader is also useful here. An embroidery frame keeps work from puckering, but check that the backing fabric is strong enough to take the stretching. A beading pad (see Clothes Renovation Kit Checklist) is also essential for pressing beaded work. If you're altering a beaded dress, the seams will have to be hammered flat to crush the beads, or else they will be too bulky. If your repair beads are in short supply, you could unpick them from the seam areas, or use them to make beaded fringing to lengthen dress hems or sleeves. Use a cool iron to press at lowest setting, and place the beaded side of fabric directly on the pad. Press from the back only. Spraying water on the seam does help to flatten; professional beadworkers sometimes work in pairs when doing this; with one pressing and the other slightly stretching the fabric.

Patchwork panels and borders

Occasionally patchwork clothes bargains appear, sometimes in panels, or as entire garments. I once saw a wonderful winter kimono going for £2 in my local charity shop; it was worked in random patchwork pieces of Twenties and Thirties printed silks that were joined with yellow silk faggoting-stitch. Some of the patchwork pieces had worn badly, but the garment was worth saving. Damaged patchwork fabric should always be replaced with similar fabrics – in most cases I use printed silk from other old dresses – or a carefully blended new fabric. New fabrics should be washed several times before sewing;

this way they blend in unobtrusively. Damaged patchwork can sometimes be reinforced from the back or front using net dyed in suitable colours. Have old patchwork drycleaned as some fabrics may not be colour-fast.

Tapestry and petit point

You may want to recycle a piece for a bag or insert a panel into a dress or yoke. The important thing to remember is that tapestries are woven on a loom and have a warp and weft. Whereas petit point (or needle point as it is called in the States) is worked on canvas. Slits in tapestry can be sewn up with Clark's buttonhole thread in suitable colours, using a fine curved needle. Make stitches straight on right side and slanting on wrong side back. Appleton's crewel wool can be used to repair petit point.

Note. Generally speaking, it's risky to wet canvas work as sized backings may shrink, so always dryclean.

Embroideries

These usually need a frame to prevent puckering. The frame hoops fit one inside the other; the area to be worked fits over the smaller ring, with the larger ring on top. Each section should be finished before moving on to the next, but check that fabric is not under too much strain. Old fabrics and beading can be fragile, so will need tacking on to a net backing beforehand. Knits, too, can stretch out of shape in no time. Always use a scrim or net to back the fabric, when embroidering direct, and tack this in place before you start work. Picking the right embroidery threads for the job is an art in itself, especially if you're trying to match up existing ones. Check the number of strands, and if necessary be prepared to home-dye to match the colours you want on old or antique clothes. Try to keep the back of your embroidery as neat as possible: some Chinese work is so neat it's almost impossible to tell the back from the front. Cut off threads and darn them into each section or colour. Never carry a thread across from one part to another as this will cause puckering. For a really three-dimensional effect you may need to pad out with wadding (I use Terylene wadding as it's washable and very light). Always press embroidery on the wrong side and, as required, manipulate work gently into shape. Do avoid pressing padded three-dimensional areas. If using a steam iron, press over a cloth. Don't forget that when washing old embroideries use distilled water (it prevents iron mould forming); and do a colour test beforehand. The best way is to iron on damp white tape or cotton-wool on an unobtrusive area. Each coloured thread will have to be tested; just one 'bleeding' colour could ruin the whole effect.

Some basic embroidery stitches

You will need to know a few basic embroidery stitches to carry out repairs to ethnic and old clothes. They can also be used to brighten up dull knitwear.

Blanket-stitch. Useful for all kinds of needlework. A running-stitch can first be worked along the line to be covered as slight padding, if desired. Stitches may also be placed closer together. This is sometimes mistaken for buttonhole-stitch where a knot rather than a loop is made.

Cable-stitch. This is worked like chain-stitch, but the needle is inserted at the side of the preceding stitch.

Chain-stitch. This consists of a series of loop stitches. The thread coming out of each loop has the needle inserted at the side. The needle is reinserted by each preceding thread loop.

Couching-stitch. Useful for repairs to oriental metallic embroidery work. Two threads or more are fastened down to the ground material by means of stitches taken across the cords, the stitches being worked straight, or on the slant.

Cross-stitch. This is quickly worked. Slanting stitches are first made from left to right, then crossed with others from right to left. Always keep the top stitches in the same direction throughout one piece of work, the crosses coming exactly one over the other.

Faggoting. This can be used as decorative reinforcing on kimono sleeve seams. Evenly spaced, it may be used to join two folded edges, selvedges, or edges neatened by turning in and tucking. Each stitch must pass through a double thickness of fabric. Faggoting consists of various kinds of twisted bars, or of a joining stitch which closely resembles the herringbone-stitch. With this kind of stitch all kinds of materials and shapes can be ornamented, and it is as pretty when used to join diagonal or curved seams as when applied to a straight edge.

Feather-stitches (also known as cat- or osier-stitch). There are three types: single, double, and treble. Useful for outlining purposes, ornamenting dresses, etc.; they can be done in fine or coarse embroidery cotton. Keep the spacing and stitch size uniform by marking out fabric first lightly with a pencil.

All three stitches are worked on the same principle: a buttonhole loop taken in a perpendicular direction. Also, each stitch can be taken rather on the slant from right to left if preferred.

Fly-stitch. This is used as a filling stitch, because it gives a light dainty effect. Bring the thread up from the wrong side, and take it to the back again a tiny distance to the right, bringing the needle out just below the two points with the thread under the needle. To complete, take the needle down on the other side of the loop.

Knotted-stitch (French knots). Bring the thread out at the required position, hold the thread down with the left thumb, encircling the thread twice with the needle. Still holding the thread firmly, twist the needle back to the starting point and insert it close to where the thread first came through. Pull the thread through to the back and secure for a single French knot, or pass on to the position of the next stitch.

Lazy-daisy stitch. This is a quick way to embroider small daisy-like flowers. The needle is brought up at the centre; the thread is held down under the left thumb, then the needle is taken down again at the centre and brought up at the tip over the loop held by the thumb. To fix the loop the needle is taken down at the other side of it and brought up at the centre again ready for the next stitch.

Long-and-short stitch. This is a form of satin-stitch for filling shapes too large or irregular to be covered by regular satin-stitch. It is useful for achieving shaded effects. Outline the shape first with stem-stitch or back-stitch. For the first row of stitching, the stitches are alternately long and short, and closely follow the outline of the shape.

160

Stitches in the following rows are worked to achieve a smooth appearance.

Loop stitch (see Blanket-stitch).

Running-stitch. This is the simplest embroidery stitch, and consists of a thread run in and out of fabric at even distances. It is effective for all-over designs.

Satin-stitch. This is a stitch that should be worked very evenly. The needle takes up the width between the lines, thus making flat stitches on the surface. Satin-stitch can have a padding of running-stitch underneath, and a layer of washable padding gives greater emphasis.

Seeding. A simple filler stitch made up from small straight, closely formed stitches of equal length which are sewn at random over a particular area.

Split-stitch. Useful for very fine outlines. The needle is taken through the preceding stitch thus splitting the thread.

Star-stitch. This is used as a filler over large areas. Stitches radiate from the centre. Pencil out the design lightly beforehand, as stitches must be kept a regular size and spaced evenly.

Stem-stitch. This is used for outlines, etc. The needle is inserted at a slight angle to its line of direction.

Attaching cord and braid

Prussian cord
This is often used as an edging especially on dressing-gowns etc.; it is sewn onto the fold edge with invisible slip-stitches. The ends of the cord should be secured by a knot to prevent them from unravelling.

Soutache
A silk-covered cotton braid, this differs from other flat woven braids in that it is moulded and has a centre line along which it can be stitched by hand or machine. It is narrow, very elastic and pliant,

and is used for the most intricate decorations. A double soutache edging is often seen on uniforms, and evening dress trouser stripes, etc.

Tubular braid

This is stitched or slip-stitched on. It is tacked on first in straight lines, or in a fancy design. Then by lifting the edge a little at a time, it can be sewn on from the inside with small slip-stitch.

Braid binding

Machine a line of stitching along the edge of the braid and secure it to the right side of a fabric. Braid binding can also be stitched over a raw edge or seam. Tack braid in position, checking that the seam or raw edge is covered evenly both sides before stitching down.

————14————
Recycled Clothes, Army Surplus and Workers' Clothes

What to collect

Old damaged lace and net curtains and tablecloths
Damaged velvet, chintz and chenille curtains
Fifties cretonne curtains in witty prints
Damaged skirts and dresses of 'Retro' crêpes
Grandad shirts
Silk headscarves
Embroidered linen place mats, chair backs and table runners; anything in Richelieu work, drawn-thread work, cross-stitch, Chinese appliqué and embroidery work
Old cotton sheets
Any shapeless or damaged dress in party or novelty fabrics
Damaged carpets, tapestries, beadwork and embroideries
Army surplus/uniforms/working gear and plain paratroop camouflage trousers, gas coats and trousers
String vests – the proper 'knitted' look kind
Safari jackets
Flying suits
Dungarees and painters' overalls
Parkas
Naval trousers and sweaters
Army overcoats
Gurkha shorts and jackets
Nurses' dresses
Overalls
Waiters' jackets
Chefs' trousers

163

Japanese workmen's trousers
Chairman Mao jackets

Nowhere are Conspicuous Thrift ethics more clearly demonstrated than when yesterday's classic clothing becomes today's high street fashion. An example of this is when men's traditional pinstripe morning dress trousers and waistcoats are re-cut into ersatz, pinstriped cotton versions for women, complete with such obsolete tailoring details as fly buttons and braces. Similarly, paratroop trousers with reinforced crotches, pockets for front-line battle provisions, bullets and supplies, and once available only from army surplus shops, are now widely copied, with varying styling concessions to 'macho' toughness and practicality.

Recycled fabrics can also trigger couture fashion. London dress designer, Marisa Martin, has built up an international reputation with lace dresses skilfully blended from antique and new lace pieces to create elegant variations of the 'Edwardian Beauty'. Yet similar lace dresses can be created by those who have some basic dressmaking ability and a magpie instinct for collecting old lace, as well as seeing the possibilities of recycling old net curtains. The advent of the electric sewing machine, with its zig-zag stitch and battery of sophisticated embroidery attachments, has done much to boost the appeal of recycled faded denim and somewhat tired crêpe de chines. 'Made over' again, with new, brightly coloured ribbons, broderie anglaise and lace trimmings, wearers of these recycled garments declare their sophisticated eye for bohemian, Ballet Russe-inspired patterns, colours and fabrics. Again, the 'Eighties Gypsy' look is not cheap when bought ready-made from an antique clothes shop, but with a little sewing expertise and some patience, it is a style well within the reach of most pockets. Furthermore, no special dress patterns are necessary, and it is a look which is unlikely to be copied by high-street fashion shops geared mainly to new fabrics.

Old chenille curtains and tablecloths in mellow yellows, coffees, and faded tapestry rose designs in soft pinks and magentas – all gain new charisma when transformed into jackets, cloaks, skirts and dresses. Silk headscarves and handkerchiefs can be quickly cobbled together to make instant evening dresses, with a row or two of shirring elastic around the waist; the scarves' finished edges conveniently dispensing with any need to hem or face. Lace-trimmed handkerchiefs can be recycled to make a camisole top. Even old carpet can become clothing. Carpet bags and waistcoats gain considerable cachet bound with leather and backed with silk or corduroy. But here more sewing expertise is needed and leatherwork tools are essential if your carpet bag is to look professional.

More brutalist recycled fashion looks may simply consist of turning fleecy cotton T-shirts inside out to expose bare, interlock seaming and cutting off the long sleeves. Indeed, removing sleeves from any blouson-jacket seems to instantly confer that rugged, bare-arm look popularized by James Dean and Elvis Presley. But these cut-out sleeves should also be kept in accordance with true recycling ethics. They may come in useful as future replacement cuffs for a worn anorak, or be put back on when fashion decrees sleeved blousons again.

Your fashion identity

To look their best, recycled clothes must be extra well put together: recycled fabrics must be clean and pressed; any home sewing and finishing should be ultra neat and professional. Otherwise, one is likely to be denounced 'a walking jumble sale'. Adopting recycled clothing as your main wardrobe usually means extra care and attention on the peripherals of hair and make-up. Accessories, even second-hand ones, must be polished and pristine or the whole effect quickly looks tacky. Remember that the origin of your recycled finery should never be 'Conspicuously Obvious', and if you can afford it splash out on a new belt, extra pretty tights or hair ornaments.

When it comes to army surplus, boiler suits, chefs' trousers and the like, practically anything goes – the beauty of utility garments being their intentional no-nonsense design for a particular function. These functional clothes look positively glamorous worn out of their specific work context, so dress them up with masses of chunky jewellery, flat pumps or high heels – the effect can be highly original. To look their best wear utility clothes several sizes too big; belt in waists tightly, roll up trouser legs and you'll probably be in fashion for years to come. The same applies to genuine Jack Tar naval tops, a perennial summer classic when teamed with crisp white, or navy cotton, pants or jeans – or finely pleated white or navy skirts. Khaki army parkas and gas capes make conveniently casual all-the-year-round overcoats; over-dyed a bright kingfisher, or pink, they team up well with ethnic lurex scarves, leopard-printed accessories, and separates.

Clothes renovation kit checklist (see Essential Sewing Kit, Chapter 2)

Elastic.   Shirring elastic for quick waists on recycled scarf dresses.

Eyelet punching kit.   With large rings for lacing bodices, fly fronts, waistcoats, etc.

Leather tools.   Useful for trimming if you're making your own carpet bag.

Needles.   Leather needles, and heavy-duty sewing-machine needles for coping with tough denims, leather, etc.

Seam ripper.   Essential when dissecting old clothes for their fabrics and fastenings. It's also much safer on your fingers and fabrics than a razor blade.

Sewing machine.   If you can afford one, use an electric sewing machine with a zig-zag attachment.

Stain removers.   For removing recent greasy stains on old army gear, use Polyclens Plus paintbrush cleaner, Frend or Shout.

Tailor's chalk.   For marking fabrics.

Ribbons, ric-rac, braids for trimming.

Washing, drycleaning and stain removal (see Chapters 3, 4 and 5)

Taking garments apart

It really is surprising how much fabric can be got out of ready-made garments. The only snag I've found is that if you wish to re-cut something slightly at variance with the original pattern, old darts and seams may get in the way. However, when a particularly beautiful fabric is at stake, patterns have to be adapted to accommodate.

The following points are useful to bear in mind when taking old garments apart:

1 Try to carry out a job as neatly as you can. Allow around six hours for ripping, pressing, recutting and tacking into a new style.

2 Old pattern pieces should be good enough to use as a template for something else. Press each seam before it is joined to another piece;

clip little cuts on the selvedges of seams on curves and they will then lie flat.

3 Velvet may be difficult to use, because it has a nap. Because of this, it must be cut one way and therefore presents problems if you wish to use, say, velvet curtains economically.

4 Don't try to remove old embroideries as holes made by the original needle and thread will show and the fabric underneath will probably look different anyway. It is better in this case to cut out the whole embroidered panel and recycle for something else. The same applies to beadwork panels.

5 After undoing the seams of your garment, always try to wash and press the fabric pieces. If you wish to change the colour, do so at this stage.

6 When ripping seams, look out for very small stitches on fragile, old fabrics. Even a seam ripper may damage here, so be prepared to cut through instead.

7 Decide whether the wrong or right side of a fabric is best for a garment. Mark each piece with tailor's chalk to show the fabric grain, and draw a line around any worn areas.

8 Save old buckles, belts, zips and other fastenings – these may come in useful for future recycling. Try not to pull buttons off; clip them carefully to avoid cutting fabric.

9 When making patchwork flounces, or making things up using several different fabrics, check that the colours are fast. If they are not, then you will need to have your finished garment drycleaned. But, as a general rule, avoid mixing fabrics needing different washing treatments, and use fabrics of similar weights so that patchwork flounces or borders hang, or sit, well on a garment.

Special effects

Fabric paints

Decorated T-shirts and jeans have been with us for some time, but less usual are hand-painted skirts, blouses and dresses. Newcomers to the fabric-painting game, however, would be wise to experiment with various techniques beforehand, using old pieces of plain sheeting.

Today's fabric paints, pastels and some felt pens, usually wash and dryclean well, so that a plain white skirt, or dungarees, can become moving works of art. Choose the technique to go with the design of your choice. For example, give a white dirndl skirt recycled from an old sheet Carmen Miranda appeal by painting on splashy, bold jungle fruits and flowers, using a combination of felt pen and fabric pastels. Shirts can go tropical, too, with giant palm trees. Motifs borrowed from Russian folk art also offer exciting design possibilities. The secret of successful fabric painting is to be bold and positive – happily the techniques involved favour this approach. Fabric paints also offer useful camouflage for certain stubborn stains, for painting Richelieu embroideries, and for re-tinting small areas of faded colours.

The most suitable fabrics for painting are white and pastel shades of cotton and silk, but linens also look good when painted. Dark backgrounds may need to have white fabric paint applied first to give the necessary opacity. Manmade fabrics may also be painted, so can polyester/cotton mixtures. Thick woollens, tweed, acrylic and jersey knits, are not suitable for this kind of decoration. Laces and nets look pretty when painted and, indeed, this was a favourite technique during the Twenties. When it comes to cleaning any hand-painted fabric, antique and old varieties will probably need specialist attention. Today's fabric paints, however, simply need pressing with a hot iron and a damp cloth to make them colour-fast.

When colouring or hand painting any fabrics the following points apply:

1 Check the fabric is free of any special finishes – starch for example. New fabrics must always be thoroughly washed and rinsed to remove any dressing used in their manufacture, otherwise colours may not adhere or fix properly.
2 See that a fabric is wrinkle-free – all creases must be ironed out. You may have to stretch out and pin articles before starting work.
3 Place a piece of polyurethane sheet underneath the fabric while painting; and if painting an item which cannot be opened up, i.e. a pillow case or T-shirt, place polythene sheeting inside to prevent marking the back.
4 Draw pencil outlines very lightly, or use special felt pens. Keep paint colours on the dryish side because too much water will cause colour to spread beyond the intended areas. Richelieu embroideries on linen can be dampened slightly before painting. Masking tape

is useful for marking out straight lines; a stencil brush or plant spray atomizer, are ideal for filling in stencilled patterns.

5 Stencils can either be cut from stencil board with a sharp cutting knife, or bought ready-made from good art shops. However, for fabrics I find cutting designs out of clear adhesive film (Transpaseal) gives better results than the traditional stencil board. There is less chance of any paint colours seeping underneath, and designs have a sharper edge. The film peels off easily afterwards. Alternative painted effects can be achieved with masking tape cut-outs and spray-painting the fabric freehand, using a plant atomizer spray and 2 teaspoons of Dylon Color-fun fabric paint to ½ litre (1 pint) of water. Spray-painting fabrics gives a lovely effect, perfect for producing clouds and subtle graded effects on silk. Spatter effects are also possible: simply spray through a fine sieve for an interesting textured effect. But watch out for drips and keep the spray atomizer upright as you work. Always start with the lightest shades when using any fabric colours, and gradually work through to dark. Allow each colour to dry before starting the next.

6 Fabric pastels are simple and easy to use. The effects vary from 'naive' wax crayon children's drawing, to more sophisticated oriental effects using autumn leaves. To achieve this latter effect, just rub a pastel on a slightly dry leaf vein side up. Place the waxed side down direct on to your fabric, put a piece of white tissue-paper on top and iron over. Pastels can also be used with stencils.

Batik

Batik is a traditional method of patterning fabrics using hot wax as a resist with cold-water dyes. The patterns are built up by applying wax to the areas where the fabric colour is to be retained, and then dyeing the material. Apply hot wax again where the new colour is to be retained and dye a darker shade, and so on until the design is completed. Finally the wax is removed by pressing the fabric between sheets of newsprint and then washing in soapy water.

Simplified batik. As hot wax needs careful handling a simplified method of applying a resist is to use watered-down Dylon Color-fun fabric paints with a flour and water paste. This is not suitable for fine work but is safer for children to use. The same method can also be used to simulate a passable army camouflage or a leopard-skin design.

Stretch the fabric across a drawer or batik frame (an old picture frame will do). Mix flour and water to a paste consistency and paint it onto the fabric where you do not want to colour the material. Leave to dry. Dilute Color-fun fabric paint with water, and paint on to the fabric starting with the lightest colour. Use a combination of greens for the army camouflage background, and yellow for the leopard spots, and paint around the dried flour areas. Then dry, cover the painted material with a clean dry cloth and press with a hot iron to fix the colour. Wash the fabric thoroughly to remove dried flour. When dry, paint the white areas with diluted Color-fun, using darker colours: rusts and black for the camouflage; black and brown for the leopard spots.

Tie and dye

This is one of the easiest ways to pattern fabrics, and you can achieve a random marbled effect by screwing up and securing fabrics into a tight ball. Dye, using a Dylon cold-water dye – diluted charcoal, or brown, gives the most authentic marbling. Untie, crumple and bind again before dyeing a darker shade or another colour. When dry, paint in the veins with Color-fun fabric paints.

Sewing repairs

Reversing a collar

To turn a collar, first slip the point of a seam ripper under the stitches joining the collar and the neckband, gently pulling the point along under the stitches as you go. Be careful that you do not cut the fabric. When you have removed the collar, fold it in half, and put a pin at the centre fold. Next fold the neckband in half, pinning the centre. Turn the collar to its good side and reinsert it into the neckband, checking that pins in the collar and the neck are centred correctly. Pin the ends of the collar in place, and fasten it at the centre of the neckband with another pin. Pin all the way along the neckband and then tack, making sure that the underside of the band is caught by the stitches. Machine stitch carefully along the original stitching line.

Repairing shirt cuffs

If the shirt has double cuffs, remove them with a seam ripper. Turn the cuff over with the worn side inside and patch worn areas with

170

cotton tape. Pin, tack and re-sew renovated cuff carefully along the edge. If the shirt has badly frayed single cuffs bind the edge with bias binding in a colour matching the shirt or the most prominent stripe. Ease the binding around the corners so it lies perfectly flat. Unless you are expert with a sewing machines binding attachment, tack on before stitching.

Alternative cuffs.   Thread shirt sleeve with elastic. Finish lower edge with a hem (or facing) wide enough for elastic,, leaving an opening in seam. Edge-stitch fold of hem. Insert elastic, lap ends and fasten. Slip-stitch opening.

Accessories: 'Little Things Mean a Lot'

What to Collect

Footwear

Court shoes with stacked leather heels, high vamps in good calf
leathers, two-tone co-respondent-style brogues

Evening styles in satin, brocade and lace; novelty finishes and
leathers, i.e. lizard, water snake, zebra, ostrich, python and patent

Evening shoes with strappy sandals in bronze, gold and silver calf;
glitter finish – anything metallic or trimmed with sequins,
diamanté

Winkle-pickers (circa 1960) with stiletto heels

Sling-backs with open ('peep') toes, wedge heels

Flattie styles including ballet pumps

Gucci shoes

Granny-style lace-ups, bar-strap, tap-dancer shoes

Footwear belonging to national dress, i.e. Chinese embroidered slippers, Japanese wooden-soled geta, Indian and Arabian slippers
with turned-up toes, beaded moccasins, ghillie pumps and clogs

Boots

Classic leather-lined riding boots in plain black calf

Genuine cowboy boots also leather-lined with fancy stitching and
stacked Cuban heels

Theatrical boots in suede

Embroidered Tibetan and Afghan boots

Traditional Wellingtons

Pixie boots, ankle boots trimmed with fur

172

Men's shoes

Anything handmade in Italian, French and Spanish leather
Oxford brogues – and brogue golfing shoes
Black patent lace-ups

Bags

Shoulder bags in good condition, especially Italian or any Spanish
leather with tough, saddle-stitched calf, lots of pockets and good
leather linings
Clutch bags in unusual skins (but mint condition) i.e. crocodile,
lizard, zebra, snake, etc.
Evening bags in unusual shapes and fabrics – anything beaded,
sequinned or embroidered, dorothy bags, purses, pochettes; watch
out for tapestry or ethnic bags
Fun bags in clear plastic with joky motifs; raffia and straw beach
carry-alls; knitting bags with wooden handles and school satchels
Carpet bags, leather holdalls, briefcases and Gladstone bags
Hatbox cases
Art Deco minaudières
Luggage in smart sets, and any surplus canvas and leather cases

Gloves

Any leather ones, particularly those with leather linings in good
condition: washable suede gloves, crochet cotton gloves and
mittens, ethnic woollen gloves from Mexico or Afghanistan, driving
and sheepskin gloves, Arran and Fair Isle. Evening gloves in full-
length white kid, suede, satin, lace or shortie satin gloves

Scarves and shawls

Any Liberty-printed silk scarf
Kashmir, Chinese and Spanish embroidered silk shawls (even if
damaged)
Shetland lacy shawls
Mohair, Fair Isle and cashmere scarves
College and old school scarves
Fifties silk souvenir scarves from different countries
Russian rose-patterned peasant shawls
Lace shawls
Silk and cotton cravats

Belts

Any good leather ones
Sam Browne military and webbing belts
Beaded and embroidered styles; dinner dress cummerbunds

Ties

Boot-lace and 'Slim Jims' in stripes and spots, or in suedes, lurex
and other novelty fabrics, satin kipper ties, ties with joky motifs,
old school ties, pony club ties
Bow ties in any shape or colour. White evening dress ties

Costume jewellery

Anything in tortoiseshell lacquer, bone, etc.
Hair combs
Kilt and tie pins
Joky brooches
Earrings
Chains, cultured and synthetic pearls, wooden and glass beads
Ethnic brass, copper and ivory bracelets and necklaces
Anything made in diamanté, coral, jet, turquoise, amber

Hats

Anything in straw including panamas, boaters, coolie styles
Felt cloches and men's trilbies, fedoras, turbans, air-force caps, stet-
sons, skull caps – twenties sequinned hats, fez and other ethnic
caps
Topees
Toppers, beaver and Homburg, Fifties cocktail and cling feather hats

Miscellaneous accessories

Fans, sunglasses, feather boas, fox furs, dress clips, umbrellas and
parasols, walking-sticks and canes
Buttons and buckles, handkerchiefs, braces, spats

There is no doubt that accessories can make or mar an outfit. During
the Fifties, fashion magazines were always bossily insisting that
women had exact matching bags, gloves and shoes – anything else
was quite unacceptable. Turning up at an interview or a wedding
with non-matching accessories was a fashion *faux pas* one never lived

down. Those without the correctly coloured shoes, gloves and bags were briskly told to stick to sensible black or brown. Coloured accessories were risqué: shades of Soho attached to red shoes; white shoes made your feet look big and were considered common by couture fashion pundits. Men couldn't escape the accessories debate, either, they could be shunned at dinners and ignored in clubs for wearing brown shoes with navy trousers. As with clothes, accessories were for a specific function: golfing shoes for golf, riding boots for riding, and so on. 'Mix 'n match' colours also had strict rules: 'blue and green should n'er be seen', etc. Redheads were advised endlessly on the shade of lipstick they should use – in case it clashed with their hair, dress or jewellery.

Opinion is still divided about accessories, only today it's about quality and cost. One camp stoutly believes in spending their all on the latest chic continental leather, while economizing on chainstore clothes. Others argue that today's ersatz leather accessories, at a tenth of the price, defy all but closest scrutiny, and they prefer to put their money on a designer dress instead. Neither view counts for much when it comes to secondhand accessories as prices are so low. In fact, they are hardly worth quibbling over, when you consider a once-worn pair of handmade gold kid evening shoes, originally costing an average week's salary, can be scooped up in a local charity shop for as little as two pounds.

Many people, even those in favour of Conspicuous Thrift clothing, will draw the line at purchasing secondhand footwear. These fears have some foundation, and obviously care has to be taken when buying (see General fitting and hygiene later in this chapter). I couldn't, however, advise secondhand footwear for children, but at least money saved by adults in this clothing department can go towards new children's shoes with less strain on family finances. I have been wearing secondhand footwear for years, and feel bound to say that it has always been new footwear that's given me most problems.

Most charity shops and secondhand clothes specialists select their stock rather carefully, so the chances of boots, sandals or shoes being in poor condition are fairly remote. Obviously, it makes sense here to avoid anything badly misshapen or with broken zips, unless it is a particularly good bargain in other ways. The same applies to uppers that have departed soles, wobbly shanks and tacky, stained linings. But if the leather, style or fit is good, and provided the faults are minor ones, many accessories are worth repairing. Certainly changing the colour is no problem, and makes an immediate difference. Today's ranges of shoe paints and dyes offer some wonderful colours and effects.

It also pays to shop around your local shoe-repair shops to compare services – these can differ enormously depending on the area.

Small splits and holes in leather uppers can be invisibly patched; handles can be replaced; and bag corners can be re-stitched, although this may be better tackled by your local saddler. Simpler leather repairs may be carried out at home with the appropriate leather needle and some waxed thread. Some specialized shoe repairers, notably those still making bespoke shoes, may be able to remodel completely to make fashionable heels in matching or contrasting leather. Relining and remodelling a real crocodile bag is also possible, though this proves a costly and specialist repair – over £200 or so at the last count. Replacing crocodile handles is less pricey if imitation croc is used. Generally speaking, bargains in exotic skin are thin on the ground and, unless perfect, cost a small fortune in repairs.

Other accessories such as gloves, umbrellas, hats and scarves are also well worth looking out for. The best sources for these are some of the better organized charity shops. I've picked up a wide variety of things, including an unworn Fifties coolie-style sunhat, Fair Isle berets, designer silk ties, Sam Browne belts, paisley print men's silk scarves, kid gloves, evening length black suede gloves, and a pretty brolly or two. And all for under 50p a time.

Finding the best in costume jewellery bargains means training your eye to hone in on the usually disordered array of knick-knacks on a market stall or in a charity-shop window. Ethnic jewellery, sunglasses, hair combs, buttons and artificial flowers may cost a few pence here. Don't be put off by limp, fake blooms. These can be successfully revived by steaming for a few seconds with boiling water; fraying edges can be treated with spray-on starch, fray preventative or colourless nail varnish. Pure silk scarves going for a song because of some small hole can be patched or invisibly mended if it's antique. Special bargains such as a Kashmir or embroidered shawl may need specialist repairs and cleaning. As will hats and gloves, although be warned that very few cleaners undertake this kind of work and prices are high. Provided you're careful, some of these things can be cleaned and repaired at home. And it will be well worth the trouble if you've something like a battered panama hat to rescue – a new equivalent might cost around £50 to purchase. While on my clothes-searching sprees, I've come across equipment for mending and restoring at knock-down prices. Look out for traditional solid wooden boot shapers and shoe-stretchers, hat blocks and glove stands. The contents of old sewing-boxes can often reveal interesting repair materials, such as lace bobbins, silk threads, and needles unobtainable from any other source.

Your Fashion Identity

Accessories are really the key to a total, individual look. They can quite literally dress any outfit up or down at the drop of a hat; and can create illusion, lighting up your best points and playing down your worst. After all, who is to know legs are less-than-perfect when clad in well-cut boots, albeit secondhand ones? But proportion does have a lot to do with whether accessories look right or not. Even Fifties fashion dictates were correct in pointing out the absurdity of tiny women wearing Osbert Lancaster-style cartwheel hats (redolent of fairies under a mushroom), or that spindly legs in boat-like court shoes confer instant 'Minnie Mouse' looks. I think a change of colour, and the way a scarf or belt is tied, can give a good deal away. As can little things like trimmings on a hat, a brooch or hairslide. And a new set of buttons can bring an existing outfit more up-to-the-minute than a whole new wardrobe.

Footwear

General fitting and hygiene points

Secondhand shoe sizes tend to be in the four to seven range, but occasionally extra-slim, small and large fittings do turn up. Foot-care experts are adamant that people should not be tempted to buy shoes that are too small, although shoes half a size bigger than your normal foot size is acceptable. When trying shoes on always stand up in both shoes and walk about because by the end of a hot day feet lengthen by 12 mm (½ in) (the same goes for the feet of pregnant women). It is best to try on shoes around midday (early-morning feet are deceptively small), and remember that by evening they may have increased by half a size. A well-fitting shoe should be half an inch longer than your foot, with plenty of room for toes to move.

177

Useful aids for reducing sloppy-fitting shoes are to wear thick woolly tights or socks and lambswool insoles. For extra comfort there are heel grips and pillows to prevent unnecessary heel rub; heel shields can protect hosiery from holes by heels, while metarsial supports are a boon for tired arches. On leather shoes where the fit is otherwise perfect but the shoe rubs slightly, say on a big toe joint, applying a shoe-stretcher preparation to the lining can help. This does not make a shoe bigger, the stretcher has a chemical action which merely thins the leather – so don't overdo it! Full-size insoles reduce a shoe by half a size or more; half-insoles allow more room. If soles are deodorized they also offer protection against possible 'inherited' irritations. Spraying secondhand footwear with specially formulated anti-bacterial agents for shoes and feet will also prevent the risk of infection. These are available at chemist shops. Open-toed sandals are considerably safer from the hygiene point of view than closed boots, but provided all footwear is checked, sprayed and worn together with protective deodorized insoles, the chances of foot infections are greatly decreased. Leather deodorized insoles treated with Actifresh, last a good deal longer than foam rubber ones.

Changing the colour

Real leather and suede can be dyed a darker colour with special dyes, with the colour range mainly confined to the darker browns, blues, greens, reds and black. Do bear in mind that the original colour of leather and suede affects the final result, so always test beforehand on an inconspicuous part of the shoe (inside the strap or heel, for example).

In recent years shoe paints have improved enormously and, provided instructions are followed to the letter and surface preparation is carried out properly, painted footwear, bags and belts should last out the season. The advantage of shoe paints is that they can also be used on manmade (plastic) or leather accessories. Always check that surfaces are clean and grease-free or your colour will not adhere.

It is important to realize that different brands of shoe colour are not necessarily interchangeable. Indeed, they may use quite different ingredients. In addition to the applicator provided, you will also need a no 2 size water-colour paintbrush (available from art shops) to paint in any awkward areas and for thin lines. For really professional results, remember two or three thin coats of shoe colour diluted with

178

a little water will look better and last longer than one thick coat. Some fascinating designs can liven up otherwise boring shoes. For example, leopardskin spots, tiger or zebra stripes can be painted on to a background colour (beige) and allowed to dry before stippling on spots of brown or black shoe paint with a dryish brush. (It helps to have a piece of fabric or fur as a pattern to follow.) One bottle of shoe paint covers approximately one pair of shoes, depending on the style and how many coats are required. A pair of knee-high boots will probably need at least two bottles. Leave painted footwear, bags and belts to dry out overnight between coats, and protect shoe colour with a final layer of protective transparent sealer. Other interesting colours can be achieved by mixing silver or gold into ordinary opaque shoe colours for a metallic, pearlized look.

Scuffed uppers and heels on footwear can be greatly improved with special colour coatings. Very bad chips in heels can be filled in with plastic wood or plastic epoxy-resin putty. Allow to dry before painting with an appropriate shoe colour.

How to dye canvas shoes with Miss Dylon Instant Shoe Colour

1 Shoes must be cleaned first.
2 Dilute the bottle of Miss Dylon Instant Shoe Colour with 25 per cent water, mix thoroughly and then apply to the shoes with the brush.

Note. It is not necessary for pre-conditioner in the pack to be used on canvas shoes.

How to dye satin shoes with Dylon multi-purpose dye

1 Shoes should be clean and free from stains as the dye will not hide bad blemishes. Pad the inside of the shoes with paper.
2 Pierce the tin and shake the dye powder into a jug. Add 1 pint of boiling water. Stir until the powder is fully dissolved.
3 Lightly damp the surfaces of the shoes with clean water. Dip a small, clean brush (an old toothbrush is ideal) into the solution. Shake off the surplus liquid, then work the brush all over the shoes with a light, circular movement. Allow to dry.
4 If necessary, repeat the process, remembering that each application of the dye deepens the colour.

SHOE-CARE CLEANERS AND DRESSINGS

Footwear material	Shoe-care product	Shoe-cleaning method
1 Glazed leather Softee patent Glow patent Synthetic patent Wet look Synthetic or real calf	Patent and wet look aerosol	Remove soiling with damp cloth, when dry apply recommended dressing.
2 Pearlized leather Glow calf	All Leather Shine	Remove soiling with damp cloth, taking care not to scratch. When dry apply polish sparingly. Polish with a soft dry cloth.
3 Smooth polished leather (calf, kid and side leather) in all colours	Ladies' – matching colour shoe cream Men's – Wren's shoe polish, Padawax, or Aniline Cream All Leather Shine	Remove dry dirt with brush, and heavy soiling with damp cloth. When dry apply polish sparingly. Polish with a soft dry cloth.

4 Grain leather Bison Buffalo Pebble grain, etc.	Ladies' – matching colour shoe cream Men's – Wren's shoe polish, Padawax, or Aniline Cream All Leather Shine on Ladies' or Men's A protector can be used to prevent stains	Remove dry dirt with brush, and heavy soiling with damp cloth. When dry apply polish sparingly. Polish with a soft dry cloth.
5 Smooth man-made materials (i.e. Corfam) in all colours	Leather Care All Leather Shine Neutral shoe cream	Remove dry dirt with brush, and heavy soiling with damp cloth. When dry apply polish sparingly. Polish with a soft dry cloth.
6 Waxy aniline leather Waxy buffalo	Matt leather aerosol cleaner Aniline Shoe Cream	As above. Please note, these leathers darken when dressings are applied. Use thinly and evenly.
7 Genuine snakeskins	All Leather Shine or neutral shoe cream	Great care needed. Clean as 5 above. Apply polish, being careful not to raise scales with applier or polish cloth.

8 Suedes Brushed pigskin Velvet suede	(a) *Protection*. Protector to prevent oil and water staining (b) *Cleaning*. Wire or nylon bristle brush. Suede aerosol shampoo. Suede spray (c) *Stain removing*. Mal solvent grease remover	Protect new shoes with (a). For general purpose cleaning use (b). Brush to remove all dry soiling then clean with suede shampoo. Allow to dry and brush up the nap with suede brush. For grease stains use Mal sparingly, removing grease by two or more applications.
9 Nubuck Velvet calf	Neutral shoe dressing or spray	Spray on cleaner and clean away any obstinate stains with a clean lint-free cloth. When dry raise nap with abrasive paper.
10 Fashion fabric Canvas Hessian Denim	Fabric and canvas spray Fabric and canvas cleaner	Clean any bad soiling from shoe with damp cloth. Wet shoe, apply cleaner and work foam into fabric. Rinse and allow to dry.
11 Brocade	Fabric and canvas spray Art gum rubber	As above. Light soiling marks can be removed with art gum rubber.
12 White canvas White buckskin White leather	Meltonian Superwhite	Clean badly soiled shoes with a damp cloth. Apply dressing and allow to dry.

13	Lustre Bronze Silver Gold	All Leather Shine or neutral shoe cream	Remove dry dirt with brush, and heavy soiling with damp cloth. When dry apply polish sparingly. Polish with a soft dry cloth.
14	Children's leather shoes	Kids' Stuff Wren's shoe polish Padawax	As above. Badly scuffed shoes may need more than one application. Let shoe dry between each application.

This chart is by courtesy of Meltonian Shoe Products. The products listed are their brand names. Some are made by other manufacturers, i.e. fabric and canvas cleaners.

Looking after leather

General leather care

Whether your shoes or boots are new or secondhand, they will look better and last a good deal longer if you wear them on alternate days. Handbags in daily use should have a weekly clean out; grubby fabric linings should be brushed first, then treated for grease and lipstick stains with a spot remover. And any bags benefit from being padded-out with acid-free tissue to keep their shape when not in use. Footwear can be kept far better using shoe or boot trees; some are impregnated with a deodorizer such as Actifresh, so they do a double job of keeping shoes fresh and hygienic at the same time. Fingers of leather gloves should also be padded out with acid-free tissue to keep their shape.

Never dry wet leather or suede footwear, handbags or gloves, in front of direct heat. Instead, pad out with newspaper and leave to dry out slowly for two or three days if necessary.

Leather brushes

Bristle ones for shoes should be clean, so check for cloggy, stale polish and soak in white spirit until the polish disappears. Wash in hot water and heavy-duty detergent, rinse through in warm then cold water, and leave to dry out. Suede brushes should also be checked for dust and dirt. It is a good idea to have both wire and rubber brushes: wire for treating tougher suedes and heavier staining; rubber for fine suede and light marks. Brush in a circular movement to raise the suede nap.

General points

There are three basic tanning processes:

1 The oldest technique is the mineral method which involves steeping skins in salt and alum.
2 The vegetable method, using the tannin found in leaves and wood.
3 Chamoising, where the leather is treated with oils and fats and brains of other animals.

Other techniques involve leather being dyed, embossed or plated to give it a shiny surface. There is also 'boarding', which brings out any natural leather grain patterns; enamelling which gives a patent finish; and scraping which gives a suede.

Cleaning

Most leather, unless specifically designed not to be wetted (e.g. certain kids, suedes, and aniline calf in delicate shoes and gloves), benefits from a simple clean with soap and water using a branded toilet soap such as Lux. Crocodile, particularly, benefits from this. Working soap into a lather and rubbing it well into the surface with finger tips should remove most surface grease and dirt. When the leather is dry, the shine and grease is put back with a colourless neutral dressing or a dressing appropriate to the leather type (see Shoe-Care chart). There are also a number of branded preparations for removing spots and stain marks, such as salt stains from walking in the snow, and these are to be recommended rather than homemade remedies. Unless marked or labelled in some way, most leather gloves are not washable and need special cleaning; washable leather gloves can be treated with a special glove shampoo (see Directory). Leather luggage should be treated with a good hide dressing; one suitable for upholstery also works for luggage, but not for leather handbags as the oil could stain clothing. Avoid secondhand, old leather luggage and brief-cases with red or pinkish markings all over the surface. This condition, known as 'red rot', although treatable in the early stages, makes items brittle and fragile and unusable later.

Protective finishes

These are useful for rendering clean fabric, leather and suede accessories water and dirt-resistant. They may darken material and must only be used on clean or new surfaces or else dirt will also be irretrievably sealed in. Fashion shoes are not normally made water-resistant, but the use of protective finishes can help do this. Wax coatings are invaluable when treating old, battered leather finishes. The following recipe for feeding and treating brittle dull leathers will also prolong life. Light-coloured leathers should be tested beforehand as colour may darken.

Gloves

Repairing leather gloves

Gloves frequently tear at the thumb and finger intersections, and at the wrist opening if they are long evening ones. If the leather or suede is strong enough, seams can be repaired with whip-stitches or buttonhole-stitch (Basic embroidery stitches, Chapter 13). Use a triangular, pointed glover's needle. Rub a little beeswax on the thread to make it easier to pull through.

Where leather is torn, a patch can be made; if possible, try to match the leathers closely. Turn the glove inside out. Clean the surface around area to be patched, and the patching leather, with white spirit, before sticking down with contact adhesive.

Dyeing gloves

You cannot change the colour of leather gloves as dye processes are specially formulated against perspiration and wet weather. However, satin, cotton, crochet, lace and nylon gloves can be dyed. Use a Dylon Multi-purpose dye, one tin will treat 225 g (8 oz) dry weight fabric. But for light articles such as gloves, only a proportion of the dye must be used.

1 Pierce the tin and shake the dye powder into a jug. Add ½ l. (1 pint) of boiling water and stir until dissolved. Use half a cup of solution to each pair of gloves. Add this to enough hot water to cover the gloves in a container, e.g. a saucepan. Add 1 dessertspoon of salt.
2 Wash the gloves and leave wet, then immerse in the dye solution. Bring to near boiling. Maintain this heat for ten minutes, keeping the gloves moving.
3 If the shade is not dark enough add small quantities of the dye solution until the desired colour is obtained. But remember that colours appear darker when wet.
4 Rinse until the water is clear of colour, and dry as usual.

Hats

General cleaning and care

Hats are difficult for those trying to clean at home, but few specialist cleaners seem willing to undertake the job. Thus, DIY cleaning is probably the only way. Wetting hats, either with water or other chemicals, is going to result in crowns and brims losing their shape. The best solution is to have an adjustable hat block to hand; otherwise use an upturned china mixing-bowl padded out with fabric to fit the hat crown. Always remove trimmings before cleaning.

Felt hats, put on a hat block, can be dry-cleaned with a paste made from magnesia and distilled water. This should be brushed on and left to dry; when brushed off, any dirt should brush out with it.

Panama hats also need blocking. Discoloured, soiled panamas can then be gently scrubbed with a nail-brush dipped in spirit soap lather. The hat can subsequently be rinsed in clear water and glycerine. Excess moisture should be blotted up with tissues and the hat can be left to dry in the sun. Straw hats that have lost their stiffness after a soaking can be re-stiffened with a varnish made from gum arabic or shellac. But do keep the brim flat under a weight. For tears in the crowns of old panamas, try an iron-on tape on the wrong side. For tears in coarser straws, try stitching with a straw needle and a polyester thread.

Berets can be washed, according to fabric fibre, in liquid detergent and stretched out to dry over a plate of suitable diameter.

Feathers and trimmings. Water and dry-cleaning fluids could make these limp; adhesives may also dissolve if mounted on a canvas backing. So dryclean with french chalk, powdered magnesia or fuller's earth. Leave overnight and brush out the powder with a soft brush. Feathers (including ostrich) that can be removed may be washed in warm, soapy water. Rub with the finger tips until clean, and rinse in cold water. A thin starch solution in the final rinse adds body. Feathers should then be shaken lightly, laid out on an absorbent surface and gently pulled back into shape. When thoroughly dry, cover with a sheet and beat lightly with a fly swat to separate the fronds. For dyeing feathers, see Chapter 7.

Cleaning costume jewellery, buttons, bag frames, etc.

Costume jewellery soon starts to look dull if it is not cleaned regularly – rings, particularly, seem to suffer from the general round of household chores. Good costume jewellery should be checked at regular intervals for loose clasps and catches, and necklaces should be looked at to see if re-threading is necessary. Professional jewellers clean ultrasonically: jewellery is put into an electric tumbler containing special fluids which removes grease and moisture and finished afterwards with an electric buffer. It's an inexpensive service, but you can save a few pounds by cleaning yourself and taking care to see that pieces don't get too dirty in the first place.

Most jewellery responds to a simple clean up, either with washing soda and a bar of soap, or with liquid detergent. Goddard's do a brand cleaner formulated for the purpose. Powder detergents should never be used as these are abrasive and can scratch surfaces. Fine sawdust can be heated gently in a baking tin and is a useful mild cleaner for delicate stones, such as pearls and opals. A medium-soft toothbrush with pared-down bristles is also handy for getting into the crevices; a chamois leather is useful for a final polish. Soaking rings for a few minutes in methylated spirit, or eau de Cologne, offers an effective cleaning alternative to the soap and water method; but check that the gemstones are suitable and that the settings are not the enclosed type, because these special fixings could dissolve. Remember, too, that worn patches on silver- and gold-plated pieces can be re-dipped by jewellers.

But there are exceptions to simple soap-and-water treatments mentioned above. And, although the following list includes cleaning gold and silver, precious stones such as diamonds, rubies, etc., have been omitted as these are all better cleaned professionally. Articles such as parasol handles, bag frames, powder compacts and haircombs may be made of several materials, and care must be taken to see one cleaning method does not conflict with another.

Agate.   Clean in soap and water. Polish dry with a soft cloth.

Amber.   Clean in soap and water. Polish with a dry cloth.

Antique glass beads.   Clean in warm, sudsy water and add a drop of ammonia or methylated spirit to the final rinse for extra sparkle. Clean breaks in a glass bead can be repaired with Loctite glass adhesive.

Bakelite.   Trade name for a group of plastics first developed in the 1860s and much seen in Art Deco jewellery, buttons and belt buckles. Items can be fragile so avoid wetting or soaking. Surface dirt and grease can be removed with a paste of baking powder and water. Brush this off when dry. Cracks can be repaired with a clear adhesive such as Uhu. Polish with Renaissance micro-crystalline wax.

Bone. (See ivory)

Brass. Most of today's jewellery is lacquered to prevent tarnishing but even this does not prevent long-term tarnishing. Remove the old lacquer with brass polish, then wipe over the clean surface with methylated spirit before painting on a new coat of clear lacquer. A specially prepared cellulose varnish for protecting metal can be bought from most hardware shops. When cleaning brass trimmings on leather, i.e. military belts, spurs etc. always try and avoid staining because marks can be impossible to remove. Safer to use is powdered wood ash (from a log fire) or powdered charcoal. Buff brass with a little of this on a soft cloth.

Casein. Old buttons abound in this material which is manufactured from milk. Casein dissolves and fades when soaked so remove buttons before washing. (One test to find out whether a button is a casein one is to place a hot needle on the back; it will smell like burnt milk.) To clean surface dirt and grease make a paste of baking powder and water and brush off when dry. Casein buttons are best removed before drycleaning.

Coral. Clean by sponging in warm water and detergent. Remove ingrained dirt with whiting or powdered chalk or pumice. Polish with Renaissance micro-crystalline wax polish. Repair breaks with a contact adhesive.

Diamanté. (See paste jewellery)

Electro-plating. This is a process which is applied to base metals, such as brass, German silver or bronze. A thin layer of a more valuable metal, such as silver, gold, rhodium, copper or nickel, is electrolytically deposited onto the base metal. English electroplating is marked EPNS (electro-plated nickel silver), or EPBM (electro-plated Britannia metal). To clean electro-plated articles, rub with french chalk moistened with methylated spirit plus a few drops of ammonia. Use a soft cloth and repeat several times until the tarnish is removed. Electro-plated articles tarnish easily, so keep in a dry place and wrap in acid-free tissue. Never use harsh abrasives to clean, or dip into silver liquid cleaner, because the plating will literally

189

vanish before your eyes. Dents and bad scratches have to be repaired professionally, as does worn plating.

Enamel. The opaque variety turns up in Chinese inlay buttons, pendants and rings, and in quite a bit of modern jewellery. Don't use detergent to clean. Use warm, soapy water and a biological powder such as Bio-tex. Items that contain other materials and stones such as pearls should be cleaned professionally because there may be a paste backing. A few drops of Vulpex mixed with distilled water can clean badly cracked and ingrained, soiled enamel surfaces. Repeat if necessary. Hydrogen peroxide may also be used to bleach out stained cracks, but this can be risky as dirt may be holding the pieces together and enamel can come away from metal backing. Tiny chips on damaged enamels can be restored by painting with Dryad's cold enamel. Unfortunately badly damaged transparent enamel jewellery is difficult to repair, and, unless the piece is of particular value, is probably not worth the cost of professional repairs.

Gilt. Badly soiled bargains can be washed in warm, sudsy water; then dried and polished with a soft cloth.

Gold. Washing in warm detergent and lightly brushing crevices and chain links works for many pieces, but where precious stones and delicate ring settings are involved gold should be professionally cleaned and buffed. Jeweller's rouge (see Directory) and a cloth specially impregnated with cleaning agents is also a useful gold cleaner. Hagerty Gold Cleaner is also specially formulated for the purpose (see Directory).

Horn. Horn buttons are sewn on quality raincoats, Scottish knits, duffel and loden coats. Wash quickly in warm, soapy water; never soak. Dry quickly. I have repaired cracked and chipped horn buckles with an epoxy-based putty resin paste, such as Loctite Handy Strip, and then painted over with Humbrol enamel (grey). Doing this repair, however, means the buttons or buckles will not dryclean.

Humbrol enamels. (See modelling paints)

Ivory. In one form or another – from fans to cane tops – ivory and bone crop up in junk shops fairly frequently. Old pieces may be

190

rather yellow but this should be left as patina. You can tell real ivory by the striations (lines) that radiate out from the centre of a tusk as in a tree trunk. These can be seen clearly and cannot be imitated. Items can be cleaned by lightly brushing in a soap-and-water solution. Never soak, and always dry immediately. Cracks can be drycleaned with spirit soap mixed in white spirit. Brushing onto the ivory removes soiling; rubbing with white spirit afterwards gets rid of any residue. Cracks and repairs in valuable ivory pieces should be treated professionally. Polish with a micro-crystalline wax. If you must bleach non-valuable ivory, soak in a diluted solution of hydrogen peroxide, or in salt and lemon juice.

Jade. Two types most commonly found in jewellery are nephrite and jadeite. The colour variations range from greyish white to shades of yellow, blue, pale and dark greens. Wash in warm soapy water, rinse thoroughly and dry with a soft cloth. Small breaks can be repaired with a clear epoxy resin adhesive. Valuable pieces should be professionally repaired.

Jet. Jet is fossilized wood which closely resembles shiny black glass; and it was popular as mourning jewellery in Queen Victoria's time. French jet is an inexpensive substitute and is in fact black glass. To clean real jet, simply rub with fresh breadcrumbs. Avoid immersing or soaking in water, although gentle rubbing with warm, soapy water will shine up pieces.

Jeweller's rouge. (See gold, mother-of-pearl)

Lacquer. Lacquer frequently appears in decorated Japanese hair combs. The best way to clean grease from the teeth is to brush them with a spot cleaner, such as K2r, and then brush off immediately. Never use water, or soak hair combs, because the lacquer will peel, and the painted and gilded decorations start to chip off. Scratches and chips on damaged combs can be touched in with red or black shellac polish. Polish with Renaissance micro-crystalline wax.

Marcasite. Marcasite is made up from small pieces of iron pyrites cut to resemble gemstones and is usually set in silver. Clean by rubbing with an impregnated silver cloth or piece of french chalk, then brush off the powder with a dry toothbrush. Very soiled pieces can be brushed gently with a paste made from french chalk, methylated spirit and a few drops of ammonia. Always keep marcasite jewellery away from heat or the sparkle will be impaired.

Mica. Early sequins were often made of this material; Indian shisha sequins still are. Wash with water. It is, however, advisable to seek professional drycleaning advice. Washing could cause material to disintegrate.

Modelling paints. These are cellulose-based paints which are useful for painting out chips and disguising fillers. They are also good for repainting plastic frames of sunglasses, but the paint may react with the plastic if it is removed with a cellulose cleaner or nail-polish remover. Buttons and buckles painted with modelling paints are not drycleanable, so must be removed before cleaning.

Moonstones. These are sometimes backed with black paper. Remove before washing in warm, soapy water.

Mother-of-pearl. This comes mostly from the shell linings of fresh- and salt-water molluscs, e.g. oyster and nautilus. Jewellery, buttons, fan handles and powder compacts are made from it. Soiled pieces can easily be revived with a paste made from water and precipitated, or refined, whiting. This should be rubbed in and left to dry, before polishing off with a soft cloth. Finish by washing in warm, soapy water; rinse and dry.

File small chips with a fine nail file or emery board and polish with Jeweller's rouge (see Directory for stockists). Damaged pieces can be replaced by cutting out new pieces, but it needs a fine fretsaw and a good deal of patience. Keep mother-of-pearl items well away from acids as these will damage. Real mother-of-pearl buttons can be identified by the striations (ridges) on the back.

Nail polish. In the same way as modelling paints, nail polish is useful for touching up and painting small pieces of costume jewellery, spectacle frames, etc.

Paste jewellery. These stones are usually stuck into a setting and for this reason may be easily damaged. Try cleaning with an impregnated cloth. Seek professional advice over damage and major cleaning (see Directory).

Opals. Opals need careful handling as they are highly porous. Never wear opal rings while washing up. Have them cleaned professionally.

Pearls. Cleaning methods rather depend on value. Valuable pearls should be cleaned by an expert; ordinary pearls can be cleaned by placing them in a small tin, covering them with powdered magnesia, and then shaking the tin gently. Polish afterwards with a soft cloth. Pearl can also be washed in lukewarm soapy water, but this sometimes weakens the thread so is not recommended. Other pearl-cleaning alternatives include using a mixture of starch and ground rice. Discoloured pearls can be whitened in a mixture of Reckitt's Blue bag and powder starch. Colour-tinting inexpensive pearls is also possible. Dissolve a quarter of a tin of Dylon Multi-purpose dye powder in ½ litre (1 pint) of boiling water and leave them to soak for ten minutes. The best treatment for pearls is to wear them next to your skin as they absorb the skin's natural oils and are meant to gain colour and lustre. Imitation pearls are delicate and prone to peeling. Always rub gently with a soft cloth or chamois leather to remove surplus dust and dirt. Paint out small chips in damaged coating with pearlized nail polish. Keep pearls wrapped away from other jewellery as the coating is liable to be scratched by other items. Never wear pearls when using hairspray, perfume or putting on make-up.

Perspex (polymethyl methacrylate). This is used a great deal in modern jewellery, and sometimes complete handbags (minaudières) are made of it. It is a rather delicate material as it scratches easily and breaks. Wash in hot soapy water; very badly soiled perspex and surface scratches can be treated with metal polish or a special perspex polish or micro-cystalline.

Pinchbeck. Pinchbeck is a brass alloy consisting of 83 per cent copper and 17 per cent zinc. It is known as 'poor man's gold' because of its colour. Clean as for brass.

Plastic. Plastic jewellery, handles, buttons, compacts, etc., can be cleaned in warm water and washing-up liquid. Use washing-up liquid neat on very soiled areas. Polish with Mr Sheen furniture polish.

Platinum. This metal can be cleaned with a special platinum cleaner.

Re-stringing. Valuable pearls and other semi-precious stones should be strung professionally. Clear nylon beading thread is suitable for beads and costume jewellery. Clasps and catches on necklaces should be checked regularly. New ones can be bought from craft shops (see Directory).

Silver. Not every silver item sports a hallmark and you may have to have a piece identified by a jeweller. Some pieces, chain-mesh evening bags, for example, should not be cleaned with Goddard's Silver Dip because it's too harsh. Try a foam pad silver cleaner, or put aluminium foil (a milk-bottle top) into a plastic washing-up bowl and add 2 tablespoons of washing soda. Put tarnished silver into this and after some chemical reaction (fuming and effervescing) the tarnish will disappear. Dents and severe corrosion will have to be treated professionally. Keep silver wrapped in acid-free tissue to prevent re-tarnishing; Goddard's do a specially impregnated cloth that is a good instant silver cleaner after the initial cleaning has been completed. Be careful to check that no silver polish or any metal polish is left on the shaft of drop earrings, as this can cause an earlobe infection.

Tortoiseshell. Derived from turtle shell, this appears in combs, bag handles, compacts and spectacle frames. Clean in soapy warm water; dry it quickly and polish with Picreator's Renaissance micro-crystalline wax (see Directory).

Turquoise. Polish with a soft damp cloth as they are porous and liable to break in water.

Watches. Cleaning depends on the particular metal. Generally cleaning with a soft cloth or leather is enough. Never try to clean inside a watch; and don't sleep with your watch on – take it off and place it on its back, checking that the surface is not too cold, because this may cause condensation. If you accidentally submerge a non-waterproof watch in water, open up the back and plunge it into a cup of oil – any type will do. This will prevent rust. Take it to a jeweller as soon as possible.

Wood.   Chunky buttons, ethnic beads and inlaid bangles in various African hardwoods can be polished up with a silicone wax furniture polish (Mr Sheen). Unvarnished wood in beads and buttons can also be stained or tinted a colour with Dylon Multi-purpose dyes, leaving to soak in dye solution for 20 minutes. Repair cracks and holes with plastic wood.

Glossary of Chemicals, Cleaners, Finishes and Repair Materials Useful to Conspicuous Thrifters

Where possible always use branded items. These are safer to apply because they are specially formulated for domestic use and come in manageable containers. The only snag is that the strength may be weaker than the chemicals bought at the chemists, and they may not be as effective in dealing with any problem stains. Always wash your hands immediately after use and work in a well-ventilated room; check also that containers used in mixing are of the right material. Some acids and solvents corrode metal and plastic almost instantaneously. Keep containers away from children and do not mix them up; never put a chemical into an old lemonade bottle where contents might be swallowed. Most of the chemicals listed here can be purchased through your high-street chemist, supermarket, art and health food shops or conservation material suppliers (see Directory). Where a remedy indicates one part of a chemical to three parts water, the term 'part' refers to the container used in measuring. The same measure must be used throughout, for example: 1 tablespoon to 3 tablespoons; 1 cup to 4 cups. The term 'vols' refers to the amount of oxygen produced by one volume of solution.

Acdo Glo-white. A branded fabric whitener and colour brightener available from household counters in the chemists.

Acetic acid. Is the acid constituent of vinegar and a useful stain remover used in this form. Available from the chemists in a 9 vol solution it is an effective solvent for organic substances and can sometimes be used to restore fabric colours damaged by alkalis, i.e. perspiration. It is mildly corrosive so avoid direct skin contact. In a dilute form acetic acid is widely available as distilled 'white' malt vinegar from any local supermarket. A cupful added to a washing-up bowl of final rinsing water rids woollens of detergent residues and keeps them soft and fluffy.

Acetone. A colourless, volatile liquid and petroleum derivative; it is also a powerful paint and varnish solvent. Apply cautiously as action is almost instantaneous (it can, however, be slowed down by diluting with turpentine substitute). Highly flammable, acetone should be stored carefully and never used to remove stains on viscose, nylon, rubber-backed, plastic fabrics or materials. Available from the chemists in its pure form and also in all branded products of nail polish remover to which an oily substance, i.e. lanolin has been added and which in some cases may leave a slight residue.

Adamite. A branded washing product specially formulated for woollens from haberdashery counters.

Alum (potassium aluminium sulphate). Is used as a mordant (dye fixative) in dyeing of fabrics and leather: Dryad's powdered alum is available from specialist art and craft shops. Can be a useful brightening agent for faded wool when dissolved with 30 g (1 oz) cream of tartar, 8 g (¼ oz) alum to every 500 g (1 lb) of wool in the final rinsing water. It can also be mixed to a paste with distilled water to brighten some tarnished metallic braids.

Ammonia (spirits of hartshorn). A gaseous compound of nitrogen and hydrogen. Most DIY shops and chemists sell ammonia in a 10% solution in water. Ammonia is an alkali useful for removing grease and dirt. It also neutralizes fruit and blood stains but in common with many DIY stain removal substances it may lighten colours. Always work in a well-ventilated room as fumes are overpowering. Keep bottles in a cool place, never in sunlight. Dilute in 3 parts water. Never mix with other chemicals.

Amyl acetate (banana oil). A colourless liquid that smells of pear drops. It is a useful fabric stain remover but is highly flammable with strong fumes so do not use in a confined place or near a naked flame. Available from selected chemists.

Banana oil. (See Amyl acetate)

Benzene. A volatile, colourless liquid derived from coal-tar, it dissolves fats, oils, phosphorous, sulphur, rubber and iodine and is therefore a versatile fabric spot cleaner and stain remover. Highly flammable, it gives off a toxic vapour, so do not use near a naked flame or in a confined space. Available from selected chemists.

Bio-tex. A branded biological pre-wash and soaking aid that is also useful for cleaning stains from enamels.

Blue bag (Reckitt's Blue). An indigo or ultramarine laundry blue used to optically 'whiten' yellowed fabrics when added to the final rinse of a hand or machine wash. It is manufactured by Reckitt & Colman in its traditional fabric dolly bag and also in a convenient liquid form for adding to washing machine loads.

Borax (sodium pyroborate). Available as Laundry Borax from the chemists. It is a mild

197

alkali for removing grease and stains. Heavily soiled white cottons and linens can be soaked in a solution of borax (mix 9 tablespoons to 3 gallons of water) for 30 minutes.

Bran. Used to dryclean fur and fabrics and widely available from chemists and health food shops.

Brasso. Branded product of brass polish.

Brobat. (See Sodium hypochlorite)

Calaton. Brand name for soluble nylon powder produced by ICI and sold in small packs by Picreator. (See Directory)

Camphorated chalk. This can be used for drycleaning and protecting white furs and ermine tails from insect damage. Textile conservators suggest mixing chalk to a cold water paste and leaving to dry. Brush to remove.

Carbon tetrachloride. A chloroform derivative and a volatile, colourless liquid. It is the basis of many drycleaning fluids and is widely used as cleaning fluid by this name as it is an excellent solvent for grease and oils. Handle with care and never near smoke, heat or a naked flame as a dangerous vapour can form. Always work in a well-ventilated room. Some fabric colours may be affected so always make a spot test first when cleaning. Can also be bought at the chemists, and is an ingredient of Targon grease and tar remover.

Chloramine. Available from chemists and also used for bleaching iron mould. Mix with distilled water.

Citric acid. Bleaching agent suitable for ink stain removal and light mildew stains on wools and silk.

Comfort. A branded product of fabric conditioner.

Contact adhesives. These bond immediately and like superglues need positioning correctly first time when sticking broken jewellery and plastic laminates. Handle with care when working and keep room well ventilated; keep away from naked flame as they are highly flammable. Many branded products about of which Evo-Stik and Dunlop Thixofix are widely available from DIY shops.

Copydex. A natural latex adhesive useful for sticking fabrics without leaving a stain. A special solvent, however, is available from the manufacturers (see Directory) should it be spilt on fabrics.

Cream of tartar. (See Potassium hydrogen tartrate)

Cyanoacrylate adhesives. The new so-called 'superglues', they stick a variety of materials from leather and some plastics to china and wood but surfaces have to be absolutely clean and dust-free (use white spirit or acetone to clean). Handle with care as contact with skin and eyes can permanently injure.

Dabitoff. Branded product of spot cleaner. (See also Iron sole plate cleaners)

Decosol. Branded product of vinyl cleaner

Distilled vinegar. (See Acetic acid)

Distilled water (de-ionized water). Unlike ordinary tap water which can contain different amounts of calcium sulphate, calcium bicarbonate, magnesium and chlorine, distilled water is free from impurities which make it hard and reduce the effective cleaning properties of soap. So always use distilled water when washing fragile fabrics, i.e., lace and silks, particularly in the final rinse as it prevents further iron mould spots forming. Buy your distilled water from a chemist, not a garage.

Domestos. Branded product of household bleach

Dryad's cold enamelling kit. A useful way of repairing chips on enamel jewellery (see Directory).

Dygon. A branded product of dye stripper and stain remover for non colour-fast dyes. It is based on sodium hydrosulphite.

Epoxy-based putty resins. (See Directory, Loctite Handy strip)

Eucalyptus oil. This is effective for de-greasing hatbands and for removing tar stains from fabrics that cannot be wetted. Place an absorbent piece of fabric behind the stain. Paint on the oil with a brush, place another piece of absorbent fabric on top before ironing at hottest setting.

Fabric conditioners. These reduce static electricity, bulk out fibres and generally impart a pleasant fragrance and feeling to tired fabrics and woollen knits. In liquid form they are generally added to the final rinsing water but one brand (Bounce) comes in small sheets which are placed between clothes when in the tumble drier. Comfort and Lenor are the best-known brand names but many supermarkets now do their own-label products. Fabric conditioners also reduce creasing in manmade fabrics, i.e. polyester, so ironing is easier.

Fabric protectors. These reduce a fabric's tendency to absorb grease and water and act as a water and dirt repellent; they do not waterproof. Mostly available in a convenient spray-on aerosol and are specially good for protecting light coloured fabric (canvas and satin) shoes, anoraks. Three brands, 3M's Scotchgard, Dylon's Rain & Stain Repellent and Grangersol's Fabsil may stiffen and darken fabric very slightly. So always test on a corner of fabric first. Use only on clean fabrics and never on vinyls or leather. (Satin shoes treated with fabric protectors cannot afterwards be dyed.)

Filtration fabric. A screening fabric used as a protective overlay for fragile fabrics, tapestries and embroideries during preliminary vacuum-cleaning before washing. Available from Picreator (see Directory).

Five-Star Glove Shampoo. Branded product specially formulated for washing washable suede gloves. Available from glove departments and larger haberdashery stores (see Directory).

Fray preventatives. For shattered (silk) fabrics and garments with fraying seams early treatment will extend the life of a garment so that it can still be worn occasionally.

Textile restorers use soluble nylon, see Calaton, made up into

199

a 5% solution in warmed industrial methylated spirit. Clear nail polish is often used for frayed edges of artificial silk flowers, and as a temporary stop for runs in tights and stockings, but unlike Calaton it is not washable or drycleanable. There may be some stiffening and fabric discolouration so test on an inconspicuous piece of fabric beforehand.

French chalk. A powdered soapstone available from the chemists as a white powder and also available from haberdashery counters in solid block form for marking alterations. It is a useful grease absorbent. It can be sprinkled on to a stained fabric, rubbed into the stain and then brushed off to remove the stain. Alternatively it can be mixed with carbon tetrachloride to make a cleaning paste. French chalk can also be used as a mild abrasive polish.

Frend. A branded product of pre-wash and stain remover.

Fuller's earth. A surface dirt and grease absorbent powder used in simple DIY dry cleaning. It is brownish in colour and therefore not suitable for white or light coloured fabrics.

Glass Bond. A branded adhesive for mending clean breaks in glass beads etc.

Glycerine. A by-product of soap and used as a solvent, to dissolve most water-soluble substances and metallic oxides. When removing stains, use to 2 parts water and check that any dry glycerine is thoroughly washed off with water; residues cannot be later removed by grease solvents.

Glycerine toilet soap. This is suitable for removing surface dirt and grease from leather prior to polishing. (See also Vulpex soap.) Wipe over leather with a soft cloth well wrung out in a solution of glycerine toilet soap.

Ground rice. A gentle drycleaner when mixed to a paste with fuller's earth and water. Leave 2–3 hours before shaking out.

Gum arabic. Traditionally used for adding body to old silk to regain former lustre. It is available from art shops and ½–1 teaspoon should be mixed to a pint of water; items can be left to soak for 2 minutes.

Hagerty Gold Cleaner. Branded product (see Directory).

Handy Strip. A branded product of plastic putty based on epoxy resin and a useful filler for repairs to badly chipped shoe heels; also plastic jewellery, buckles, buttons etc. Manufactured by Loctite, it is available from DIY shops.

Heel and sole enamels. These mostly comprise a water-based enamel which can be colour-matched to restore time-tarnished heels to their original new look.

Humbrol enamels. A range of modelling paints suitable for painting metals and plastics and available in tiny tins, from DIY and modelling shops (see Directory).

Hydrogen peroxide. A clear, colourless solution used for bleaching scorch marks from wool (coat stain with glycerine first) and also for lightening silk. It is available from the chemists in three strengths: 100 vols, 20 vols and 10 vols. It is sold in tinted glass bottles and needs to be stored in a cool, dark place.

Hypo. (See Sodium thiosulphate)

Impregnated cloths. These are useful for dealing with light tarnish on silver but are not really intended for removing heavy tarnish. Goddard's Long Term Silver Cloth should not be washed and should be stored away from grit and dust.

Iron sole plate cleaners. These remove sticky residues left by iron-on adhesive webbings. Several branded products exist but some may not be suitable for Teflon-coated sole plates. Dabitoff sole plate cleaner manufactured by Kiwi (see Directory) and sold in supermarkets is suitable for all types including Teflon-coatings.

Javelle water (eau de javelle). (See Sodium hypochlorite)

Jeweller's rouge. A special polishing cream for gold jewellery. Available from most jewellers and craft shops.

K2r. Branded product of stain remover.

KP4. A branded washing powder for heavily soiled clothes.

Leather restorers. Scuffed, worn areas on garments and shoes can be disguised in a variety of ways either by using a shoe colouring paint such as Lady Esquire or Miss Dylon, or by treating with a special coloured polymer self-shining polish, i.e., Scuff-Kote. Connolly's Coloured Lacquer and Picreator's Renaissance Leather Reviver are also suitable for disguising but none of these products is suitable for suede shoes which can only be recoloured with suede dyes.

Lemon juice (natural). A very delicate bleach and can sometimes be used to lighten some light rust marks and recent ink stains.

Lenor. A branded product of fabric conditioner.

Lighter fuel. Good for removing petroleum-based adhesives from price tags often thoughtlessly stuck to garments; is also convenient for removing grease-based stains from silk ties. But never rub at fabric: dab gently. Keep away from naked flame.

Loctite Super Glue. (See Cyanoacrylate adhesives)

Magnesium carbonate (powdered magnesia). This is an excellent grease absorbent for cleaning white woollens, felt and furs. It can be mixed to a paste with distilled water or carbon tetrachloride and used for cleaning felt hats and white kid gloves. Simply rub the paste on and leave to dry out before brushing off.

Methyl alcohol. (See Methylated spirit)

Methylated spirit (methyl alcohol). This is composed mainly of ethyl alcohol (wood spirit), fuel and paraffin oils together with a violet aniline dye to discourage anyone from drinking. Colourless industrial methyl alcohol is available from the chemists in small quantities for stain removal as the violet dye may stain light and white non-washing fabrics. It is a useful

201

solvent for removing ballpoint, felt pen and wax stains and for cleaning bone, ivory and glass jewellery. It is flammable so use and store carefully.

Micro-crystalline wax. (See Renaissance)

Milk. Sometimes used in old recipes for stiffening lace. It is also a good *real* patent leather cleaner.

Milton. A brand name for sodium chloride (salt) and sodium hypochlorite. A sterilizing solution used for soaking baby clothes and nappies but is also effective on adult underwear.

Movol. (See Oxalic acid)

Mystox Solution A versatile branded bactericide, fungicide and insecticide for dealing with a number of problems related to textiles and leather. It is also a permanent moth-proofer and can be used as a mildew preventative on non-washable fabrics; also to treat persistent perspiration odour in jacket linings and underarms. It is available from Picreator (see Directory).

Napthalene. This is a crystalline hydrocarbon distilled from coal-tar; it has a strong odour and is extremely volatile.
Manufactured commercially as an insecticide and moth preventative, e.g., mothballs.

Nylon monofilament. (See Filtration fabric)

Oxalic acid. A weak, but poisonous acid found in high natural concentrations particularly rhubarb leaves. It is sold in the chemists in white crystal form. Mixed in a 3% solution in distilled water it will remove rust, ink and iron mould stains from most fabrics and leather. Always rinse thoroughly after use as it can burn, so protect hands, clothing and furniture. Sold under the trade names of Rustol or Movol.

Ox gall. A clear, colourless solution still extracted from genuine oxen gall, aids fabric penetration. A little added to the final rinsing water can sometimes reduce excessive colour running (bleeding) in some brown and grey dyes. It is available from art shops.

Parazone. A branded product of domestic bleach.

Petrol. (See Lighter fuel)

Perspex cleaner/polish. Useful for polishing up jewellery and minaudières from the Fifties and Sixties. Manufactured by ICI, it is available from furniture shops.

Polyclens Plus. Branded paint brush cleaner and a useful multi-purpose stain solvent for a number of grease-based stains and chewing gum. Available from DIY shops.

Potassium hydrogen tartrate (cream of tartar). Can be effective on mildly tarnished metallic trimmings. Make a paste with distilled water. Brush off when dry.

Potato flour. Warmed slightly in a baking tin in a moderate oven, it can be used to dryclean white and pastel-coloured woollen shawls or fabric shoes. Items can be wrapped in aluminium cooking foil to retain heat longer and increase cleaning action. Brush off before cool. Potato flour is available from delicatessens and supermarkets.

Reckitt's Blue. (See Blue bag)

Renaissance Micro-crystalline wax. For polishing and protecting every kind of material from leather, metal and tortoiseshell to ivory, bone, horn and coral. It is the only wax polish made entirely from processed oil-based micro-crystalline waxes. Available from Picreator, the manufacturers, and selected craft shops (see Directory). Renaissance Leather Reviver, from the same company is a lanolin-based revitalizing treatment for dry neglected leather.

Rice water. Traditionally used by the Japanese for starching cotton kimono (yukata). Simply dilute a quantity of the water in which rice has been boiled and soak items for about 10 minutes.

Rust removers. For cottons and linens see Oxalic acid; for woollens, silk and manmades see Stain Devils' range and Chloramine T.

Saponaria (soapwort, soap root, latherwort). Herbal cleaner used since Roman times for washing fabrics. It is still good for old, fragile items that can be wetted. But as with any cleaner, always test first for colourfastness. When the saponaria is made up it may not keep long (mildew forms on the top) so only make as much as you need at the time, or store in the refrigerator. Available from Culpeper (see Directory).

Seal 'n Shine. A branded product for protecting shoes etc., painted with Miss Dylon shoe colours. It is also good for giving old leatherware a protective shine.

Shellac. A varnish made from natural resins and suitable for reglazing panama and other straw hats. Available from art and specialist craft shops.

Shout. A branded pre-wash and stain remover

Silver Dip. A branded product for cleaning silver.

Silver sand. Is useful for cleaning sable, skunk and pony skin. It should be heated in a baking tray in a moderate oven. Leave on for 20 minutes before brushing off.

Soap jelly. This can be used for washing any fabric that would be damaged by rubbing. Simply grate some household bar soap such as Fairy or Sunlight into an old saucepan and heat slowly until dissolved. When cool it forms into a stiff jelly ready for use. Use with soft water (rainwater) for effective results.

Soda (sodium carbonate, lye). This acts as a de-greasing agent and water softener. Add before soap powder to water of 60° C (140° F) but causes yellowing of white woollens and silks.

Sodium bicarbonate (commonly known as bicarbonate of soda). A mild alkali for removing acid stains.

Sodium hydrosulphite. This chemical is contained in a convenient form in the Stain Devils range of stain removers for treating rust and iron mould. It is also an ingredient of Dygon colour and stain remover.

Sodium perborate. Useful for bleaching (brightening) coloured fabrics as well as removing stains (non-protein ones) either by washing at high temperatures or soaking overnight and for this reason is already contained in many branded detergent products.

Sodium pyroborate. (See Borax)

Sodium thiosulphate (photographer's hypo). A useful solvent for removing iodine stains.

Soft Touch. A branded product of liquid detergent for washing woollens and delicate new fabrics.

Soluble nylon. (See Fray preventatives)

Spirit soap. A form of soap for dry-cleaning textiles (see Vulpex)

Stain Devils. A branded range of DIY stain removers to deal with almost every fabric stain. Available from supermarkets and good haberdashery counters. See Directory.

Supakleen. A branded product of oxygen-based bleach for heavily soiled white overalls.

Super Glue. (See Cyanoacrylate adhesives)

Super White. A branded whitener suitable for whitening all fabrics.

Swade Groom. Branded product for cleaning suede clothes.

Talcum powder. The purest form is baby powder and it is sometimes used as an effective cleaner for light coloured fabrics that cannot be wetted.

Targon. Branded product for removing oily, tar and creosote stains from fabrics.

Tartaric acid. Is available from the chemists and useful for treating heavily tarnished metallic braids and lamé fabrics. Always rinse off thoroughly after use.

Tenestar. A branded washing product specially formulated for silk. It contains a bactericide that deals with perspiration. Available from haberdashery counters in department stores (see Directory).

Transparent Lacquer. Branded product for protecting brass and copper (jewellery) from tarnishing. Manufactured by Rustin's (see Directory), when chipped it can be removed with Strypit paint remover.

Turpentine. Genuine 'turps' is distilled from pine tree gum and is a good solvent for paint stains. It is available from art shops in a refined form and is a good deal more costly than 'turps substitute' (white spirit) sold in DIY shops which may contain traces of other solvents.

Uhu. A branded product of clear adhesive suitable for sticking fabrics. It is not washable or drycleanable.

Vinegar. (See Acetic acid)

Vinyl cleaners. These are usually found in car and garage accessory shops and are available in spray-on and bottle form in the Decosol range. White spirit is also a good vinyl cleaner but leaves surface less glossy.

Vulpex Liquid Soap. Uniquely soluble in either water or white spirit for normal washing or 'drycleaning'. Used by professional conservators in museum work on all types of materials. Cleaning action is easily controlled by degree of dilution or steep time. Manufactured by Picreator (see

Directory) who will supply 100 ml or 1 litre bottles.

Whiting (precipitated). This acts as a mildly abrasive polish for mother-of-pearl and can be made by mixing a little ground french chalk in distilled water. Also available from art and craft shops.

White spirit (turpentine substitute). Is distilled from petroleum and can be used as a solvent for oil paint, grease stains and for cleaning vinyl. Inflammable so store and work away from a naked flame.

White vinegar. (See Acetic acid)

Woolite. A branded product specially formulated for woollens.

Yellow soap. A coarse soap, less refined and therefore more alkaline than soft soap, i.e. toilet soap. It is suitable for applying direct to a fabric and is recommended for treating heavily soiled areas. Sulphur soap is available from most hardware shops.

Directory

One of life's great pleasures for Conspicuous Thrifters is collecting old and antique costumes and maintaining them in good condition. The more knowledge obtained about materials, sewing techniques and conservation methods, the better equipped you will be to look after them. It has to be said, however, that renovating any badly damaged antique costume bargains or a relative's heirloom should always be considered very carefully at the outset. Specialist repairs and restorations are costly, time-consuming and can even work out a good deal more expensive than buying perfect examples. Poorly executed work not only looks déclassé but may devalue a garment considerably.

Bearing this in mind, you should then try to be as coolly objective as you can over your abilities before deciding to go ahead with any DIY cleaning and repairs. Fortunately, this country has enormous resources in costume and textile conservation. Many people working in these fields may either be able to undertake the work themselves or at least suggest suitable craftsmen. A number of costume museums have their own conservation departments and, increasingly, antique costume dealers are employing specialist craftsmen. Museums, however, can only date, identify and suggest ways of cleaning and storage; only auction houses such as Christie's will value items. If you cannot manage a personal visit to the costume museum concerned, send in large colour or black-and-white prints, together with an s.a.e., and they will do their best to identify. On a point of courtesy, always remember to send the s.a.e. when contacting any of the organizations listed in the following pages.

To back up the information here, further books should be consulted for a more comprehensive, historical and technical study (see Further reading). Visiting museums and costume collections where you can study pieces similar to your own is helpful, but watching an expert embroiderer or tailor at work or attending special sewing classes is probably the best way of all to improve your skills.

All details are correct at time of going to press. The publishers and author take no responsibility for errors. Prices mentioned are only a guide, and cheques or postal orders should not be sent before details of goods, services or courses are verified in writing. Telephone numbers have been given where useful or possible.

Antique costume sales

The auction houses listed below will value items and place bids for absent clients. Allow approximately three months for placing in catalogues and selling items.

Bonhams (Costume and Textiles) Montpelier Galleries, Montpelier Street, London SW7 1HH (01) 584 9161

Sales approximately every three months throughout the year. Catalogues.

Christie's (South Kensington) 85 Old Brompton Road, London SW7 3LD   (01) 581 2231

Every Tuesday at 2pm. Viewing on Mondays from 9.30am to 7pm; Tuesdays from 9.30am to 12pm. Catalogues.

Phillips Son and Neale Ltd 7 Blenheim Street, London W1Y 0AS   (01) 629 6602

Approximately every month. Viewing from 9am to 4.30pm Tuesdays and Wednesdays. Catalogues

Sotheby's (Chester) Booth Mansion, 28 Watergate Street, Chester CH12 NA Chester (0244) 315531

Occasional costume sales throughout the year. Viewing is around a week before sales. Catalogues.

Sotheby's (Belgravia) 19 Motcomb Street, London SW1X 8LB   (01) 493 8080

Occasional sales throughout the year but only for good Chinese costume and early needleworks.

Museums of Interest

Visitors to the museums listed here would be advised to telephone first about opening times and days, as these can vary considerably. Appointments to view certain special collections or to use the facilities usually need to be verified in writing with the keeper of the department concerned. It is not unusual for some costume museums to charge admission fees and in the current economic climate Conspicuous Thrifters may well consider, where possible, becoming a 'Friend' and giving a small donation, thus ensuring free admission. The list is by no means comprehensive, there are numerous regional museums also displaying important costume collections, but space is limited here.

London

Bethnal Green Museum
Cambridge Heath Road, London
E2 9PA   (01) 980 2415/3204/4315

Children's costume gallery from 1750–1920; wedding dresses and bridal accessories 1770–1970; also fancy dress and Mary Quant children's wear.

Museum of London
London Wall, London EC2Y 5HN
(01) 600 3699

The costume collection divides into everyday, ceremonial, uniforms, royal clothing, theatre and accessories as well as haute couture.

Victoria & Albert Museum
London Wall, London, SW7 2RL
(01) 589 6371

The Dress Collection shows a fairly comprehensive range of fashionable dress from the 17th century. Also fine examples of 20th-century haute couture. The accessories are beautifully displayed; fans, gloves and hats are in chronological order. There is also an extensive lace collection, and galleries displaying Middle Eastern and oriental dress. The museum library has a well-stocked costume and textiles section.

Avon

The American Museum in Britain
Claverton Manor, Bath, BA2 7BD
Bath (0225) 60503

Not strictly a costume museum as such but the patchwork quilts and glass-beaded pincushions merit a visit.

The Assembly Rooms, Alfred Street, Bath, BA1 2QH
Bath (0225) 61111

Comprehensive collection from 16th century to present day; beaded baby bonnets are a treat. Excellent costume bookshop.

The Costume Fashion Research Centre
4 The Circus, Bath, BA2 7BD
Bath (0225) 65025

Late 18th century; also 20th-century haute couture: Nina Ricci and Dior; utility shoes and Fifties frocks.

Blaise Castle House Museum
Henbury, Bristol
Bristol (0272) 506789

Late 18th century to present day. French haute couture, also Seventies blue denim collection.

Bedfordshire

The Cecil Higgins Art Gallery
Castle Close, Bedford, MK40 3NY
Bedford (0234) 211222

Good lace collection. Clothes from 1900 to present day with local dressmakers represented.

The Luton Museum
Wardown Park, Luton, LU2 7HA
Luton (0582) 369471

The Luton 'Life Gallery' celebrates Luton's hat industry with a hat collection – look out for plaited straw models.

Bucks

Buckinghamshire County Museum
Church Street, Aylesbury
Aylesbury (0296) 82158/88849

Some lace. Collection depicts more social aspects of costume from early 1900 to present day.

Devon

Allhallows Museum
High Street, Honiton
Honiton (0404) 487307

Lace collection and demonstrations of lace making.

The Pauline de Bush Collection
Killerton House, Broadclyst,
Exeter, EX5 3LE
Exeter (0392) 881345

National Trust owned collection mostly seen in tableau. Look out for Thirties cocktail party and Twenties nursery clothes.

Royal Albert Memorial Museum
Queen Street, Exeter
Exeter (0392) 56724

Haute couture collection contains some Twenties beaded dance dresses also accessories and Honiton lace.

Devonshire Collection of Period
Costume
High Street, Totnes
Totnes (0803) 862423

Private collection of 1900–present-day costume.

Essex

Chelmsford and Essex Museum
Oaklands Park, Moulsham Street,
Chelmsford, CM2 9AQ
Chelmsford (0245) 353066

Uniforms (military and otherwise) also some Fifties and Sixties fashion.

Herefordshire

Hereford City Museum
Churchill Gardens, Venn's Lane,
Hereford, HR1 1DE
Hereford (0432) 6812

20th-century fashion, vintage Biba and Ossie Clark; also Twenties and Thirties. A 20th-century children's collection that is reckoned to be very comprehensive.

Merseyside

Merseyside County Museum
William Brown Street, Liverpool,
L3 8EN   Liverpool (051) 207 0001

Between-the-wars costume and some Parisian couture; also examples of Sixties and Seventies student work.

Midlands

Leicestershire Museums, Art
Galleries and Record Service
96 New Walk, Leicester, LE1 6TD
Leicester (0533) 554100

Between-the-wars collection; the Symington swimwear display also contains underwear, hosiery etc.

The Gallery of English Costume
Platt Hall, Platt Fields, Rusholme,
Manchester, M14 5LL
Manchester (061) 224 5217

Largest collection outside London from 1900 to the present day. A wide selection of haute couture. The hat collection includes designs by Otto Lucas. Library and study collection by appointment only.

City Museum and Art Gallery
Chamberlaine Square,
Birmingham, B3 3DH
Birmingham (021) 235 2834

Good examples of 18th-century costume and everyday 20th.

Norfolk

Bridewell Museum of Local
Industries
Bridewell Alley, St Andrew's Street,
Norwich, NR2 1AQ
Norwich (0603) 611277

Mr Starling's collection of children's handmade shoes – the unique work of a Norwich shoemaker in the 1930s.

Stranger's Hall Museum of
Domestic Life
St Benedict's Street, Norwich,
NR2 4AL
Norwich (0603) 22233/611277

Collection showing the social aspects of clothing; also Paisley shawls.

Northamptonshire

Central Museum and Art Gallery
Guildhall Road, Northampton,
NN1 1DP
Northampton (0604) 34881

Largest shoe collection in the UK, it celebrates the town's main industry. Appointments are advisable as only a small part is displayed.

North of England

Castle Howard Costume Galleries
Castle Howard, York
Coneysthorpe (065 384) 333

Reputedly the largest private UK collection, from 18th-century to the present day.

Lotherton Hall
Aberford, Nr Leeds
Leeds (0532) 818259

Mid-18th century to the present day. The 20th-century collection includes examples by Bill Gibb, Kaffe Fassett and Zandra Rhodes.

City of Kingston-upon-Hull
Museum and Art Gallery
Georgian Houses, 23–24 High
Street, Hull   Hull (0482) 222737

Exquisite collection of beaded Twenties dresses and jackets by Hull dressmaker, Madam Clapham.

Nottinghamshire

Museum of Costume and Textiles
43–51 Castlegate, Nottingham,
NG1 6AF
Nottingham (0602) 411881

Costume collection mainly displays work of local dressmakers. Also on show is a collection of machine and handmade lace and children's whitewear.

Scotland

Perthshire

Museum of Scottish Tartans
Comrie   Comrie (0764) 07647 779

Largest collection of tartans and Highland dress; also library, and demonstrations of dyeing and handspinning.

Renfrewshire

Paisley Museum and Art Galleries
High Street, Paisley, PA1 2BB
(041 889) 3151

Comprehensive collection of Paisley shawls.

Surrey

Weybridge Museum
Church Street, Weybridge,
KT13 8DE   Weybridge (97) 43573

Wedding dress collection from 1824–1955 worn by local brides. Also RAF and WAAF uniforms.

Sussex

The Fashion Gallery
Royal Pavilion Art Gallery and
Museums, Brighton, BN1 1UE
Brighton (0273) 603005

Haute couture evening clothes. The collection also strives to show social aspects and the occupational influence of costume.

Worthing Museum and Art Gallery
Chapel Road, Worthing,
BN1 1HD   Worthing (0903) 204229

Collection from mid-18th century to 1920, with some 'utility' clothing and uniforms.

Wales

The Welsh Folk Museum
St Fagin's, Cardiff, CF5 6XB
Cardiff (0222) 569 441

Collection ranges from 18th century to 1970. There is also some 'utility' clothing with authentic alterations and Fifties and Sixties ballgowns with accessories.

Worcestershire

Worcestershire County Museum
Hartlebury Castle, Hartlebury,
Kidderminster, DY11 7XX
Hartlebury (0299) 250416

The collection dates from 1900–1950 and includes examples of maternity and mourning clothes and accessories. Good library.

Antique and clothes shops

These days most large towns and nearly all the university cities have ubiquitous high street 'nearly new' shops, dress agencies or antique shops with a sideline in old or antique cast-off clothes. Indeed many antique markets now seem a permanent fixture in city residential areas and most seem to have at least one stall specializing in old lace garments, embroidered and Kashmir shawls, oriental clothes and antique jewellery and accessories. Unfortunately the nature of the more easy-going, less established secondhand shops tends to be ephemeral, and short-term leases mean they may have vanished by the time this book appears. Where possible, *check* opening times before visiting – admittedly difficult where no telephone number is listed. You may have to take pot luck. The following list has been compiled with the help of the current Yellow Pages for the appropriate areas. To find more shops than those listed may well mean your fingers will be walking under various headings such as Antique Shops, Dress Agencies, Secondhand Dealers and Wardrobe Dealers (actual furniture wardrobe dealers may be included in this section) and Surplus Stores. Outside London individual specialists are not exhaustively listed, nor is this list a personal recommendation of shops mentioned.

London

American Classics
400 & 404 King's Road, London
SW10 0LR   (01) 351 5229

Mainly Fifties imported American clothes, men's tweed overcoats, battered leather jackets, chinos (military fatigues).

Annie's Antique Clothes
10 Camden Passage, London
N1 8ED   (01) 359 0796

Victorian to Forties clothes; also wedding dresses.

211

The Antique Textile Co.
100 Portland Road, London
W11 4LO   (01) 221 7730

Upmarket Kashmir shawls, 18th-century clothes, strictly not for DIY restorers.

Being There
4 Charlton Place, Camden Passage,
London N1 8ED   (01) 354 1285

Twenties beaded dresses, Fifties ballgowns. Stilettos.

Blax
8 & 11 Sicilian Avenue,
Southampton Row, London
WC1 2QD   (01) 404 0125

No. 8 concentrates on ladies' and men's evening wear, c. late Twenties to Fifties including every kind of accessory. No. 11 stocks mainly menswear of the mid-Twenties to late Fifties and Sixties. Again, every kind of accessory including cufflinks and tiepins.

John Burke
20 Pembridge Road, London
W11 3HL   (01) 229 0862

Gents' morning and evening dress, bow ties, cummerbunds.

Catherine Buckley
302 Westbourne Grove, London
W11 2PS   (01) 727 4937

Lace dresses; also beaded clothes. Repro Victorian posy hats.

Capricorn
118 Kensington Park Road, London
W11 2PW   (01) 727 6985

Lace dresses; also beaded Twenties frocks.

Chrissie & Pia
The Kensington Palace Barracks,
Kensington Church Street, London
W8   (01) 937 4015

Evening/bridal dresses, whitewear, lace. Some accessories.

Cornucopia
12 Upper Tachbrook Street,
London SW1V 1SN   (01) 828 5752

Huge assortment of clothes c. 1910–1960; also accessories.

Demob
47 Beak Street, London W1R 3LE
(01) 734 2746

Accessories, vintage Gladstone bags, crocodile attaché cases etc.

Dodo
185 Westbourne Grove, London
W11 2SB   (01) 229 3132

Victorian nightwear, Twenties and Thirties lingerie, Forties dresses/blouses.

The Dress Pound
125 Notting Hill Gate, London W11
(01) 229 3311

Upmarket agency selling Couture and Designer clothes in good condition and not more than two years old.

Etcetera
236 Portobello Road, London
W11 1LT   (01) 727 1632

Some old Japanese kimonos.

Flip
125 Long Acre, London WC2E 9PE
(01) 836 9851
also at 191 King's Road, London
SW3 5ED   (01) 352 4332
and 96/98 Curtain Road, London
EC2A 3AA   (01) 729 4341

Secondhand American clothes from the Forties to the Sixties; relined old Japanese kimonos, Donegal tweed overcoats, army mackintoshes.

Fripplers,
187 Portobello Road, London
W11 2ED   (01) 221 0451

Frocks, also recycled fashion, embroidered shawls, some accessories.

Glamour City
54 Battersea Bridge Road, London
SW11   (01) 223 7436

*Overcoats, dinner jackets, Forties and
Fifties clothes, also evening wear.*

Green's Antiques Galleries
Kensington Church Street, London
W8 7LN   (01) 229 9618

*Victorian originals, also nightwear,
underwear, christening robes, shawls.*

Laurence Corner Ltd
62 Hampstead Road, London
NW1 2NU   (01) 388 6811

*Mecca for government surplus clothes, old
and new. Next door sells theatrical costume
and antique dress uniforms.*

Lost Weekend
90 Nutbrook Street (off Fenwick
Street) Peckham, London
SE15   (01) 639 5240

*Esoteric selection of clothes: Thirties
(unworn) underwear; felt hats; silk
frocks.*

Lunn Antiques
86 New King's Road, London
SW6 4SQ   (01) 736 4633

*Exclusive selection of lace, Victorian
clothes, Welsh working skirts.*

Marisa Martin
110–112 Parkway Units, Camden
Town, London NW1 7AN
(01) 267 7714

*Antique lace conture numbers; telephone
for an appointment to view showroom.*

Melody Sacks
108 Parkway, Camden Town,
London NW1 7AN   (01) 482 1902

Antique lace wedding dresses a speciality.

Phrox
240 Portobello Road, London
W11 1LL   (01) 229 4532

*Forties, Fifties and Sixties clothes, and
some accessories.*

Radar
284 Portobello Road, London
W10 5TE   (01) 960 8712

Fifties and Sixties clothes and accessories.

Stumbles Lace and Linen
28 Artesian Road, London W2 5DA
(01) 221 6482
(also at 131 East Street, South
Molton, North Devon, EX36 3BU
South Molton (07695) 3279

*Period clothes, lace and embroideries,
whitewear and accessories.*

Thrift Shop
67 Falcon Road, London SW11
(01) 228 2322

Jeans, flying jackets.

Virginia's
98 Portland Road, London
W11 4LN   (01) 727 9908

*Victorian whitewear, kimonos, Twenties
beaded dresses, also accessories.*

London markets can also be
splendid hunting grounds for
Conspicuous Thrifters for bargains
in recently discarded clothes,
designer labels and junk fabrics as
well as antique numbers, but if you
want to scoop these you need to be
an early riser – most of the bargains
have gone by 7.30am.

Antiquarius Antique Market
15 Flood Street, London SW3
*Open 10am–6pm, Mondays–Saturdays.
Indoor market not strictly as Conspicuous
Thrift as the others but, none the less, a
place for antique-clothes hunters seeking
top quality items.*

Camden Lock
Commercial Place, Chalk Farm
Road, London NW1

*Open 9am–dusk, Saturdays–Sundays.
Mainly Fifties and Sixties clothes.*

Camden Market
Camden High Street, London NW1

Open 9am–dusk, Saturdays–Sundays.

Chelsea Antiques Market
245/252 King's Road, London SW3

*Open 10am–6pm, Mondays–Saturdays.
Indoor market—some Victorian, Forties
clothes, etc.*

Covent Garden Market
Floral Hall, London WC2

*Open 9am–8pm, Mondays only for
antique clothes, Victorian whitewear,
shawls, accessories and jewellery.*

Kensington Market
Kensington High Street, London
W8

*Open 10.30am–6pm,
Mondays–Saturdays. Indoor market
selling a cross-section of American sports,
army surplus and some Fifties and
Sixties clothes.*

Portobello Market
Portobello Road, London
W10–W11

*Open 7am–1pm Fridays, 7am–dusk
Saturdays. Street market with enormous
range of clothes, from haute couture to flea
market.*

Bath

Great Western Antiques Market
Bartlett Street, Bath

*Antique dresses and accessories are for
sale on Wednesdays.*

Birmingham

Students go to the 'Rag Market',
Birmingham's equivalent of the
King's Road for bargains.
Annabel's in Main Sutton Road is
also a good hunting ground.

Gemini Nearly New Fashions
50 Chester Road, Sutton Coldfield
Birmingham (021) 354 6350

*Designer label and makes like Jaeger,
Country Casuals and Laura Ashley.*

Bournemouth/Poole

As New
1 Church Road, Parkstone
Parkstone (0202) 742917

Upmarket dress agency.

Flappers
457 Poole Road, Branksome, Poole
Poole (0202) 767083

Forties frocks, lace etc.

Holly's Dress Agency
1 Cinema Building, Palle Road,
Westbourne, Bournemouth
Bournemouth (0202) 762179

Small selection of good quality clothes.

Petre
5 Poole Hill, Bournemouth
Bournemouth (0202) 26114

Varied selection of clothes.

Brighton/Hove/Lewes

As Good As New
19 Upper Market Street, Hove
Brighton (0273) 725854

Celia Charlotte's Antique Lace
7 Malling Street, Lewes
Lewes (07916) 3303

Mecca for the Glyndebourne set and for anyone looking for authentic beautiful examples of period lace. The owner is a lace expert and has a stall in Covent Garden on Mondays.

Heather's Kids' Gear Old and New
4 Queen Street, Arundel
Arundel (0903) 882900

Established children's shop selling classic smocked dresses, velvet collared coats, riding gear, ballet, school uniform and maternity wear.

Ivy's
23 Church Street, Brighton
Brighton (0273) 28587

Quality secondhand gents' clothing. Shop run by the Brown family since 1939. Morning and evening dress, toppers, bowlers and umbrellas.

Bristol

Clifton Antiques Market
24/28 The Mall, Clifton, Bristol
Bristol (0272) 741627

Look out for Paula Coles's stall selling lace and shawls.

Lavender Hill
Clifton Road, Bristol
Bristol (0272) 737675

Established shop selling Forties frocks and a good general selection of separates and accessories.

Cambridge

The Cambridge open-air market on Mondays has some antique lace.

Tiger Lilly
84 Mill Road, Cambridge
Cambridge (0223) 68442

Varied selection of clothes on offer.

Canterbury

Ritzy Bits
Palace Street, Canterbury
Canterbury (0227) 52558

Period clothes.

Thrift (V. Heslop)
19 Castle Street, Canterbury
Canterbury (0227) 66792

Dress agency selling upmarket clothes.

Cardiff

The market on Thursdays and Saturdays sells some antique clothes, whitewear and accessories.

Wild & Woolly
2 Mackintosh Palace, Roath,
Cardiff   Cardiff (0222) 487309

Pre-1950 clothes. Telephone first to check on opening times.

Edinburgh

Look out for the shops run by Paddy Barris in St Stephen Street and in the Grass Market on Fridays.

Gladrags
17 Henderson Row 3, Edinburgh
Edinburgh (031) 556 8899

Varied selection.

Hand in Hand
3 North West Circus Place,
Edinburgh
Edinburgh (031) 226 3598

Pre-1950s clothes. Also some accessories and oriental textiles.

Guildford

The Antiques Centre
22 Haydon Place, Guildford
Guildford (0483) 67817

Some lace, Victorian whitewear etc.

Recollections
90 Haydon Place, Guildford
Guildford (0483) 503449

Upmarket dress agency offering a wide selection.

Leeds

Carousel Junior Clothes Agency
78 Street Lane, Leeds
Leeds (0532) 666625

Children's clothes, upmarket ballgowns etc.

Premier Dress Agency
74 Street Lane, Leeds
Leeds (0532) 606680

Viewing is by appointment only.

Liverpool

A. Barker
168 Duke Street, Liverpool
St Helens (0744) 33458

Upmarket agency with makes such as Jaeger.

Just-a-Second
19 High Park Place, Southport
Southport (0704) 25556

Offers a selection of nearly new clothes for the whole family.

Manchester

Bargain-hunters go to Afflex Palace, an indoor market in Church Street and two shops in Burton Road, West Didsbury.

Butter Lane Antiques Centre
40a King Street, Manchester
Manchester (061) 834 1809

Antique lace, beaded dresses and period clothes.

Camisole
All Saints, Oxford Road,
Manchester

Stocks clothes from the Thirties but concentrates mainly on Sixties and Fifties. Some old diamanté jewellery amongst the new.

Norwich

Norwich Antique and Collector's Centre
Quayside, Norwich
Norwich (0603) 612582

Pat Fox's stall has authentic Victorian period costume.

St Giles Antiques
51 St Giles, Norwich
Norwich (0603) 28535

Antique clothes.

Oxford

Clothes Peg
40a Abingdon Road, Oxford
Oxford (0865) 43836

Owner Margaret Mansell stocks a varied selection of clothes for the family.

Dizzy Second Hand Clothes
14 Worcester Street, Gloucester Green, Oxford   (For tel. no. *see* Pom Pom)

Stocks a varied selection – good on cocktail numbers. Men's overcoats and dressing gowns. Occasionally antique dresses.

First Class Returns
66 St Clements, Oxford
Oxford (0865) 251147

'Model' evening gowns, popular at student commems.

Pom Pom
30 Walton Street, Oxford
Oxford (0865) 41426

Emphasis on Forties frocks, knitwear, accessories.

Second Gear
25 Little Clarendon Street, Oxford
Oxford (0865) 50759

Nearly new shop with a varied selection, including some footwear.

Unicorn
5 Ship Street, Oxford
Oxford (0865) 48130

Varied selection, particularly separates.

WS Surplus Supplies Ltd
43 George Street, Oxford
Oxford (0865) 41433

Some secondhand naval including sailor collars, also usual fatigues, parkas and raincoats.

Sawbridgeworth

Herts and Essex Antique Centre
The Maltings, Station Road,
Sawbridgeworth, Herts
Sawbridgeworth (0279) 725809

Some antique textiles and costume, also linen.

Harrogate

Bloomers
41 Cheltenham Crescent, Harrogate
Harrogate (0423) 69389

Twenties and Thirties clothes, also whitewear, linen and accessories.

Ann Wilkinson
12 Cheltenham Parade, Harrogate
Harrogate (0423) 503567

Mainly furs, some linen.

Charity organizations

For details concerning charity shops in your area, particularly those belonging to organizations such as the Red Cross, Age Concern, Dr Barnardo's, and the YMCA, look in the Yellow Pages. Otherwise write to charity headquarters at the addresses listed below for details.

MIND (The National Association
for Mental Health)
Church House,
Newton Road,
London W2 5LS

Oxfam
The Press Office,
274 Banbury Road,
Oxford OX2 7DZ

Salvation Army
International Headquarters,
101 Queen Victoria Street,
London EC4P 4EP

Sue Ryder Foundation
Cavendish,
Suffolk CO10 8AY

War on Want
467 Caledonian Road,
London N7 9BE

Specialist/Advisory organizations

Some of those listed may charge fees for their services or research etc, and these may be restricted to bona fide members. If writing remember to enclose s.a.e. for a reply.

The Association of British Launderers and Cleaners (ABLC) The Customer Advisory Bureau, Lancaster Gate House, 319 Pinner Road, Harrow Road, Middlesex HA1 4HX

Professional body that arbitrates on behalf of complaints against members; around 75% of cleaners belong. They can also put you in touch with specialist cleaners in your area.

The British Button Society White Cottage, Warren Lane, Stanway, Colchester, Essex W3 3LW

Can identify old buttons (members only), also suggest ways to conserve. Publishes a bimonthly magazine called Button Lines.

British Leather Manufacturers Research Association Kings Park Road, Moulton Park, Northampton

Can identify leathers and suggest ways to conserve. They charge for their services.

The Consumer's Association 14 Buckingham Street, London WC2N 6DS

Publishers of Which *magazine, offering useful surveys on gadgets, services and products. Back numbers are available to members only.*

Costume and Fashion Research Centre (Museum of Costume, Bath) 4 The Circus, Bath, Avon BA1 2Q8

Can identify – see Museums of interest.

Council for Small Industries in Rural Areas (CoSIRA) 141 Castle Street, Salisbury, Wiltshire

Finances courses in some crafts for those wishing to start country workshops or revive a dying craft.

Cotton, Silk and Manmade Fibres Research Association Shirley Institute, Wilmslow Road, Didsbury, Manchester 20 8RX

Publish a magazine called Textiles. *They may be able to answer queries or put you in touch with others in the textile conservation field over care and repairs.*

Crafts Council 12 Waterloo Place, London SW1Y 4AA

Has a register of working craftsmen in Britain and Wales. The Conservation Section may also be able to advise over textiles.

Dylon International Ltd Consumer Advisory Service, c/o Annette Stevens, Sydenham, London SE26

Deals with all aspects of home-dyeing using Dylon dyes, Miss Dylon Shoe Colours, K-2r spot remover etc. Useful leaflets are available.

The Embroiderers' Guild Apartment 41a, Hampton Court Palace, East Molesey, Surrey KT8 9AU

There are now 100 UK branches and many others worldwide. They organize workshops and courses for members.

European Commission for the
Promotion of Silk
50 Upper Brook Street, London
W1Y 1Q
Can send leaflets on the care of silk.

The Fabric Care Research
Organisation
Forest House Laboratory,
Knaresborough Road, Harrogate,
Yorkshire HG2 7LZ
*May be able to identify and suggest ways
to clean fabrics.*

The Fan Circle
c/o The Chairman, Victoria &
Albert Museum, London SW7 2RL
*Can identify and suggest ways of
conserving fans.*

The Guild of Cleaners and
Launderers
24 Pickersley Avenue, Malvern
Link, Worcester WR14 2LR
*Professional and technical society for those
engaged in the laundry and cleaning
industries.*

Home Laundering Consultative
Council Secretariat
Wellington House
629 Upper St Martin's Lane,
London WC2H 9D2
Can send leaflets on washing symbols.

Irish Linen Guild
Lambeg Road, Lambeg, Lisburn,
N. Ireland
*Can send useful care and stain-removal
leaflets for linens.*

Lace Guild
White House, Lowe Lane, Franche,
Kidderminster, Worcester
*Promotes the knowledge of lace making,
collecting, history etc. Publications
available to members only.*

Lever Bros
Lever House (Consumer Advisory
Service), 3 St James's Road,
Kingston-upon-Thames, Surrey
K2 2BA
*Can answer queries on washing using
their products. Will send leaflets on stain-
removal and branded products.*

National Association of Shoe Repair
Factories (NASRF)
60 Wickham Hill, Hurstpierpoint,
Hassocks, Sussex BN6 9NP
*Professional body that can deal with
complaints on behalf of its members and
the public.*

Picreator Enterprises Ltd
44 Park View Gardens, Hendon,
London NW4 2PN
*Can send leaflets on conservation products
and suggest cleaning and care methods.*

St Crispin's Boot Trades
Association Ltd
St Crispin's House, 21 Station
Road, Desborough,
Northamptonshire NN16 2SA
*Professional body that arbitrates over
complaints on behalf of members and the
public.*

Textile Conservation Centre
Limited
Apartment 22, Hampton Court
Palace, East Molesey, Surrey
KT8 9AU
*Can identify old textiles and embroideries
and suggest ways to clean and conserve
them.*

Wool Industries Research
Association
Headingly Lane, Leeds LS6 1BW
*Can identify and suggest ways to clean
and conserve woollen textiles.*

Repair Services

Most of the firms listed are London-based, but many of them will undertake mail order repairs. Other specialized local repair services – such as embroiderers, quilters, weavers and saddlers (who may restitch leather luggage) – can be located through the Council of Small Industries in Rural Areas (CoSIRA). The Yellow Pages directories also list services under various headings: Tailoring – Repairs and Alterations, as well as Umbrella Makers and Repairers, Shoes, Jewellery, etc. Any mentions, however, should not be taken as recommendations and wherever possible it is advisable to ask for written estimates before commissioning work. This can save embarrassment later should fees prove higher than anticipated. For other repair sources see Specialist organizations and courses.

Embroideries/tapestries/lace/antique costume

The Grange Training Centre
Great Bookham, Leatherhead,
Surrey   Bookham (31) 52608
Charity workshop employing handicapped girls. They will finish off embroideries, tapestries and embroider existing items to match i.e. collars and cuffs.

Philippa Scott
30 Elgin Crescent, London
W11 2JR   (01) 229 8029
Specializes in cleaning and repairing some Middle Eastern costumes and textiles, also fans and feathers.

The Royal School of Needlework
28 Princes Gate, London SW7 1QE
(01) 589 0077
Strictly for heirloom repairs but they sometimes undertake selected private commissions, i.e. invisibly mend an antique Kashmir shawl.

Footwear

Jeeves Snob Shop
7 Pont Street, London SW1X 96J
(01) 235 1101
Will completely overhaul footwear.

London Cobblers
1 Wellington Place, St John's
Wood, London NW8 7PE
(01) 722 8424
Can repair all kinds of footwear including sporting; also renew stacked leather heels, patch and waterproof uppers and replace boot zips.

Henry Maxwell & Co. Ltd
11 Savile Row, London
W1X 1AE   (01) 734 9714
Riding boots restitched.

James Taylor & Son
4 Paddington Street, London
W1M 3LA   (01) 935 5917
Established handmade shoe makers since 1859. New heels fitted etc. Prices on application.

Furs and leather alterations/cleaning

London Suede & Fur Cleaning Co.
Ltd
Broadwalk Lane, London NW11
(01) 458 7373
Offers an extensive cleaning and repair service for furs, suede, sheepskins and leather.

Suede Services Ltd
2a Hoop Lane, Golder's Green,
London NW1   (01) 455 0052

*Will clean and repair furs, suedes and
sheepskins. M.O. service.*

Gloves

Pullars of Perth
35 Kinnoull Street, Perth,
Tayside   Perth (0738) 23456

*Practically the last remaining cleaner of
leather and fabric gloves.*

Handbags/luggage

Bland and Son
24b Notting Hill Gate, London
W11 3JE   (01) 229 6711

Repair luggage (see also Umbrellas).

Handbag Services Co.
16 Beauchamp Place, London
SW3 1NQ   (01) 589 4975

*Will remodel crocodile handbags from
around £100, also repair petit point
evening bags and couture luggage.*

Harrods (Souvenirs Department
'Initially Yours')
87–135 Brompton Road,
Knightsbridge, London SW1
(01) 730 1234

*Will initial luggage and small leather
goods, a useful camouflage for
irremovable stains. (Allow about 3 days.)*

Mayfair Trunks
3 Shepherd Street, London
W1Y 7LD   (01) 499 2620

*Specialize in luggage repair and some
handbags.*

Hats

The following cleaners clean hats
but do not reblock or stiffen:

Marie Blanche
154 Battersea Park Road, London
SW11   (01) 622 0151

Mayfair Laundry
Stirling Road, Acton, London W3
(01) 992 3041

Take 7
194/196 Stamford Hill, London N16
(01) 800 6780

Invisible mending

British Invisible Mending Service
32 Thayer Street, London
W1M 5LH   (01) 487 4292

*Can perform near-miracles on badly
damaged fabrics. They can also suggest
ways to camouflage. Prices on
application.*

Jewellery

Timothy Blades
54 High Street, Ross-on-Wye,
Hereford and Worcester
Ross-on-Wye (0989) 64560

*Modern jeweller who can also repair old
jewellery.*

Mervyn Bradley
27 West Hill, Dartford, Kent
Dartford (0322) 78650

Repairs and remodels old jewellery.

Cavey McCallum & Co. Ltd,
The London Diamond Bourse, 100
Hatton Garden, London
EC1N 8NX   (01) 242 5517

*Normally deals with trade inquiries but
can arrange to set, match or find precious
and semi-precious stones – even to carve*

a special cameo. Telephone Christopher Cavey for an appointment.

Eaton's Shell Shop
16 Manette Street, London
W1Y 5LB   (01) 437 9391

Stock semi-precious stones, coral, jade, amber, lapis, jet and mother-of-pearl but do not cut to size.

Gregory Botley & Lloyd
8/12 Rickett Street, London SW6

Gemologist's paradise with a wide selection. No cutting service.

Liberty's Jewellery Department
Regent Street, London W1
(01) 734 1234

Will restring and clean pearls; replace and repair stones etc.

Sloane Pearls
4a Sloane Street, London SW1
(01) 235 9163

Will restring top quality pearls. Also alter old-fashioned necklaces into modern styles, repair and replace clips.

Re-glazing chintz

Starcraft Cleaners
394 Finchley Road, London NW2
(01) 794 9367

For best results, chintz has to be fairly new; old chintz, however, can be stiffened but glaze is not so apparent.

Shirts – collars/cuffs replacement

A. Rahman Shirt Manufacturers
190 Westgate Road, Newcastle-on-Tyne   Newcastle (0632) 329636

Redoubtable conspicuous thrifter, Mr Rahman, replaces worn cuffs and collars in white polyester cotton. Alternatively he will take it from the shirt tail so no one will know! Price in 1984: £2.00. P & p 60p extra.

Umbrellas – re-covering/repairs

Adbank Ltd
8 Chiswick Common Road, London
W4   (01) 995 9718

Repairs and re-covers umbrellas, also belts and bags.

Bland & Son
24b Notting Hill Gate, London
W11 3JE   (01) 229 6711

Can re-cover (in nylon only) in a choice of 9 colours. M.O. service.

Clifford Johnson
35 Wellhouse Drive, Leeds 8
Leeds (0532) 401901

Repairs broken spokes and ribs. Will also re-cover in any fabric to customer's requirements. Antique and theatrical parasols, sunshades and golfing umbrellas also serviced; also M.O.

James Smith & Sons Ltd
53 New Oxford Street, London
WC1A 1BL   (01) 836 4731

Will re-cover in black nylon.

Frances Leather Goods
55 Upper Gloucester Road,
Brighton, East Sussex
Brighton (0273) 24492

Repairs antique and new umbrellas also small leather goods.

Wedding veils

Liberty's (Wedding Dress Department)
Regent Street, London W1
(01) 734 1234

Can refresh and remount old or antique lace veils on tiaras.

Manufacturers

R. P. Adam Ltd
Riverside Road, Selkirk, Edinburgh
TD7 5NA

Adamite – a highly concentrated cool water shampoo suitable for handwashing woollens and fine fabrics.

Artemis Products Ltd
684 Mitcham Road, Croydon
CR9 BAB

Distributors for Pebeo crafts products whose range includes fabric paints (gold, silver and fluorescent colours), liquid embroidery, fabric felt pens; also solvent and water-based enamels for jewellery.

Astley Dye & Chemical Co. Ltd
Malt Street, Bolton, Lancs.
BL1 8PP

Acdo Glo-white – whitens and brightens fabrics. For expert consumer advice, address queries c/o Helen Why, ACDO Service Bureau, Bolton.

Beecham Uhu
Brentford, Middlesex

Clear adhesive suitable for sticking fabrics and leather.

Bio-tex, *see* Jenks Brokerage

The Boots Co. Ltd
Nottingham NG2 3AA

Own-label products and chemicals mentioned in this book can be purchased in their branches throughout the UK.
 Boots 'household products' departments stock distilled water, a number of useful stain removal products, also detergents, glycerine soap, soda, ammonia, Milton, fabric conditioner, etc. The prescriptions counter usually stocks tartaric acid, oxalic acid, magnesium carbonate etc.

Bostick Ltd
Ulvercroft Road, Leicester
LE4 6BW

Bostick Clear adhesive is the only UK adhesive for fabrics that is washable and drycleanable.

Coats Ltd
12 Seedhill Road, Paisley PA1 1JT

Manufacture embroidery cottons and Drima sewing threads, needles and sewing booklets. Catalogue.

Connolly Brothers (Curriers) Ltd
39/43 Charlton Street, Euston Road, London NW1 1UE

Ceebee Hide Food is good for cleaning worn leather luggage. Also helpful leaflets on cleaning available.

Copydex Ltd
1 Torquay Street, London W2 5EL

Manufacturers of Pac clear adhesive and Copydex latex adhesive, used for sticking fabrics without marks. A special solvent is available for mishaps, send s.a.e. for details. Craft booklet also available.

DDD Ltd
Watford, Hertfordshire WD1 7JJ

UK distributors for Stain Devils, a comprehensive range of DIY stain removers.

Dabitoff – stain remover and ironsole plate cleaner – *see* Kiwi Products

Decosol Ltd
Shelf, Nr Halifax, Yorkshire

Special range of cleaners for vinyl.

Dryads
PO Box 38, Northgates, Leicester
LE1 9BU
Wide range of art and craft products including fabric paints, lace-making and enamelling kits.

Dunkleman
The Manor House, Gold Street,
Desborough, Northamptonshire
Manufacturers of deodorized insoles, shoe and boot shapers. Catalogue.

Dylon International Ltd
Worsley Bridge Road, Sydenham,
London SE26 5HD
Products include K-2r, Color-fun fabric paints, dye, cold-water dyes, Multi-purpose dyes, Polyester, Colourfast dyes, Miss Dylon shoe colours, Dygon, Soft Touch, Super White etc. For consumer queries write to Annette Stevens Consumer Advisory Service. Booklet also available.

Fabrella
56 The Boulevard, Crawley, Sussex
Proofing solution for umbrellas.

Five-star Glove Shampoo
Shepborne Road, Yeovil, Dorset
BA21 1SA
This can be used to clean washable suede gloves and gloves in fine fabrics.

H. Gaddum & Co. Ltd
3 Jordangate 1, Macclesfield,
Cheshire
UK distributors for Tenestar silk cleaner.

Goddard & Sons Ltd
Frimley Green Road, Frimley
Green, Camberley, Surrey
GU16 5AJ
Manufacturers of Silver Dip, Jewellery

Care, impregnated cloths for cleaning silver, etc.

Grangersol,
Imperial Way, Watford
Manufacturers of Fabsil water repellent finish suitable for most fabrics.

Gütermann, *see* Perivale Gütermann

Hagerty Cleaners for gold, silver etc
– see Prescott Clock & Watch
Company

Handy Strip – *see* Loctite

Humbrol Enamels Ltd
Marfleet, Hull, North Humberside
Modelling paints suitable for painting plastic jewellery, buttons etc.

International Chemical Company
Ltd
11 Chenies Street, London
WC1E 7ET
Manufacturers of Targon – grease and tar solvent.

Jenks Brokerage Ltd
High Wycombe, Bucks
UK distributors for Bio-tex prewashing agent. For consumer queries write to Bio-tex Information Bureau, PO Box 116. Leaflets also available.

Johnson Wax Ltd
Frimley Green, Surrey
Manufacturers of Shout and Dry-Clean stain removers. Leaflets available.

Kiwi Products
Parkwood Industrial Estate,
Maidstone, Kent
Manufacture Dabitoff hot iron sole plate cleaner stick, useful on all types of sole plate including Teflon-coated ones. Other products include Dabitoff stain remover, Kiwi and Tuxan shoe polishes. Leaflets

on stain removal and care of fashion shoes.

K-2r, *see* Dylon International

Kleeneze
Hanman, Bristol BS15 3DY
Bristol (0272) 670861

Manufacturers of Supakleen oxygen-based additive bleach, which is particularly effective on heavily soiled, white new fabrics and overalls in conjunction with Kleeneze KP4 washing powder for automatic washing machines. For washing coloureds, use KP4 on its own. Available from Kleeneze agents. Leaflets available.

Lady Esquire, *see* Punch

Lever Brothers Ltd
Lever House, 3 St James Road, Kingston-upon-Thames, Surrey KT1 2BA

Manufacturers of many detergents including Drive, Stergene, Lux, etc. Write to the Consumer Advisory Unit over washing queries with any of the above products and 'labelled' garments.

Loctite UK
Watchmead, Welwyn Garden City, Hertfordshire AL7 1JB

Manufacturers of Handy Strip (epoxy resin-based putty), Super-Glue 3 (contact adhesive) and Glass Bond (special glass adhesive).

Henry Milward & Sons
Needle Industries Ltd, Needle Division, Studley, Warwickshire B80 7AS

Established firm of 200 years standing with a most comprehensive needle range, including ones for straw, gloves, quilting and full ranges of hand sewing needles. Leaflet available.

Movol
66 Harrow Lane, Maidenhead, Berkshire SL6 7PA

Sold in small phials this is probably the handiest solution to removing light rust and iron mould. M.O. service

Newey Goodman & Co. Ltd
Sedgley Road West, Tipton, West Midlands, DY4 8AH

Manufacturers of practically every kind of fastener from little invisible poppers to hooks and eyes in enormous sizes. Write in for Newey leaflet pack for up-to-date information.

Netlon Ltd
Kelly Street, Blackburn BB2 4PJ

Plastic garden netting (fine gauge) is useful for drying delicate or beaded antique dresses flat, also woollens.

Pin garment over a frame of some kind (an old picture frame) and rest it over the bath where the water can drain safely away. Available from garden centres and hardware shops.

Offray Ribbon
31 Carter Walk, Tylers Green, Buckinghamshire

Huge range of ribbons from narrow (3mm) velvets and polyester satins to elaborate evening metallic woven jacquards (20mm) wide. Also useful, a trimming called 'velvet tubing', plus novelty spotted, tartans, picot-edged and crisp petersham ribbons. Good range of leaflets available on crafts such as ribbon weaving, making ribbon flowers, bridal accessories etc.

Orkin Ltd
Central Buildings, 24 Southwark Street, London SE1 1UG

UK distributor for Swade Groom, a useful cleaner for suede clothing.

Pentel
Unit 1, The Wyvern Estate,
Beverley Way, New Malden, Surrey
KT3 4PF
Range of fabric dying pastels. Some of their felt pens are suitable for using on fabrics. Leaflets available.

Perivale Gütermann Ltd
Wadsworth Road, Greenford,
Middlesex UB6 7J6   (01) 998 5000
Thread manufacturers whose seam engineering department can answer technical sewing queries. Leaflets also available.

Picreator Enterprises Ltd
44 Parkview Gardens, London
NW4 2PN
Manufacturers of Renaissance products: Micro-crystalline wax, Leather Reviver, small distributors for Mystox solution Celation (soluble nylon) and Vulpex spirit soap. Leaflets available.

Polycell Products Ltd
30 Broadwater Road, Welwyn
Garden City, Hertfordshire
AL7 3AZ
Polyclens Plus brush cleaner is useful for a number of stain-removal jobs. Leaflet available.

Prescott Clock & Watch Company
Ltd
Prescott House, Humber Road,
London NW2 6ER
Hagerty gold, silver and pearl cleaners.

Proctor & Gamble Ltd
PO Box 1EE, Newcastle NE99 1EE
Manufacturers of Ariel, Dreft and Tide.

Punch Shoe Products
Punch (Sales) Ltd, Lower Farm
Road, Moulton Park,
Northampton NN3 1XF
Manufacture Lady Esquire shoe paints and suede dyes; also shoe stretcher, heel enamels and many products to do with shoe care.

Reckitt & Colman
Reckitt Products (Household),
Reckitt House, Stoneferry Road,
Hull HU8 8DD
Manufacturers of Meltonian shoe products, Frend pre-wash stain remover, Reckitts Blue.

George Romney (Bama) Ltd
No. 8 Industrial Estate, Steeple
Road, Mayland, Chelmsford,
Essex
Bama insoles and protective footwear.

Russell Hobbs Ltd
PO Box 1, Blythe Bridge, Stoke-on-
Trent ST11 9LN
Manufacturers of irons. Helpful leaflet on ironing available.

Rustin's Ltd
Waterloo Road, London NW2 7TX
Their transparent lacqueur and lacqueur remover are suitable for coating brass and copper jewellery to prevent tarnish.

Scholl (UK) Ltd
182 St John Street, London
EC1P 1DH
Footcare products include spray-on shoe and foot deodorizers; heel cushions, deodorized insoles etc. Leaflets available.

Scotchgard
3M UK Ltd, Skimped Hill, 1
Bracknell, Berkshire RJ12 1JU
Fabric dirt and moisture repellent. Leaflets available.

Scovill Dritz
Whitecroft Scovill, Lydney,
Gloucestershire

Sewing products, including belt puncher kits.

Selectus Ltd
Beddulph, Stoke-on-Trent,
Staffordshire

Manufacturers of Velcro (nylon pile tape, also known as touch-and-close fastening). Leaflets.

Stain Devils, *see* DDD

Sunbeam Products,
Sunbeam Electric Ltd, Rutherford
Road, Daneshill West,
Basingstoke, Hampshire
RG24 0QY

Special iron sole plate cleaner and solution for use in steam irons.

Vilene Highline Range, Sewing Aid
and Craft Products,
Vilene Ltd,
PO Box 3, Geetland, Halifax, West
Yorkshire HX4 8NJ

Manufacturers of Vilene interlinings, iron-on adhesive webbings: Wundaweb, Bondaweb, Foldaband, Wundatrim also Vilene clean iron sole plate cleaner. For queries and leaflets write c/o The Publicity Department.

Wilkinson Sword Ltd
Sword House, Totteridge Road,
High Wycombe, Bucks HP13 6EJ

Manufacturers of quality scissors, pinking shears.

Winsor & Newton
Whitefriars Avenue, Wealdstone

Manufacturers of art materials. Their products also include gum arabic, whiting, etc.

Woolite International Ltd, Howard House, Gippeswyk Avenue, Ipswich, Suffolk IP2 9AE

Woolite is a specially formulated detergent for washing woollens and delicate fabrics.

Specialist shops and suppliers

Always send an s.a.e. when contacting any of the organizations listed below. Some of the catalogues and brochures are priced and postage is also extra.

ANI Art Needlework Industries Ltd
7 St Michael's Mansions, Ship
Street, Oxford OX1 3DG

Wool samples, also tapestry suppliers.

John Bell & Croydon
54 Wigmore Street, London W1

Stock selected chemicals in small amounts for cleaning: i.e. amyl acetate, Chloromine T etc.

Brodwaith Embroidery
5 Lion Yard, Dolgellau, Gwynedd
LL40 1DG

Comprehensive range of needlework materials, also books. M.O. service.

Button Box
44 Bedford Street, London
WC2 E9HA

Wide selection of plain and colour (fast-dyed) mother-of-pearl buttons also novelty plastic and some glass. M.O. catalogue.

Button Queen
19 Marylebone Lane, London
W1M 5FE

The Button Collector's shop for those seeking the elusive regimental or exclusive 18th-century semi-precious coat button; also real horn, mother-of-pearl, leather, wood.

227

E. A. & H. M. Bull Ltd
Lawling House, Manningtree Road,
Strulton, Ipswich 1PQ 28W

*Can re-cover buttons and belts in
customer's own fabric. Extra fast service
available. Send for leaflet.*

Cass Arts & Craftsmith (also
branches at Richmond and Slough)
The Marlows, Hemel Hempstead,
Herts

*Wide range of embroidery materials
including silks, wool yarns and
needlework.*

Cobra
Unit 5, Portobello Green, 281
Portobello Road, London
W10 5TU

*Everything for studding leatherware eg.,
brass, chrome or coloured glass dome
heads, hexagons. Also fancy metal
buckles, belts made to order.*

Creative Beadwork
Unit 26, Chiltern Trading Estate,
Earl House Road, Holmer Green,
High Wycombe, Bucks

*Everything for the beadworker. M.O.
catalogue.*

Charles Cooper (Hatton Garden)
Ltd
23 Hatton Wall, London
EC1N 8JH

*Suppliers of jeweller's rouge; also fittings
for old jewellery; silver cleaners.*

Culpeper (14 other branches
throughout UK)
21 Bruton Street, London
W1X 7DA

*Old established herbalist and stockists for
Saponaria. M.O. service*

Danish House
16 Sloane Street, London
SW1X 9NB

*Craft shop run by the Danish Handicraft
Guild. Sells Flower thread (naturally
dyed), embroidery cottons.*

Delabere House Embroideries
Moreton-in-the-Marsh,
Gloucestershire GL56 0AS

*Filoselle and Filoflos silks, Appleton's
crewel wools. M.O.*

Dryads Shop – *see* Reeves

Duttons for Buttons
32 Coppergate, York, N. Yorkshire

*Vast selection, including antique buttons,
also general haberdashery, lace and craft
suppliers. M.O.*

Eaton Shell Shop
16 Manette Street, London
W1V 5LB

*Wide selection of semi-precious stones:
mother-of-pearl, coral, shells, cane,
wicker and raffia suitable for mending
accessories. M.O. service, but no
catalogue.*

Ells & Farrier
5 Princes Street, Hanover Square,
London W1R 7RB

*Bead suppliers of all kinds, also sequins,
braids etc. M.O. bead catalogue is a
work of art. They can also dye beads to
match any fabric colour.*

The Enamel Shop
21 Macklin Street, London
WC2B 5WH

*Specialist shop for everything to do with
enamel work.*

Falkiner Fine Papers
117 Long Acre, Covent Garden,
London WC2E 9PA

DIRECTORY

Specialist shop for bookbinders, but basement department stocks leather skins in beautiful fast colours – some are suitable for patching and decorating clothes.

The Gate Art
29 Seaside Road, Eastbourne, Surrey
Wide ranges of embroidery cottons, including DMC ranges.

Harrods
87–135 Brompton Road, Knightsbridge, London
SW1X 7XL

The 'Top People's Store' has much for Conspicuous Thrifters: the embroidery department sells novelty sequins, beads and a wide range of threads; the haberdashery department has as comprehensive a range of elbow pads as you will find, also rarities such as diamanté trimming by the metre for replacement shoulder straps on that little black dress.

John Heathcoat & Co. Ltd
54 Great Marlborough Street, London W1V 1HL   (01) 437 9898
Stock special silk net for mounting delicate fabrics, repairing wedding veils, tutus etc.

T. M. Hunter
Sutherland Wool Mills, Brora, Scotland
Wide ranges of woollen yarns suitable for repairing knitted garments.

In Stitches
48 King's Road, Brentwood, Essex
CM14 4DW
Embroidery shop stocking DMC lace bobbins and threads etc.

David E. Jacobs Ltd
Baxter House, Richmond Road, London E8   (01) 935 3377
Suppliers of pigskin leather for patching repairs.

Kaplovitch Fabrics
43 Vicarage Lane, London E15
(01) 534 3725
Silk nets for mounting fragile fabrics, repairing wedding veils, tutus etc.

John Lewis Ltd (and 20 branches throughout the UK)
Oxford Street, London W1A 1EX
The haberdashery department is a Mecca for Conspicuous Thrifters – everything here from macramé beads, wools, ribbons, hat veiling, nylon pile tapes, dress shields, shoulder pads, belt puncher kits, buttons – some unusual novelty designs – and silk embroidery threads. The fabrics department stocks a huge assortment of traditional satin linings, to ready-made quiltings and fur fabrics, also terylene waddings, glazed furnishing chintzes.

Liberty's (and 20 other Liberty fabric shops throughout the UK)
210/220 Regent Street, London
W1R 6AH

Interesting and unusual haberdashery department has a good selection of wools, threads, Offray ribbons etc. The fabric department offers quality Art Nouveau printed vicuna wools, Tana lawns, silks and many other novelty fabrics useful for updating garments.

Macculloch & Wallis Ltd
25 Dering Street, London
W1R 9AA
Brass and stainless steel lace pins – these are extra long and do not rust – useful for pinning and mounting lace when drying

or displaying as they do not leave rust marks.

Morgan's Haberdashery
28 Chepstow Corner, Chepstow Place, London W2 4XA

Can cover fabric belts and buttons in original Forties styles in your own fabric. Send s.a.e. for details. Shop also sells lining fabrics, old buttons and retro leather buckles for mackintoshes.

Necklace Maker,
Unit 25 Workshop, Portobello Green, 281 Portobello Road, London W10 STU

Tiny, specialist craft workshop-cum-gallery for bead artworks, jewellery. Also stockists for antique Czech glass beads, French jet (glass), Victorian jug, bugle and rocaille; good selection of threads for stringing, clasps etc. M.O. catalogue.

Needle Needs
20 Beauchamp Place. London SW3 1NQ

Comprehensive range of embroidery materials for specialists.

Nice Irma's Ltd
46 Goodge Street, London W1P 1FJ

Wide selection of Ikat cotton weaves and Indian embroideries, also velvet patchwork and Indian woven slub cottons, block-prints etc. M.O. catalogue.

Patchwork Dog & Calico Cat
21 Chalk Farm Road, London NW1

All kinds of quilting materials including special cotton fabric, threads, templates etc for the professional quilter. Also good range of books on quilting, M.O. for leaflets.

Picreator Enterprises Ltd
44 Park View Gardens, Hendon, London NW4 2PN

Conservation materials specialist and Royal Warrant holder who will supply in manageable amounts, i.e. 500 ml and 1· litre plastic bottles: Mystox solution, Calaton (Soluble Nylon), Renaissance Leather restorer, Vulpex; also filtration fabric and Renaissance Micro-crystalline wax. M.O. service only.

Reeves Dryad Ltd
178 Kensington High Street, London W8 7KG

Stock a wide range of fabric paints, dyes, shoe colours and art materials such as gum arabic, shellac, whiting etc. Dryads craft shop (downstairs) stocks enamelling kits, leaflets etc.

Roberson & Co
77 Parkway, London NW1 7PP

UK stockists for Talens' Silka fabric paints

Rowneys & Co Ltd
12 Percy Street, London W1A 2BP

Wide range of artist's materials, gum arabic, whiting etc.

Royal School of Needlework Shop
25 Princes Gate, London SW7 1QE

Very wide range of embroidery threads, from Au ver à soie and Japanese silks to Egyptian gas cotton; linen threads in wide colour ranges, lace equipment and metallic thread suitable for repairs to oriental embroidery. M.O. catalogue available.

Rymans (shops throughout the UK) stock acid-free tissue

Silken Strands
33 Linksway, Gatley, Cheadle, Cheshire SK8 4LA

Stock Indian rayon floss embroidery threads and metallic threads, also Shi Sha mirror (mica) sequins in silver, gold and green. M.O. only.

The Silver Thimble
33 Gay Street, Bath, Avon
BA1 2NT

Tapestry materials, wools, and embroidery silks.

Teazle Embroiderers
35 Boothferry Road, Hull, North Humberside HU3 6UA

Specialists for embroidery materials: metal threads, braids, kid leathers etc.

H. S. Walsh & Sons Ltd
243 Beckenham Road, Beckenham, Kent BR3 4TS

M.O. service supplying small packs of jeweller's rouge.

Warehouse
39 Neal Street, London WC2H 9PJ

Selection of beads useful for embroidery and costume jewellery.

WHI Tapestry Shop
85 Pimlico Road, Lower Sloane Street, London SW1W 8PH

Stocks wool and a selection of materials for embroidery.

Yarncraft
112A Westbourne Grove, London W2 5RU

Wide range of yarns (including chenille) for weavers, and knitters, also stockists for Russell Dyes and specialist craft books.

Specialist and interest courses

The growing interest in all kinds of craft activity has led to a boom in classes and courses from those provided by the ILEA and listed in *Floodlight* (obtainable from newsagents) to privately run summer schools in the country offering working craft-holidays inclusive of board and lodging. Details of local craft courses can be found on local library noticeboards, or through advertisements in national newspapers and craft magazines. Some craft shops also organize their own classes, *see* Specialist shops and suppliers and Specialist advisory organizations. The following organizations are best contacted by writing rather than telephoning. Courses and prospectuses may also be subject to sudden change.

The Campden Needlecraft Centre
High Street, Chipping Campden, Gloucestershire
Evesham (0386) 840583

Specialist shop stocking an exceptionally wide range of materials for the embroiderer. Classes are mostly one-day but gold work is a two-day class. Other subjects include beading, needlepoint and quilting.

Central School of Fashion
37 Foley Street, London W1P 7LB

Offers expert tuition in designing and cutting all clothing; also fashion drawing classes. Write for a prospectus.

Council for Small Industries in Rural Areas (CoSIRA)
141 Castle Street, Salisbury, Wiltshire

Runs courses for those wanting to take up traditional country crafts. Write for details.

Mardie Gorman
Needlepoint School, 31 Trevor Square, Knightsbridge, London SW7 1DY

Basic course comprises three consecutive mornings from 10.30a.m.–1.30p.m., stitching a sample cushion and learning 30 stitches. Homework is expected, however, and a more advanced course is available where old and new techniques are taught; also repairs and application to clothes and accessories.

The Embroiderers' Guild
Apartment 41A, Hampton Court Palace, East Molesey, Surrey KT8 9AU

Organizes classes and workshops for members throughout their 100 branches in Britain.

The Enamel Shop
21 Macklin Street, London WC2B 5NH

Day courses on Saturdays for those wishing to try their hand at this craft; unfortunately repairs to existing pieces may not be possible.

The English Lace School
Honiton Court, Rockbeare, Nr. Exeter, Devon

Mainly residential weekly courses starting on Tuesdays at 10 a.m. and finishing mid-day Saturday. Most of the English laces are taught by regional teachers; also some Flemish lace. There is a separate lace conservation course and would-be students are encouraged to bring their old lace for repair.

Stefany Heatherwick
Unit 25, Portobello Green, 281

Portobello Road, London W10 ST2

Holds beadwork classes in her beading workshop.

Anne Hulbert
Creative Ventures in Cornwall, Tremayne, St Mark Menege, Helston, Cornwall

Offers residential courses in a variety of sewing techniques, including beadwork, quilting. Also fabric painting and understanding your sewing machine. Send for a brochure.

Ladies Work Society Ltd
Moreton-in-the-Marsh, Gloucestshire GL56 0A5

Organizes workshops and evening classes locally in tapestry etc.

The Quilters' Guild (see also the Patchwork Cat & Calico Dog – Specialist shops)
'Clarendon', 56 Wilcot Road, Pewsey, Wiltshire SN9 5EL

Members hold quilting bees and courses throughout the country. All aspects from trapunto to plain patchwork are covered.

The Royal School of Needlework
25 Princes Gate, London SW7 1QE

Holds classes on all aspects of embroidery, including oriental. Also beadwork, appliqué and lacemaking

Styal Workshops
c/o Anne Blackburn, Quarry Bank Mill, Styal, Cheshire SK9 4LA

Courses on general textiles, lace, spinning and felt making.

West Deane College
Chichester, Sussex

Run specialist courses in conjunction with the British Antique Dealer's Association.

Also short residential courses in basic weaving, embroidery etc.

The National Federation of Women's Institutes
39 Eccleston Street, Victoria, London SW1W 9WT
(01) 730 7212

Runs residential weekend and longer courses at Denman College, Marsham, Oxon for WI members and husbands only.

Subjects covered include dressmaking, tailoring, embroidery, making the most of your sewing or knitting machine, lace making etc.

Yarncraft Lodge Enterprises
112A Westbourne Grove, London W2 5RU

Organize knitting and weaving classes in the shop's workroom. Beginners catered for as well as experienced pupils.

Bookshops

Bayswater Books [Yarncraft]
112A Westbourne Grove, London W2 5RU   (01) 229 1432

Good selection of craft books, particularly those to do with knitting, weaving etc.

R. D. Franks Ltd
Kent House, Market Place (Great Titchfield Street), Oxford Circus, London W1N 8EJ   (01) 636 1244

Comprehensive stock of fashion

magazines and books for anyone in the fashion industry or interested in making clothes.

The Bookshop
The Museum of Costume, The Assembly Rooms, Alfred Street, Bath BA1 2QH
Bath (0225) 61111

Comprehensive range of books relating to the history of fashion.

Further Reading
Accessories

Beadwork, Pamela Clabburn, No. 57 Shire Albums. (Shire Publications Ltd, Cromwell House, Church Street, Princes Risborough, Aylesbury, Bucks HP17 9AJ

Buttons Diana Epstein, Studio Vista, 1968

Discovering Old Buttons, Primrose Peacock, No. 2/3 Discovery Series, reprinted 1984

Hats in Vogue Since 1910, Christina Probert, Thames and Hudson, 1981

The Kashmir Shawl, John Irwin, HMSO, Victoria & Albert Museum, 1973

Shawls, Pamela Clabburn, No. 77, Shire Albums.

Shoes in Vogue since 1910, Christina Probert Thames & Hudson, Condé Nast, 1981

Straw Plait, Jean Davis, No. 78 Shire Albums, 1981

233

Crafts

Dictionary of Dyes and Dyeing, K. G. Ponting, Mills & Boon, 1980

Fabric Dyeing and Printing (2) Stuart and Patricia Robinson, Dryad Press, Northgates, Leicester LE1 4QR

Leatherwork: A Step-by-Step Guide, Mary and E. A. Manning, Hamlyn, 1974

Stitch In Time, Knitting and Crochet Patterns of the 1930s and 1940s, Duckworth, 1972

Tie & Dye Made Easy, Anne Maile, Mills & Boon, 1971

Vegetable Dyeing, Alma Lesch, David & Charles, 1970

Wild Knitting – edited by Susannah Read, Angela Jeffs and Jane Sarton, Mitchell Beazley, 1979

An excellent range of small craft booklets edited by Kit Pyman, particularly those on goldwork, smocking and patchwork are published by the Search Press Ltd, Wellwood, Tunbridge Wells, Kent TN2 3DK

The Good Housekeeping Book range on various crafts: needlepoint, crochet, embroidery, patchwork and appliqué, knitting and traditional knitting is also highly recommended.

Dressing/fashion/style

Cheap Chic, Catherine Milinaire and Carol Troy, Omnibus Press, 1973

Collector's Book of Twentieth Century Fashion, Frances Kennet, Granada, 1983

A Man's Book – Fashion in the Man's World in the 1920s and 1930s. ed. by Jane Waller, Duckworth, 1977

Dressing Right, Charles Hix, St Martin's Press, New York, 1978

Dressing Thin, Dale Gooday, Omnibus Press, 1980

Vogue: More Dash than Cash, Kate Hogg, Hutchinson, 1982

Guides

Antiques Trade Gazette
116 Long Acre, London WC2
Subscription only, but a comprehensive source on antique fairs and auctions.

Good Museums Guide, Kenneth Hudson, Papermac, Macmillan, 1980
Detailed information about some of the museums used here plus opening times.

Where can I get. . .? Beryl Downing, Penguin, 1983
Lists services of various kinds including those to do with clothing repairs.

London Street Markets, Kevin Perlmutter, Wildwood, 1983

Markets of London, Alec Forshaw, Penguin, 1983
Two useful guides for those interested in tracking down clothes bargains.

Time Out magazine
Lists jumble sales in London every week.

Lace/lingerie

The Identification of Lace, Pat Earnshaw, Shire Publications, 1980

The History of Lace, Margaret Simeon, Stamer & Beel, 1979

Lace Our Heritage, Madeleine Van Hornwick, Joan Duckworth, Farthing Cottage, Churches Yard, Olney, Bucks, 1982

Sewing techniques

The Bag Book, Ericson & Ericson, Van Nostrand Reinhold Ltd, 1976

The Basic Stitches of Embroidery, N. Victoria Wade, HMSO, Victoria & Albert Museum, or HMSO book shop, Holborn, London WC1

'Everything About Sewing Lingerie and Loungewear', 'Everything About Sewing Fur and Fur-like Fabrics', 'Everything About Sewing Trims' from *Vogue Patterns*, Suzanne Olsen, Butterwick, 1972

Fabrics, Ann Ladbury, Sidgwick & Jackson, 1979

Good Housekeeping Step-by-Step Encyclopaedia of Needlecraft, Judy Brittain and Sally Harding, Ebury Press, 1979

Heirloom Sewing Techniques, Judith C. Wood, Box 7152 Marietta GA 30065, USA, 1980

Making Things Fit, Ann Ladbury, Severn House Publishers, and ITB Books, 1976

Mend It! Maureen Goldsworthy, Mills & Boon Ltd, 1979

Needlework and Embroidery, Therese de Dilmont and Mary Gostelow, Alphabooks, 1982

Sewing, Ann Ladbury, Mitchell Beazley, 1978

Using Your Sewing Machine, Women's Institute Books, 39 Ecclestone Street, London SW1 9NT

Washing/cleaning/care

Crinolines and Crimping Irons, Victorian Clothes: How they were Cleaned and Cared For, Christina Walkley and Vanda Foster, Peter Owen, 1978

How To Cope At Home, Barbara Chandler, Ward Lock, 1980

How To Clean Everything, Alma Chesnut Moore, Tom Stacey, 1972

Spot Check, Barbara Chandler, Ventura, 1980